324.941
JON

CAMPAIGN 1997

Nicholas Jones has had twenty-five years' experience as
a journalist with the BBC, as Labour Correspondent
and currently as Political Correspondent. His previous
books are *Strikes and the Media* (1986), *Election '92*
(1992) and *Soundbites and Spin Doctors* (1995).

CAMPAIGN 1997

Nicholas Jones

HOW THE GENERAL ELECTION WAS WON AND LOST

(U.W.E.)

17 OCT 1997

Library Services

UWE BRISTOL
WITHDRAWN
LIBRARY SERVICES

*IND*IGO

First published in Great Britain 1997
by Indigo
Indigo is an imprint of the Cassell Group
Wellington House, 125 Strand, London WC2R 0BB

© Nicholas Jones 1997

The right of Nicholas Jones to be identified as author of this work
has been asserted by him in accordance with the Copyright,
Designs and Patents Act, 1988.

A catalogue record for this book is available from the British Library.

ISBN 0 575 40116 8

(U.W.E.)

17 OCT 1997

Designed and typeset by Production Line, Minster Lovell, Oxford
Printed and bound in Great Britain by
The Guernsey Press Co Ltd, Guernsey, Channel Isles

All rights reserved. No part of this publication may be reproduced
or transmitted in any form or by any means, electronic or mechanical
including photocopying, recording or any information storage or retrieval
system, without prior permission in writing from the publishers.

This book is sold subject to the condition that it shall not, by way of trade
or otherwise, be lent, resold, hired out, or otherwise circulated without the
publisher's prior consent in any form of binding or cover other than that in
which it is published and without a similar condition including this
condition being imposed on the subsequent purchaser.

97 98 99   10 9 8 7 6 5 4 3 2 1

Contents

Picture credits

'Punch and Judy' by David Giles/PA News Photo Library
'John Prescott' by David Jones/PA News Photo Library
'The Battle of Knutsford Heath' and 'The carefully choreographed
    "spontaneous outpouring"' by Dan Chung/Popperfoto/Reuter
'Alastair Cambell and Tony Blair' and 'Brian Mawhinney' by Ian Waldie/
    Popperfoto/Reuter
'Peter Mandelson and Fitz the bulldog' by Paul Hackett/Popperfoto/Reuter
'Charles Lewington' by Dylan Martinez/Popperfoto/Reuter
'"Don't bind my hands"' by Russell Boyce/Popperfoto/Reuter

Introduction

In an age when election campaigns are fought largely through the news media, reporters are effectively the public's front-line troops. Our task is to examine and explain the policies on which the parties hope to get elected. This book presents my account from the battlefront of the campaign of '97, with the intention of illustrating the challenges which confront us as electioneering becomes ever more sophisticated.

Labour's historic landslide victory in the 1997 general election was so decisive, and the routing of the Conservatives so comprehensive, that many political analysts have ventured to suggest that the six-week campaign made little difference to the way people voted. The opinion polls tend to bear this out. Labour's commanding twenty-point lead had been stable for months, and right up to polling day the Conservatives' projected share of the vote stuck stubbornly at around 30 per cent. So great were the troubles which beset the Conservatives that their defeat had seemed a foregone conclusion. Nevertheless, Labour had every reason to be fearful. The Conservatives retained a formidable reputation for effective political propaganda, and their power of recovery had, after all, secured them a fourth term in 1992: Neil Kinnock's defeat was a constant reminder to Tony Blair of the electorate's volatility. John Major's eventual drubbing at the hands of the voters, and the emergence of tactical voting on a scale not seen before in a British general election, resulted from deep-seated dissatisfaction with the Conservatives' record in government and their disregard of decent standards in public life. The Tories were trounced. Even so, elections are not won by chance, and Labour's 1997 victory owed much to the effectiveness of its communications strategy, Blair and his shadow Cabinet colleagues working ceaselessly to remind the electorate of the failings of Major and his ministers. For their part, the Conservatives were deserted by the popular newspapers which had remained loyal to them throughout the Thatcher years, and their failure to take full advantage of the opportunities provided by radio and television allowed Labour to reign supreme.

My book seeks to explain how Labour established and then maintained their supremacy in influencing, and even manipulating, the news media. Never before had a British political party put so much effort into presentation. Labour's success owed a great deal to the campaigning tactics of their pre-eminent strategist, Peter Mandelson, the sure touch of their campaign coordinator, the shadow Chancellor Gordon Brown, and the astute advice of Blair's indefatigable press secretary, Alastair Campbell. These three were the conductors of a formidable operation based in Labour's newly established media centre in Millbank Tower, Westminster.

Inevitably my book draws extensively on the experiences and opinions of the rival spin doctors, who could hardly be considered the most reliable witnesses of an historic political event. Nonetheless, I hope my account of the part they played, both in the long-drawn-out pre-election skirmishing and in the campaign itself, will provide a valuable insight into the techniques they used to influence public opinion. Some of what they say might seem far-fetched, to be dismissed as nothing more than point-scoring. However, in my view political spin doctors are at their most revealing when protesting about the behaviour of journalists or complaining about the way television, radio and the newspapers are interpreting events. It is at such moments that the mask slips and one can observe the true motives of the political propagandist.

1

Excalibur Unsheathed

In an era when many people find themselves overloaded with information, political parties are increasingly at a disadvantage. The communications industry has provided such a surfeit of choice that the political news of the day can be turned on and off at the flick of a switch or passed over with the flip of a page. Consequently, if a party's general election strategy is to have a decisive impact, it has to be implemented with the precision of a military campaign so as to take full advantage of any opportunity which might arise to attack an opponent. Once political parties do get the chance to test out their policies in front of the voters, they must be prepared to fight each other to destruction. Even before the opening shots are fired, there is frequently a preliminary skirmish with those who control access to the news media as the rival parties struggle to command the attention of the viewer, listener or newspaper reader. Politicians know full well that because of the competitive pressures among journalists, they are entering hostile territory here. Sometimes a rapid advance for their cause is possible; on other occasions there are casualties and a retreat is inevitable.

While military analogies might seem far-fetched for an activity which fails to excite a large proportion of the population, the language is representative of the realities of political campaigning. In the months leading up to a general election, the most highly guarded document in every party has always been what is known as the 'war book', which sets out in great secrecy the strategy to be adopted until polling day. Once the campaign is under way, a secure 'war room' is established at party headquarters. Key staff meet there regularly to thrash out tactics. There are invariably illustrations on the walls which highlight the countdown to polling day, together with the latest campaign slogans. Great play is made of the delivery of the leader's 'battle bus', ready for long hauls up the motorways to far-flung parliamentary constituencies. Each of these converted coaches is fitted out with what is described as a 'high-tech nerve centre', capable of maintaining constant and instantaneous contact with party headquarters.

Preparations for the 1997 election broke new ground for the political parties, reflected in additional terms of military vocabulary. Because of the prolonged uncertainty as to precisely when Major would go to the country, there was an inordinately long pre-election campaign. Labour and the Conservatives both stepped up their party propaganda months before there was any firm idea as to when polling would take place. Far greater resources were directed far earlier than in previous elections towards the front line of the push for publicity. During the long wait for the announcement, Labour added a new concept to the lexicon of campaign jargon. Tony Blair spoke of the way his party had been engaged for months in the 'hand to hand fighting' which was required to 'capture the news agenda of the day'. It amounted, in effect, to a form of guerrilla warfare, fought through the news media, an offensive which Labour maintained day after day and which had a devastating effect on John Major's government. Another unprecedented development was the way the main broadcasting organisations treated the interminable phoney war between the parties as if the general election had already been formally announced. Months before polling day, the main television and radio news bulletins were already going to considerable lengths to maintain a strict balance in the air time allocated respectively to Conservatives, Labour and Liberal Democrats. As a result there tended to be something almost ritualistic about the way political events were reported and the politicians were interviewed. All too often the soundbites delivered were thoroughly predictable, only adding to the air of disillusionment which many people seemed to have developed towards the whole political process.

By the time Major finally called the general election, Labour had effectively been on a campaign footing for most of the previous three years, in effect since the death in May 1994 of the then party leader John Smith. The choice of Tony Blair to succeed him had not only resulted in a rapid acceleration in the pace of change within the party, in both its organisation and its policies, but had also heralded yet another transformation in Labour's campaign tactics against the Conservatives. Labour were relentless in their efforts to turn each day's political events to their own advantage. Casualties were sometimes taken on their own side, so great was the pressure to command and then hold the attention of the news media. If it was not possible to dominate that day's agenda with one of Labour's own media initiatives, the party did its utmost to engineer unfavourable publicity for the government. As the months went by John Major became increasingly needled by Labour's success in diverting attention from his government's successes. In one memorable outburst he castigated Blair for the way Labour's spin doctors were 'running around with all sorts of daft stories, day after day, trying to tilt the news media in a particular direction'.

Major's irritation was shared by most Conservative MPs. The party hierarchy was exasperated by the apparent ease with which Labour could entice the news media into accepting and then sustaining new lines of attack on the government. While much of the damage to the Conservative cause tended to be self-inflicted, Labour's publicity machine demonstrated considerable flair in exploiting the possibilities. Countless ways were found to draw attention to the failings of the privatised utilities and the excesses of their 'fat cat' directors. By sheer dint of repetition, the word 'sleaze' became firmly associated with Tory MPs. Another rich source of ammunition for Labour's publicity team were the innumerable contradictions and evasions which tumbled from the mouths of ministers amid the Conservatives' infighting over European policy and the turmoil which surrounded the government's fast-disappearing parliamentary majority. As often as not it was a Labour propagandist rather than a diligent reporter who spotted an inconsistency or change in nuance in the government's position and then excited the news media with lurid tales about the latest ministerial 'gaffe', thus encouraging prominent coverage.

The cumulative effect of all this publicity was to entrench Labour's overriding campaign theme that the Conservatives could not be trusted with an unprecedented fifth term in power. 'Enough is enough' and 'time for a change' were the two constant refrains. Labour's undoubted achievement, at least in terms of publicity, was that they made a reality of their slogans. The momentum thus created was not only maintained but strengthened as polling day approached. Tony Blair's vision of the future, and his readiness to embrace change, could be held up in increasingly sharp contrast with the tiredness and ineffectiveness of John Major's government.

Of all the Labour strategists who contributed to what became known as the Blair 'project', Peter Mandelson could justifiably claim to have been the most consistent in the changes he was advocating. He was certainly the most influential of the leader's advisers. Looking back on my own often abrasive encounters with him, I have to acknowledge that long before Blair was elected leader he was espousing tactics and policy shifts which not only came to pass in the birth of New Labour but also proved to be highly effective in repositioning the party. Mandelson's appointment as

Labour's head of election planning early in 1996, well over a year before polling day, was a triumphant moment for an MP and former party official whose name had come to be reviled by a significant proportion of the membership. While some of his fellow MPs, especially on the left, openly detested him, inside Labour's campaign headquarters at Millbank Tower his name was revered by party workers, many of whom were in awe of his brazenness in manipulating the news media. Among his fellow practitioners in the dubious calling of political spin doctor, Mandelson had no equal. His experience far outweighed that of any of his Conservative or Liberal Democrat counterparts. For more than a decade Mandelson had either been responsible for Labour's promotional strategies or helped influence them behind the scenes. After directing the party's publicity effort for the 1987 general election, under the leadership of Neil Kinnock, he took a back seat during the 1992 campaign; then, after secretly advising Blair during the 1994 leadership contest, he finally assumed control of a publicity machine which he had helped to devise and develop and which allowed him to exercise unparalleled authority. In the New Year 1997 edition of the party's magazine, *New Labour New Britain*, Mandelson declared that the publicity operation which he controlled at Millbank Tower was the 'finest, most professional campaigning machine that Labour has ever created'. In the weeks leading up to polling day the party would be 'fighting a war on the air and on the ground . . . fighting the battle of the airwaves, as well as in the press'.

Much of the envy and resentment which Mandelson had generated over the years derived from his knack of making himself appear indispensable, first to Kinnock and then to Blair. In conversation with journalists he was usually careful not to be too open in claiming personal credit for the numerous policy changes and promotional advances which the party had secured. Rather, his technique was subtly to underline the importance of his own contribution. For example, in late 1989, shortly after announcing that he intended to stand as parliamentary candidate in Hartlepool, he outlined to me what he believed he had achieved for Kinnock while serving as the party's director of communications. The phrase which kept recurring was that he had 'delivered' for Kinnock. The first of what he described as his 'projects' was the party's 1986 'freedom and fairness' campaign. This was followed by the introduction of the red rose symbol which appeared at the 1986 party conference and was used during the 1987 election campaign. In my diary I noted down the words Mandelson had used: 'I delivered the rose for Neil . . . I negotiated its passage through the party.' Almost a decade later, when Mandelson was firmly ensconced in Millbank Tower, his colleagues were struck by the way he continued to personalise his work. They noticed again how he spoke of 'delivering' for the leader, rather than the party. Errant members of staff would be chided in a similar vein when cross-questioned by Mandelson about their performance. 'What have you delivered for Tony today?' became a regular refrain as polling day approached.

Before his unexpected death in 1994 John Smith had gone out of his way to dismantle the public relations enterprise which Kinnock had established in the leader's office and which would subsequently take on an even higher profile under Blair and his press secretary, Alastair Campbell. Smith had told me that he felt the value of personal publicity was highly overrated. Mandelson, who at that time was out of favour with the leadership, believed Smith had made a grave mistake in dispensing with a personal press officer. 'A leader needs someone to look ahead, to think about the way they are projected and promoted and to give a strategic overview. Publicity for the leader has to connect with the overall promotion of the party.' After the loss of John Smith as leader, Mandelson still had to wait a year and a half before assuming overall control and being in a position to make his own 'strategic overview' and then put it into effect; but his formidable skills were put to notable use immediately, in promoting Blair's candidacy for the leadership. Under the codename of 'Bobby', he worked tirelessly but discreetly during the weeks of the contest, promoting Blair's speeches, arranging interviews and briefing political correspondents. There was no doubt that his professional guidance was invaluable and that when it came to the handling of publicity, Blair's campaign was remarkably trouble-free.

A week before the special conference in July 1994 to announce Blair's resounding victory in the leadership election, I sat with Mandelson for half an hour on the terrace of the House of Commons. With the outcome of the poll now beyond question Mandelson was in an expansive mood, happy to reflect on what he thought were the mistakes of the 1992 campaign while at the same time keen to predict how Blair would seek to prepare the party for the 1997 election. He felt the seeds of the 1992 defeat were sown in 1991, not long after he left party headquarters in order to fight the Hartlepool seat. 'It just began to unravel. Kinnock was exhausted. Labour were no longer standing for change. Then we made mistakes in the election. Frankly, there was a lot of bungling. Tony Blair must repair that damage. He must restore a belief in what Labour stands for; convince the party that we have a message; enthuse our members; and build up a momentum for change and for the election.' Mandelson gave me his own three-point checklist for the new leader. Blair would have to put the politics into place; then the people; and finally the party machine. 'There will have to be some painful decisions,' he said.

While Mandelson did not go so far as suggesting a precise task for himself, it seemed to be implicit from the conversation that he intended to play a central role. He identified two of his own strengths as skill in managing a team and the ability to hold his nerve should the party encounter a crisis during an election campaign. To illustrate his point he contrasted his own performance in the 1987 campaign, standing firm against the then Conservative party chairman Norman Tebbit, with the way the Labour leadership 'lost their bottle' in 1992 during the controversy which surrounded the fiasco over Labour's 'Jennifer's ear' party political broadcast. In the 1987 campaign Mandelson had taken great delight in publicising an aside by Tebbit to the effect that the Conservatives would not deserve to win the election if unemployment remained at over three million. 'When Tebbit claimed he was misquoted and said Labour were lying, people all around me began to panic. They said I had destroyed Labour's campaign. Then, twenty-four hours later, a tape recording was found in a cupboard with Tebbit saying exactly that on a radio programme to Brian Hayes. If we had bottled out we would have lost our position.' Mandelson was highly critical of the way shadow Cabinet members and party officials failed to hold their nerve during the uproar which followed the 'Jennifer's ear' broadcast. 'Jack Cunningham, Robin Cook and David Hill [then communications director] all panicked. There had been bad staff work to begin with; then you bungle; then you panic; then you retreat. When you are working with politicians you must have nerves of steel.'

I knew from my own experience that Mandelson's assertion that he would always hold firm while others might buckle was no idle boast. Whenever he made a complaint about Labour's affairs being reported inaccurately or unfairly he would stand his ground to the bitter end, never giving an inch. The versatility of his routines for browbeating not only journalists and broadcasters but also their editors and programme controllers was much admired and widely copied. As soon as Tony Blair got his first high-profile job on Labour's front bench as employment spokesman in November 1989, he took full advantage of the advice and guidance being offered by Mandelson. If ever Blair got involved in a disagreement with the news media, he relied on the communications director to sort it out. Blair told me subsequently that it was this ability to penetrate news organisations and get his complaints to stick which explained 'precisely why Peter Mandelson is a star'. Once Blair had become party leader, his reliance on Mandelson was even more noticeable. Joy Johnson, a former BBC political news editor, who observed Blair at close quarters during her brief spell as Labour's communications director, was struck by the close bond between the two men. 'Blair told me that what he so admired about Mandelson was that he had balls of steel when it came to standing up for Labour against the news media.'

Mandelson had spent longer than anyone else in British politics directing a propaganda offensive deployed by an opposition party against the government of the day. Moreover, he had been operating during a period of rapid expansion within the communications industry which had seen the competing demands of a proliferation of news outlets, combined with the discipline imposed by the shortening of news deadlines, increasing the pressure on Labour. The stories which Mandelson propagated so proficiently served a multitude of purposes. The overriding objective was to promote Labour while at the same time damaging the Thatcher and Major governments. Mandelson's flair for news manage- ment was such that he also used the media to help drive forward change within the party. He had no hesitation in making use of his many contacts among political journalists to generate unfavourable coverage for anyone who sought to impede the path of Blair's supporters or was critical of the direction being taken by those who regarded themselves as Labour's modernisers. The pace was unrelenting. News conferences would be held day after day, week after week. Often these occasions were simply no more than an excuse for blatant Tory-bashing. Some, certainly, were staged in order to announce new policies; but often an event would turn out to have nothing more to offer than the unashamed recycling of existing policy positions dressed up as news.

When the 1997 election was only a matter of weeks away, Labour's education and employment spokesman David Blunkett left Millbank Tower one morning muttering under his breath about his punishing schedule. As I walked with him back to the House of Commons, together with his guide dog Lucy and assistant Conor Ryan, Blunkett said he accepted that the unveiling that morning of a new Labour poster, which claimed that the Conservatives would put value added tax on food, was a necessary part of their pre-election warm-up. 'Even so, I only wish I could spend a year doing something positive, like being a minister, rather than going to endless news conferences.' Blunkett was voicing the frustration shared by other members of the shadow Cabinet, some of whom doubted the effectiveness of the constant campaigning which by this stage had been under way for so long. They believed that instead of devoting so much time to publicity stunts the leadership should have consulted far more widely about the policy changes which were being imposed on the party and done more to ensure that the whole of the membership went along with what was being proposed. Blair had no such reservations. As party leader he knew that more often than not it would be his responsibility to take the lead in the 'hand to hand fighting' which would be required if Labour were to succeed in getting their case across to the public and in countering the pro-Conservative bias of much of the press. Not long after being elected, Blair had acknowledged quite openly the limitations of being an opposition party leader. When he awoke each morning his first task was not to consider what he might be able to do that day but rather to think about what he could say in order to promote the interests of the Labour Party. 'As ever in politics, you have to restate a message a thousand times before even a small fraction of people hear it.'

Had Labour not kept up a continuous barrage of publicity stunts, they could easily have been overwhelmed by the might of the government's propaganda machine. A well-timed ministerial announcement can easily wipe out news coverage of a significant policy launch or overshadow a high-profile interview by an opposition leader. Therefore, if Labour were to maintain the strong opinion poll lead which they had established over the Conservatives, they had no alternative but to go on renewing their appeal. Opinion surveys showed that a third of voters remained undecided and would not commit themselves as to which party they would support until much closer to polling day. Although most of the pre-election policy launches and publicity initiatives appeared to wash over the heads of floating voters, no party dared forsake them.

Labour's perpetual offensive was also aimed at fuelling the media's own appetite for a change of government. Because John Major's position had looked so hopeless for so long, and because his party seemed likely to implode at any moment, many political journalists had become impatient for his downfall, almost as though they were intent on seeing what they could do themselves to help engineer the end of eighteen years of Conservative government. Some Tory MPs suspected that most of those who worked for the news media had in fact developed their own unspoken agenda and were effectively rooting for the Prime Minister's defeat, believing that the upheaval which would follow the election of a Blair government, and the ensuing mayhem in the Conservative Party, would make for a far more momentous story than Major's survival.

By and large I thought they were right – though I considered the sentiment was largely apolitical. As journalists we wanted the closest possible election campaign, because that would provide gripping news copy; but there was no doubt in my mind that many broadcasters and newspaper correspondents sensed that the political tide was on the turn and secretly favoured a change of government. I well recall feeling a similar sense of excitement in the final months of the last Labour government. My task then, as labour correspondent for BBC radio, was to report on the industrial disputes which preceded the 1979 general election and which became known as the 'Winter of Discontent'. The disarray in Jim Callaghan's government in the face of sustained trade union pressure, together with Labour's deep-seated internal divisions between left and right and arguments over issues like nuclear disarmament, were just as debilitating as the Conservatives' split on Europe and the constant harrying of John Major's administration by Euro-sceptic Tory MPs in 1996–7. Margaret Thatcher, like Tony Blair, offered the prospect of change and the chance to defeat an unpopular government. Her campaign broke new ground politically, and the enthusiasm which this generated in the news media helped take the Conservatives to victory.

Some correspondents and columnists at Westminster have always been quite open about their party affiliations, especially if they work on newspapers with well-established political connections; as the 1997 election approached, those loyalties resurfaced and, by and large, were self-evident. However, the journalists who produced what might be considered to be slanted news stories were well known and in a minority: in my experience, most of us took pride in being regarded as 'straight' when it came to our political reporting and were careful not to reveal how we might vote ourselves. As far as I was concerned this certainly applied to my colleagues at BBC Westminster and I was surprised when, within two months of polling day, the Conservatives' communications director, Charles Lewington, launched a particularly intemperate attack on the BBC's journalists.

Writing in the *Sunday Telegraph*, Lewington castigated the Corporation for the 'eager anticipation now sweeping through the BBC at the prospect of a Labour government'. He said that for every one BBC journalist with 'common sense', there were three with 'undisguised left-wing prejudices'. It was no surprise that the BBC was 'warming to New Labour' because the director-general, John Birt, had failed to root out the 'comfortable middle-class liberal culture' that coloured the BBC's 'big-picture editorial judgements' and its 'jaundiced view of the world'. Lewington's attack was endorsed by the party chairman, Brian Mawhinney, who said that all too regularly there was an assumption in the BBC's news broadcasts that a Labour victory was 'predetermined'.

Sir Christopher Bland, the Corporation's chairman, rejected allegations of bias. He told the Broadcasting Press Guild that Lewington had failed to substantiate his 'absurd and shallow' attack which had consisted mainly of 'vague views, repeated time and again'. Nevertheless I understood Mawhinney's annoyance: the Conservatives were having great difficulty in sustaining their case for a fifth term in government. There was no doubt that the momentum for change was as infectious within the broadcasting organisations which had studios at No. 4 Millbank as it was across the road inside the offices of newspaper correspondents in the House of Commons press gallery. However, in the BBC's case there existed a vast panoply of controls to ensure that the Corporation honoured the terms of its charter and delivered a news service which maintained a strict balance between the political parties. In my judgement it was not the political inclinations of individual journalists that were influencing the news agenda of the day but the air of crisis surrounding both the government and the Conservative Party, and Labour's ability to exploit the impression that John Major was heading an administration which was falling apart.

Labour's efforts to intensify the public's perception of a loss of confidence in the government were made easier by the utter contempt for Major and his ministers which had developed among newspapers traditionally loyal to the Conservative cause. A network of sympathetic proprietors and editors had done much to sustain the Thatcher governments, but by the mid-1990s this had all but disintegrated. Labour did not bring this about by themselves: a new generation of editors seemed well disposed towards the possibility of a Labour government, and restructuring within the newspaper industry had also contributed to a reduction in the pro-Tory bias of the press. Nevertheless, Blair and his press secretary Alastair Campbell did what they could to encourage the ebbing of support for the Conservatives by mounting their own charm offensive. Campbell was ideally placed to take full advantage of this shift in loyalties.

As a former *Daily Mirror* political editor and a columnist on the now defunct *Today* newspaper when he agreed to give up journalism in the autumn of 1994 in order to become Blair's press secretary, he was well versed in the culture of tabloid journalism, where Labour were so anxious to make inroads. Almost single-handedly, he set about transforming the way a Labour leader was packaged and presented for the popular press. Articles signed by Tony Blair became a regular feature of mass-circulation newspapers like the *Sun* and the *News of the World*. Exclusive stories, articles, interviews and photo-opportunities were tailored to meet the tastes of individual tabloids. Their political editors and correspondents were offered the kind of access which previously would have been frowned on in the party. Blair and Campbell became the regular guests of newspaper proprietors and editors at lunches, dinners and other social occasions. Campbell was equally assiduous in cultivating the broadcasters, playing off one channel or programme against another with offers of exclusive interviews and stories. Blair's tactic of going abroad to make high-profile speeches was exploited to the full. Campbell knew just how to entice political editors and correspondents with the offer of what for London-based journalists would be a much coveted foreign trip. If senior journalists were sent to accompany Blair, newsrooms were more likely to give their reports top billing.

Campbell played on the expectation that Labour would win the election and the consequent anxiety of political journalists to avoid incurring his displeasure. They realised that he would almost certainly become press secretary to the new Prime Minister should Blair get to Downing Street and that he could therefore end up wielding immense power, virtually controlling the government's information service. Implicit in every taunt and rebuke which Campbell dished out to reporters who transgressed his diktats was a clear threat that there would be no favours in the future should he ever be pulling the strings in the No. 10 press office. Journalists do become dependent on their sources of information, and with Labour fostering a feeding-frenzy mentality among the media about their non-stop policy initiatives, most political correspondents were striving to remain within the favoured inner circle, fearful of what might happen if they failed to get the necessary tip-offs or missed out on the coveted personal, one-to-one briefings. Thus Campbell, insisting on a payback for the access or inside information which he offered, frequently found that he was pushing at an open door. In the cut-throat world of political journalism survival depended on being first with the news and, as he knew only too well, it was stories about Labour which were dictating the pace at Westminster. He liked to be forewarned of unexpected news developments affecting Blair and would often try to bully journalists into showing him their stories or scripts or reading them to him over the telephone. If anything was about to be printed or broadcast which was damaging to either Blair or the party, the faster Campbell and his colleagues found out about it, the sooner it could be neutralised.

While Campbell was applying himself to the astute management of the journalistic psyche, at the other end of the technological spectrum Labour were fortifying themselves with impressive new hardware. In contrast to previous campaigns, when they had often seemed defenceless against claims being made by the Conservatives, Labour's spin doctors were able to call on massive back-up resources when preparing for the 1997 election. Rapid rebuttal, developed in the United States, imported by Labour and subsequently matched by the Conservatives, had become the latest weapon in the armoury of the British political propagandist. 'Speed kills' had been the motto of the Clinton Democrats in the 1992 US presidential election, and by deploying the latest computer technology in a dedicated attack unit they had been able to outpace the far better-resourced campaign of President Bush, with devastating results. Alive to the implications of their success, and acknowledging Labour's failure hitherto to challenge the Conservatives' long-established superiority in negative campaigning, within months of becoming party leader in 1994 Tony Blair had set in train the arrangements for commissioning a similar database in Labour's media centre. In October 1995 it was purchased at a cost of £300,000. Once the equipment was installed, countless documents were scanned electronically in the process of transferring filing cabinets full of printed matter to the computer. Now, by using the appropriately named Excalibur software to search on key words, staff were able to home in on critical information, retrieving copies of political speeches, policy statements, statistics or press cuttings, ready for instant counter-attack or for use in research.

John Carr, the management consultant who advised Labour on the purchase and installation of the Excalibur system, said that it was, in essence, a 'fact generator'. In an article for the *New Statesman* he described how it sat at the heart of Labour's rebuttal strategy. 'Defensively, it enables Labour to set the record straight quickly and with confidence. Offensively, as the Americans say, it helps in formulating new initiatives and ensures that they are backed up by comprehensive, up-to-date research.' Carr's job description for Excalibur was spot-on: within a year of its purchase the speed with which Labour could challenge factual or statistical distortions or the misuse of quotations by the Conservatives had been transformed. Prime Minister's questions were regarded by Labour as the first real test of Excalibur's rapid-rebuttal capability. When John Major stood at the despatch box each Tuesday and Thursday he came armed with a folder packed with facts and figures: all the ammunition he would need at his fingertips. This information was collated in No. 10, where the Prime Minister's staff, in drafting the points which Major would make in his answers, were able to draw on the expertise and authority of the entire government machine. As a result, journalists were hardly likely to challenge the accuracy of factual material presented to MPs by the Prime Minister. Labour knew that if they were to stand any chance of making sure that their rebuttal was broadcast or printed alongside his replies to questions, they had only a matter of minutes in which to check out their own sources of information and then supply the news media with chapter and verse of their response.

Question time in the second week of January 1997 provided a perfect illustration of the speed with which Labour could now hit back. On the Tuesday of that week the Deputy Prime Minister, Michael Heseltine, stood in for Major at the despatch box. In reply to a question about the shortage of hospital beds, he said there were now '55,000 more qualified nurses and midwives than there were when the Labour Party was last responsible for the health service'. At 3.59 p.m. precisely, within half an hour of questions finishing at 3.30 p.m., fax machines in the BBC newsroom at Millbank were receiving copies of Labour's rebuttal, headed 'Heseltine caught red-handed'. A statement in the name of Brian Wilson, Labour's campaigns spokesman, quoted alternative figures showing that the number of nurses and midwives (full-time equivalents) had fallen under the Conservatives from 358,447 in 1979 to 353,128 in 1994, which was the latest available figure. Wilson called on Heseltine to issue a retraction and an apology: once again the Tories were 'telling lies to cover up their record of failure'. Two days later Excalibur was back in action after Major told MPs that under the last Labour government 'the price of fuel was rising at a rate of 30 per cent a year'. On this occasion Labour's rebuttal had clearly taken longer to compile because it was not until 4.30 p.m. that a faxed statement, again in Wilson's name, arrived at the BBC. Major was accused of 'peddling more distortions': 'electricity prices fell in 1977 and 1978' and electricity had 'cost more in real terms every year under the Tories than it did when Labour left office in 1979'.

Often the statistics being bandied back and forth were not of central importance to the political story of the day; but by issuing a constant flood of rebuttal statements Labour were forcing journalists to question the credibility of the facts and figures which ministers were giving to the House of Commons. In order to spread the word around the press gallery as quickly as possible that Labour were about to challenge one of Major's answers, the usual routine was for the party's chief media spokesperson, David Hill, to be supplied with a brief outline of the point at issue on his message pager. Hill said he was amazed how quickly political correspondents came to rely on the information being provided by Labour's rebuttal service. 'Usually within about five minutes of the Prime Minister sitting down I'd get a bleep saying that something Major had said was untrue. That enabled me to start alerting the lobby and before we'd even finished our press release, correspondents would be ringing in to Millbank Tower to ask for a copy. Journalists are inherently lazy and our rebuttal unit has made it easier for them. They're also saying our service is faster and more reliable than their own internal news libraries.'

Hill was the first to admit that the effectiveness of any computerised retrieval system depended in the first instance on the questions which were asked of it, and then on the journalistic flair necessary to make the most of what was discovered. Adrian McMenamin, the press officer who headed the rebuttal unit, was said by Hill to have 'marvellous instant recall' across a whole range of political events and personalities. 'Adrian's great strength is that when he reads or hears about something in the news, an odd fact or name can jog his memory. It's as though a light bulb has gone on in his head and Excalibur allows him to check back instantly on what happened or might have been said.' Hill cited two examples from mid-February 1997 to prove his point. The first involved a *Daily Mail* feature in which a woman chief executive, Kay Coleman, claimed that wage costs at her family-owned textile firm in Oldham would double under a Labour government because 'Tony Blair would sign up to the European social chapter'. Mrs Coleman feared she would have to move her garment-making business to Morocco where rates of pay were lower, putting 450 British jobs at risk. McMenamin thought her name sounded familiar and by running it through the computer found that Mrs Coleman had been on the platform at the Conservatives' women's conference two years earlier. The *Daily Mail* had not mentioned Mrs Coleman's political connections; by exposing these to other newspapers, Hill said, Labour had made it difficult for the Conservatives to exploit her story in any future propaganda against Labour's support for the social chapter.

An advance copy of a speech which was about to be made by the Secretary of State for Defence, Michael Portillo, provided another fruitful lead. Tucked away in the text was a reference to the 'people who work hard and play by the rules', the quiet majority who would always have a voice within the Conservative Party. McMenamin thought he had read this before and found that it repeated almost word for word a passage in *The Blair Revolution*, authored jointly by Peter Mandelson and Roger Liddle: New Labour, they had written, appealed to 'ordinary families who work hard and play by the rules'. The speech was embargoed for release at 9.30 p.m., but by 5.49 p.m. a press release was being faxed from Labour's media centre accusing 'jackdaw Portillo' of having 'filched a phrase' from Mandelson's book.

Labour's preoccupation with rebuttal, and the adroitness of those who operated Excalibur, encouraged the party's campaigns spokesman to see if their fact-checking procedures could be brought into play instantaneously during proceedings in the House of Commons. Early in March, on a point of order after Prime Minister's questions, Brian Wilson called on the Speaker, Betty Boothroyd, to investigate the failure of the Conservative MP John Greenway to declare that he was a paid consultant of the Institute of Insurance Brokers. Only seven minutes had elapsed since Greenway had asked John Major a question about the insurance industry. Wilson had been alerted on his pager: standing at the despatch box, he looked down at the small screen and read out the message which had been sent to him by Millbank Tower giving details of Greenway's connections with the insurance industry and failure to declare his interest. Wilson's bravado provoked immediate criticism from the Conservative benches. Ian Bruce urged the Speaker to ban Labour MPs from reading out pager messages sent by Peter Mandelson and the rest of Labour's spin doctors. Greenway joined in the protests, insisting that he had in fact made a full declaration in the Register of Members' Interests. The next day Betty Boothroyd said she 'strongly deprecated' Wilson's conduct. 'For any MP to be prompted in that way by an outside group is totally unacceptable . . . I am not prepared to accept the use of such instruments as an aide memoire by an MP who is addressing the House.' However, the Speaker acknowledged that she could not prevent MPs being sent information on their pagers.

Most Labour MPs sympathised with Wilson, taking the view that sending a message to an opposition spokesman via an electronic pager was analogous to the official support given to the government's frontbench team. Whenever ministers appear at the despatch box, they know they can seek the assistance of civil servants from their department who sit in a box alongside the Speaker, but out of view of the television cameras. Messages are regularly passed along the front bench to help a minister unsure about a point of detail or in need of material to answer a query raised during a debate. And although Wilson's intervention was the first to draw general attention to the use of pagers in the House, he was not the first Labour spokesman to be prompted electronically: it emerged subsequently that during the Budget debate the previous autumn the shadow Chancellor, Gordon Brown, had benefited from a similar 'hotline' between the Commons chamber and Millbank Tower. Shortly after Brown had promised that a Labour government would cut value added tax on domestic fuel, his front-bench colleague, Alistair Darling, was sent a message on his pager by Brown's press officer, Charlie Whelan, who had been told by ITN that the shadow Chancellor's pledge on VAT was not entirely audible and unsuitable for their news bulletins. Once alerted by Darling, who was sitting beside him, Brown was able to use an interruption later in the debate to repeat Labour's commitment, this time with a rather more forceful soundbite.

Labour's purchase of the Excalibur system, a full year ahead of the Conservatives, was part of a more fundamental reappraisal of the way the party deployed its research department. The tradition had always been that Labour's research staff worked on policy initiatives and assisted front-bench spokesmen: they were not seen as being an integral part of press and public relations and were not involved in negative political propaganda. Researchers at Conservative Central Office had always been given a far wider brief and for many years much of their effort had been directed towards collecting and compiling information which could be used by the news department to attack Labour – or the Liberal Democrats or the other, smaller, political parties. Conservative researchers not only looked for damaging contradictions or omissions in Labour's policies but also investigated the personal backgrounds of Labour MPs. At moments of the greatest potential embarrassment for their opponents, the Conservatives supplied news organisations with up-to-date lists of the trade union affiliations of each Labour MP and the names of those who belonged to organisations like the Campaign for Nuclear Disarmament or questionable far-left groups. Material likely to cause most discomfiture to Labour was usually held back by Central Office until the run-up to a general election when it would be published at news conferences or, if it was considered too sensitive for direct attribution, supplied in confidence to friendly journalists who were employed by Tory-inclined newspapers. Although angered over the years by the effectiveness of the Conservatives' research department, the Labour leadership had always appeared reluctant to institutionalise such procedures at their own headquarters.

Tony Blair's election as leader set in motion structural changes within his party which were so far-reaching that Labour in effect leapfrogged over the Conservatives in the art of applying new techniques for organising and delivering an election campaign. This transformation was facilitated by the decision in October 1995 to remove the media, research and campaigning staff from the party's headquarters in Walworth Road, near the Elephant and Castle, and transfer them to new premises at Millbank Tower, much closer to the Houses of Parliament. Crucially, the internal structure was also changed. Now, instead of being in separate offices on different floors, research, media and campaign staff were grouped together in an open-plan office with the heads of each department sitting around a large table in the middle of the room. For the first time Labour's media team had instant access to the party's research capability when generating attacks against the Conservatives. After working at the centre for a year, David Hill told me that his role as chief media spokesperson had turned into something akin to that of the day editor in a newsroom. Working beside him were Adrian McMenamin, who ran the rebuttal unit, backed up by Excalibur and the research department, and Jo Moore, the chief press and broadcasting officer, who organised day-to-day relations with the news media and was supported by a much expanded unit for monitoring television, radio and the press. Hill believed that by bringing together staff from these various departments, and by being the first to invest in the new computer software, Labour had 'stolen a march' on the Conservatives and were effectively a year ahead in deploying the latest attack techniques. 'We purposely laid out our media floor in the same way as a newsroom so that we could respond immediately as a team. My job as editor of the day is to keep a constant check on what's happening so that we can see both where the news coverage might be going well for us and perhaps where we are doing badly.'

At the official opening of the new centre – housed within 15,000 square feet of office space on the first floor of Millbank Tower – in January

1996, journalists were given a glimpse of what the party described as its 'state-of-the-art equipment'. Blair said it provided Labour with the best media and campaign facilities of any party in the country. Fitting out the centre, and operating it until May 1997, would cost the party £2 million; but it was 'tough, professional and it is going to work'. A report next morning in the *Independent*, under the headline 'New Labour, new media, new message?', suggested that with their high-tech resources Labour's spin doctors would be 'slicker than ever'. One footnote to the story was that the opening of the new centre had followed hard on the heels of the departure earlier that week of Joy Johnson, who had resigned after serving for just ten months as Labour's director of communications. Although she was not replaced, many of her responsibilities were taken over by Peter Mandelson, who was chair of the party's general election planning group and who immediately assumed day-to-day control of the media centre.

Access to journalists was already being restricted, but I was given a short guided tour the following month. David Hill pointed across to the rebuttal unit and said they had just downloaded on to the computer the entire five volumes of Sir Richard Scott's report on his arms-to-Iraq investigation. And Excalibur's net was being cast not only deep but wide: among the material being accumulated within the system were vast quantities of cuttings from local newspapers. 'What we have established around the country, with our regional press officers, is a news-gathering team which can hunt through the local press and feed in stories which might be used to attack the Conservatives. Obviously our emphasis will be on positive campaigning, but we've got to go on hitting the government and we think our hit unit far outstrips anything which the Conservatives can put together.'

When Hill showed me round in early 1996 he was expecting about 100 people to be working in the media centre by polling day. In fact, a year later the staff had grown to 150 and, together with volunteers, was planned to reach 250 by the start of the campaign. The rapid expansion in personnel had been accompanied by the introduction of tight security. Visits by journalists were banned. Voluntary workers were required to sign a seven-point undertaking aimed at preventing the unauthorised disclosure of confidential information or the removal from Millbank Tower of 'back-up material, graphics, data, statistics or reports' used in the course of voluntary work. Access to the computer and other systems was reserved for authorised personnel. Any unauthorised access or tampering with the computer or software rendered the offender liable to dismissal and possible prosecution under the 1990 Computer Misuse Act. The confidentiality declaration said unauthorised penetration of the computer system damaged its integrity and confidentiality which were both of high value to the party.

The tight veil of secrecy thrown around Millbank Tower intrigued and excited journalists. In a two-page investigation for the *Observer* in February 1997, Jay Rayner described his unsuccessful efforts to get inside. He quoted David Hill as saying that no reporters would be allowed to rummage through Labour's election plans. Nevertheless, by talking to insiders Rayner pieced together a graphic description of Labour's war room. 'Millbank's employees are rarely out of sight of a large calendar ticking off the days to May 1 or the sharp imperative "enough is enough" . . . It's almost a bit *1984* . . . Televisions are on all the time to enhance the feeling that it's a twenty-four-hour operation.' The *Sunday Telegraph*'s political correspondent, Tom Baldwin, had also tried to probe the workings of the media centre. He concluded that the extra security measures and round-the-clock guard on the entrance indicated that 'Tony Blair's model army is getting nervous'. He described it as the 'most powerful election machine' in British political history. 'Those working at Millbank Tower are bright, Blairite and usually in awe of Mandelson's "tactical genius" . . . There is a spartan feel . . . Despite their youth and energy, there is, apparently, little time or inclination for romance or affairs.'

During my brief visit to the centre I had taken particular note of the bank of television sets which was to be used by the media monitoring unit. Its principal role was to help the publicity staff keep abreast of the day's news coverage by watching and listening to the competing television and radio services. The monitors were also on the lookout for inaccuracies or bias against Labour in news bulletins and current affairs programmes. Reports were prepared during the day summarising the main news stories, listing their positions in the various bulletins, and including a brief synopsis of any political items or interviews. Late each evening, as soon as they received copies of the first editions of next morning's newspapers, the monitoring staff would check through the political coverage. If there were any new or exclusive stories which affected the party or could be exploited by Labour, David Hill or Peter Mandelson was alerted. If a report in one of the first editions was thought to be untrue or damaging to Labour, every effort would be made get it corrected or changed before the main editions were printed. Labour's manipulative techniques were so sophisticated that I knew this much enlarged monitoring unit was bound to have other uses; but initially, one of the most pressing concerns of the media centre was to ensure accuracy and consistency in the promotion of party policy.

The achievement of consistency required no less constant vigilance than the pursuit of accuracy. While the rapid growth in broadcasting has provided politicians with endless opportunities to be interviewed, there are inherent dangers in allowing party spokespersons to make uncontrolled and uncoordinated appearances across a whole range of radio and television programmes. The two greatest challenges facing a political publicity department are, first, to make sure that the interviewees who are representing the party can be relied on to stick to an agreed line, and secondly, to make sure they have been properly briefed in advance. Spin doctors dread senior politicians going 'off message': this kind of foray can undo weeks of patient explanation. Over the years both Labour and the Conservatives have taken great delight in supplying journalists with transcripts of damaging interviews given by their opponents. Most gaffes are delivered inadvertently because the spokesperson either makes a mistake or is unaware of precisely what has happened or was proposed. On days when there are significant political developments, ministers and their shadows can be required to give a dozen or more interviews to rival television channels and radio stations. If it is a particularly fast-moving day, they can easily find they have been overtaken by events and may be in danger of sounding out of touch. To minimise such risks, every attempt is made to ensure that interview requests are dealt with in a coordinated way. Sometimes only one politician is made available to the broadcasting organisations, as it is easier to keep a single individual fully posted on the latest developments.

Labour in 1997 were clearly intent on stepping up the scale and scope of their monitoring. Hill had told me two months before the start of the campaign that there was a staff of six working in shifts between 6 a.m. and 2 a.m. Another three people worked on transcribing news reports and interviews. I knew from my researches that this represented a significant expansion: in the 1983 general election Labour had had three party workers monitoring and transcribing radio and television broadcasts. The fruits of these labours were soon on display: stacks of transcripts began appearing alongside the heaps of press releases from government departments and political parties which were laid out every day on the press gallery table. Usually the interviews which had been transcribed were those given by Conservative ministers or MPs, the texts of which revealed the full extent of the disagreements within the Tory party about the prospects for a single European currency or differences over other aspects of government policy. The transcripts were printed on plain paper, without a Labour heading or logo, but the choice of interviews, and the uniformity of the layout, stamped their source unmistakably on them. David Hill believed speed was of the essence. 'Within an hour we can supply transcripts of all the big interviews on *The World at One*. These can be faxed immediately to party spokespeople, or if they prefer to hear what has been said we can replay tape recordings down the telephone. No frontbencher need ever go into a studio without knowing exactly what's been said already.' Hill found that political correspondents were avid consumers of the transcription service. 'The golden rule in supplying the news media is that you must never try to doctor a transcript in your favour. If something is left out the journalists won't trust you again.'

The constant monitoring of radio and television services also enabled staff in Millbank Tower to keep a close eye on the activities of MPs, candidates and party members who were critical of official Labour policy. When MPs on the left heard of the heightened surveillance they told me they feared it would allow the leadership to tighten up on dissent. Several of those who were in the habit of writing newspaper or magazine articles which questioned Labour policy had already been reminded in no uncertain terms that they should be careful to avoid undermining party unity in the run-up to the election. A debate early in the New Year over possible reforms to the annual conference threw up one small illustration of the way the monitoring unit could be used to enforce a consistent party line. Andrew MacKinlay, Labour MP for Thurrock, told me he had been asked by the BBC if he knew the names of any regular conference delegates who might have an opinion on the proposed restructuring. He suggested Nigel Smith, Labour candidate in the safe Conservative seat of Rochford and Southend East, who was leader of the Labour group on Southend Borough Council. MacKinlay said that after Smith voiced his concern about the party's organisational changes in an interview on *The World at One*, his wife Angela Smith, candidate in Basildon, one of Labour's key target seats, received a call from party headquarters pointing out that she would be 'well advised' to have a word with her husband because his remarks on Radio 4 appeared to have been 'out of line with party policy'. The Smiths' encounter with the monitoring unit showed the subtlety of Millbank Tower: the approach was made to Mrs Smith because she was the party's candidate in a highly winnable marginal constituency, and therefore more susceptible to pressure from the centre than her husband, who was contesting a seat which Labour believed they had no prospect of winning.

My own first brush with Labour's media monitors culminated in a top-level complaint to the BBC. At issue was my coverage of Labour's local government conference at Nottingham in February 1997. My reports that day for BBC television opened with pictures of a large demonstration outside the conference centre by members of the local government union, Unison, who were protesting about the announcement earlier in the week by the shadow Chancellor, Gordon Brown, that Labour intended to stick to the present government's spending targets for local authorities. The demonstrators claimed this would lead to more redundancies and a continued pay freeze for council workers. Banners were on display from the main Unison branches in the city and county councils of the East Midlands. Unison was the biggest union in the country and one of Labour's largest affiliates, and I considered the demonstration was newsworthy: local authority workers were one of the few groups who were still strongly unionised and, in view of the depth of the spending cuts, there seemed every likelihood they could be a source of continuing dissent.

As we filmed and interviewed the Unison members who were holding the banners, I was conscious of the concern this was causing to the full-time union officials who formed part of the Unison delegation to the conference. Among the demonstrators were members of the Socialist Workers' Party, who were also carrying placards protesting at the cuts. John Freeman, head of Unison in the East Midlands, agreed to be interviewed. He said the banners had been hijacked by the far left and were being abused by a small group of the union's members. When I suggested to him that if this were the case he would naturally be seeking to retrieve Unison's banners, Freeman returned to the conference centre without making any further comment.

I knew before we began filming that the planned demonstration had already caused anxiety at the highest levels of the party. At breakfast that morning in the conference hotel, Labour's general secretary, Tom Sawyer, told David Hill, who was in charge of facilities for the media, that he suspected there would be a demonstration outside the conference centre and that he feared similar protests would probably be staged in other towns which Blair might visit in the period leading up to polling day.

Sawyer, who had previously worked for NUPE, one of the unions which had merged to form Unison, believed there was little the Unison general secretary, Rodney Bickerstaffe, could do to prevent such protests. Hill's response was that if any demonstrations took place, his staff would inform the news media that they were totally unrepresentative and had nothing to do with the party.

Immediately after the transmission of my first report that lunchtime, Hill told me that he had heard from the monitoring unit at Millbank Tower about my use of the Unison pictures. While he would personally have preferred it if the BBC had not used film of the demonstration, he said, he hoped I would make it abundantly clear in any further news bulletins that Tony Blair would not take 'a blind bit of notice' of the demonstrations. I used Hill's precise words in my subsequent reports.

Word of the party's anger at the way the banners had been paraded outside the conference had been picked up by some of the demonstrators. As we prepared my teatime report a group of Unison members from Leicestershire, headed by the branch secretary Vicky Easton and her colleague Fiona Westwood, arrived at our television edit van, insisting they were genuine trade unionists and not sellers of the *Socialist Worker* newspaper, as suggested by the Labour Party. They had been sent by their branch to picket the conference in order to protest at the likelihood of up to 800 redundancies in Leicestershire. I had already done my own research into the legitimacy of the protesters by speaking personally to about twenty of them; so had my producer, Julian Joyce, and the BBC's local government correspondent in the East Midlands. Most of those holding union banners were middle-aged trade unionists, unlike the SWP newspaper sellers who were mainly in their late teens or early twenties.

After filing our final report for the main television news that Saturday evening, we were paged on the train back to London and informed that Tim Allan, a press officer in Tony Blair's office, had telephoned the BBC to demand that the Unison pictures should not be used. The bulletin editor refused to accede to his request and my report was broadcast as originally compiled. The following Monday Alastair Campbell made an official complaint to Tony Hall, head of BBC news and current affairs, to protest at the way I had, in his view, misrepresented the importance of the demonstration. Campbell stated that I had focused my report 'on a group of about twenty demonstrators', many of whom were carrying placards from the SWP. They were not representative of Labour; they had no mandate inside the party; and 'Rodney Bickerstaffe from Unison, the union whose banners stood behind them, said that he entirely disassociated the union from them'. Campbell was concerned that the Prime Minister's 'rallying speeches' were being treated by BBC television news quite differently from Blair's, both in the prominence accorded to them and in style of coverage. He considered that my failure to give a 'thorough exposition of Blair's speech', and the placing of my report as sixth item in the late evening news, underlined the different treatments applied to the speeches of Blair and Major.

I was informed subsequently by the BBC's management that after the complaint had been investigated a reply was sent to Campbell stating in 'vigorous' terms that the Corporation stood by its report. Meanwhile, Campbell had singled me out in person to inform me of his dissatisfaction with my coverage of the conference, announcing to the assembled company in the Commons press gallery, where I was standing with a group of political correspondents, that a letter of protest was on its way. This attempt to admonish me in the hearing of other journalists was backed up by an equally forthright reprimand from Charlie Whelan, press officer to Gordon Brown. I was also rebuked by Alistair Darling, the shadow Chief Secretary to the Treasury, who stopped me in the lobby to protest at the way I had allowed myself to be 'duped by the Trots'. When I explained that I had checked with the demonstrators myself to make sure they were Unison members, Darling said SWP supporters in Edinburgh regularly made up their own Unison banners. This accusation was not one that I had heard before. In my experience, most SWP supporters and sellers of *Socialist Worker* preferred to parade under their own placards. In fact, I thought Darling was being rather disingenuous in parroting Campbell's line, in view of his own experience as a councillor (he had been chairman of Lothian Regional Council's transport committee before becoming MP for Edinburgh Central). My prediction that there were likely to be further protests over local authority expenditure cuts was amply justified the following month when Labour-controlled local authorities in Glasgow and Edinburgh faced a series of strikes and demonstrations by teachers and council workers. At the head of their marches and protests banners from the local Unison branches could be seen quite clearly.

My reporting of the Nottingham demonstration had obviously provoked considerable discussion among staff at Labour's media centre, because it emerged later that some of those close to Blair believed that he might in fact have benefited from the BBC's coverage of the event. This insight into the leadership's thinking was revealed by Derek Draper, a former assistant to Peter Mandelson who had become director of Progress, Labour's newly established political education trust. We were both asked to join a discussion on the role of spin doctors hosted by the political society of King's College London. In my opening remarks I had complimented Labour's propagandists on their efficiency in removing from Blair's media image any association with the trade unions. Labour were determined at all costs to avoid reviving public memories of the party's 1979 general election defeat and their impotence at the time in the face of damaging industrial disputes. As a consequence of this strategy, I said, while Blair might be filmed playing football with schoolchildren, photographed strumming his guitar or even on one occasion pictured with a teddy bear, there was very little likelihood of his being seen before polling day fraternising publicly with union leaders. On being questioned about this by one of the students, I explained that New Labour's media strategists went to great lengths to eliminate reminders of the link between the party and the unions, as witnessed by their attempt to get the Unison pictures removed from my Nottingham report. Draper, who had attended the local government conference, first gave the leadership's account of what had happened. The reason why the party had been 'at war' with me was because it did not want the BBC broadcasting a 'dishonest image of trade unionists and sellers of *Socialist Worker* ganging up on Tony Blair'. The effect of such coverage was to suggest that Blair did not look like a Prime Minister: that explained why the task of the media centre was to keep those images off the screen, especially as the protesters were not connected to Labour. Draper then revealed that there had been a counter-argument. Apparently some of the party's publicity advisers had wondered whether it might have assisted Labour if viewers had seen that 'Blair is unpopular with trade unionists, because that is something New Labour would like to see'. But clearly the association of images in my report had been considered too dangerous to be allowed to pass unchallenged.

Labour's decision to make an official complaint to the BBC had come as no surprise to me. The view which prevailed consistently in Blair's office during the long build-up to the general election was that every effort should be made to avoid generating news coverage which linked New Labour to the trade unions; if stories emerged which were potentially damaging, the agreed tactic was to play down their significance. Another factor which may perhaps have fuelled Campbell's annoyance was that my coverage of the often tempestuous relationship between Labour and the unions had been criticised frequently by party officials in previous years.

As a labour correspondent I had reported on most of the big industrial disputes of the Thatcher years, and had always taken a close interest in the link between the union movement and the Labour Party. My switch to political reporting coincided with Blair's appointment as employment spokesman by Neil Kinnock in 1989 and the start of a fresh attempt by the leadership to reshape Labour's policies on employment and trade union law. Blair worked closely with Peter Mandelson, then the party's communications director, and, step by step, Labour began the painful task of accepting and then adopting the legal restraints on strike action which had been introduced by the Conservatives. The path the Labour leadership had taken led, not surprisingly, to conflict, and the fractious twists and turns of the ensuing years, as the unions were forced to retreat, provided plenty of stories. In terms of news management, Kinnock and Blair were keen to portray the party as being tough on the unions and freed from any danger of union leaders dictating policy. My own background knowledge of the union movement inevitably meant I was on occasion more circumspect than some of my fellow political correspondents when Blair and Mandelson outlined changes or developments in Labour's policies on industrial relations, as I could see the potential for friction. This must have annoyed Mandelson, because on one occasion he challenged me about my attitude. He said that most correspondents who had switched from industrial reporting to politics ended up 'hating the trade unions', and wanted to know why I appeared to be an exception to the rule: 'You still have time for the unions . . . that causes me trouble.'

Occasionally I was praised by Labour's spin doctors for the way I reported the firm stand Blair took as party leader against those strikes which he thought were inappropriate. After days of repeated disruption on the London Underground in the summer of 1996, over a dispute about working practices, I suggested on BBC television that this was probably the kind of disagreement Blair believed should have gone straight to conciliation or arbitration rather than precipitating a withdrawal of labour. Campbell complimented me on my 'robust' assessment. But, by and large, I found my interest in trade union affairs was considered something of a nuisance.

Campbell's aversion to news reports which associated Blair with the unions provided an opportunity for light-hearted retaliation, especially at the annual conference of the Trades Union Congress. By long-standing tradition, the Labour leader has paid a fraternal visit and has usually been the principal guest at the conference dinner. At each of the three conferences Blair visited as leader, he was escorted into the dining room by the TUC general secretary, John Monks. Photographers and television crews were instructed to wait at the entrance to get their pictures because, we were always told, there would be no other photo–opportunities. We would then ask Campbell, with a feigned display of innocence, if we could possibly film inside the dinner so that we could show Blair chatting away to the various union presidents and general secretaries. Our request always produced a pained expression on Campbell's face and on one occasion a curt riposte to the effect that there was 'no way' we would be allowed to take pictures of Blair with all those 'cigar-munching union fat cats'.

Much as Campbell appeared to loathe having to mix it with union leaders, the TUC's 1995 annual get-together provided him with a rude awakening to the reality of political infighting after the summer break and a useful trial run for the traumatic events which he knew were bound to occur at Labour's annual conference the following month. Blair had taken the entire labour and trade union movement by surprise with his announcement at the 1994 Labour conference of his wish to rewrite Clause Four of the party's constitution and thus abandon Labour's historic commitment to the 'common ownership of the means of production, distribution and exchange'. In the weeks leading up to the 1995 conference season there was renewed speculation about the leadership's intentions towards the unions because of pressure on the party to set the rate for the proposed national minimum wage at £4.15 an hour. In an interview for the *Observer* on the eve of the TUC conference, Blair said that nobody seriously believed that Labour were still the political arm of the unions. Although he was a politician and not a psychiatrist, if anyone seriously believed he would take the party back to the position it was in a decade earlier, then they 'require not leadership but therapy'.

Blair's warning angered MPs on the left, one of whom, Jeremy Corbyn, said in an interview for BBC television that he regarded the language which had been used as 'quite horrible'. The suggestion that campaigners for a minimum wage needed to see a psychiatrist was 'quite wrong and unpleasant'. My report for that Sunday's teatime news bulletin produced an irate call from Campbell. He agreed that Blair's remark about people needing 'therapy' was not the wisest thing to have said, but the party had no intention of making any further comment and he considered the BBC had no right to 'dress up' Corbyn's response as a news item.

'Corbyn could be filmed making that kind of complaint about Tony any day of the week and you're allowing him to promote the vested interests of the Socialist Campaign Group.' Gordon Brown's press officer, Charlie Whelan, who was already in Brighton for the TUC conference, told me subsequently that he had alerted Campbell to my report the minute he had seen it and had urged him to complain to the BBC immediately. 'Alastair didn't watch the news bulletin himself, or know of your report about Corbyn, but I told him he had to get it off the television straight away.' Whelan revealed that Campbell had informed him the previous Friday about what he had then described as Blair's 'slip of the tongue' over some on the left needing 'therapy'. Clearly the party leadership had been well aware that Blair's comment might cause offence, and they had also taken the precaution of thinking through ways of limiting any news coverage should the *Observer*'s interview be followed up by other journalists. Whelan's account of what had gone on behind the scenes seemed to me to vindicate the BBC's judgement that Blair's remark, and the reaction to it, merited a news report.

The complaint about my use of Corbyn's response was one of several telephone conversations I had with Campbell that weekend. He was at home writing Blair's speech for the TUC conference while at the same time trying to see something of his young family, and I sensed that he was preoccupied and irritated by constant interruptions. When I made my first call, early on the Saturday afternoon, he asked me out of the blue if I had any idea how many times he'd been rung up so far that day. When I suggested he had probably taken around twenty calls, he said that was not a bad guess: mine was his twenty-third that Saturday. There had apparently been a moan in Blair's office about the number of weekend telephone calls his staff were receiving and Campbell, who believed his line was the busiest of all, was adding them up. I had been conscious for some time of the disturbance which journalists' calls must be causing to the Campbell household. While being briefed by him at eight o'clock one weekday evening, on a speech Blair was giving next day about the plight of lone mothers, Campbell kept interrupting to say 'just wait a minute' to his daughter, whom I could hear sobbing away at his elbow, trying to attract her father's attention. Campbell did not ask for sympathy, just for some understanding of the pressure he faced. 'You journalists have no idea about the number of calls we get involving the news media. You should spend the day in our office and then you'd see the rate at which we have to take decisions affecting the news stories of the day.'

Campbell's dedication to the party, and his readiness to shoulder the burden of round-the-clock contact with the media on Blair's behalf, had been brought home to me shortly after the 1994 leadership election. Within a few weeks of taking over, Blair launched a new policy document on education which proposed changes to the A-level examination system. To his evident annoyance, early morning news reports on Radio 4 had trailed the announcement by suggesting that Labour intended to 'abolish' A levels. The radio newsroom was somewhat taken aback when Blair rang in himself after the 6 a.m. news summary seeking to correct the BBC's report. He said the aim was to broaden the 'over-specialised and rather narrow' A-level system, not abolish it. As far as I knew this was one of only a very few times – perhaps the only occasion – when the new Labour leader had felt it necessary to intervene personally in that way. A few weeks later, Campbell was appointed press officer. From the outset he made it his business to ensure that Blair was never again put into the position of having to argue about a story or negotiate directly with the news media. Campbell said it was his job to complain to journalists. 'If Tony thinks an interviewer has stitched him up or a reporter has broken an undertaking then he'll cut them dead, but I'll be the one who makes the complaint. It's important Tony doesn't get involved himself.'

Campbell told me he had learned a lot from observing the ease with which journalists had been able to poke fun at John Major during his early years as Prime Minister. On the return flight from trips abroad Major appeared to enjoy chatting away to the political correspondents who accompanied him in his RAF VC10. Gus O'Donnell, the Prime Minister's first press secretary, encouraged such fraternisation. On one occasion, after a trip to Washington, as the Prime Minister walked down the plane, O'Donnell warned Campbell, who was then the *Daily Mirror*'s political editor, that he had better keep quiet as Major was annoyed with him. 'Of course, I did the opposite,' said Campbell. 'I immediately shouted across the plane, "What's wrong, John?" He'd apparently taken offence at what I'd written in the *Daily Mirror*, because buried away in my story was a line about people in Washington not knowing who he was. He'd done a CNN television interview and the woman anchor got his name wrong, referring to him as John Majors. I was amazed he'd bothered to pick me up on it.' Campbell said he told O'Donnell afterwards how surprised he was to be have been tipped off that Major was so cross. 'Effectively it was a case of a press secretary alerting a journalist about how best to needle a Prime Minister. I don't think I shall be doing the same for

Tony.' Campbell enhanced his own reputation for mischief-making by blurting out on another VC10 flight that he had just seen Major's shirt tucked into his underpants, an image subsequently immortalised in Steve Bell's innumerable cartoons in the *Guardian*. In view of his own notoriety as a troublemaker, Campbell's constant harrying of reporters sometimes wore a little thin.

Although Blair's relationship with the unions hit the headlines again during the 1996 TUC conference, there was no question on this occasion of the news media being criticised. In fact the opposite seemed to be the case, with Labour's spin doctors doing all they could to encourage journalists to speculate as much as they liked about the possibility of Labour introducing new legislative curbs on industrial action and perhaps eventually going as far as breaking the formal link between the party and the unions. Plans carefully laid by the TUC to present its annual gathering in Blackpool as a showcase for what John Monks described as an 'era of new unionism' came to nothing, as the conference degenerated into a week of unalloyed union-bashing by Labour's modernisers. David Blunkett, the education and employment spokesman, opened up New Labour's assault on the TUC by using an article in the London *Evening Standard* to outline plans for 'binding arbitration' in public sector disputes. Strike action by postal workers had caused disruption throughout the summer and, together with other stoppages on London Underground and the railways, had brought the number of days lost through industrial action to its highest level for six years. Labour were proposing to start consultations on ideas for ensuring that workers were given an opportunity to hold a fresh secret ballot if an employer had made a substantial new offer. Initially Blunkett denied that his proposals would require further legislation, but union leaders believed this was effectively what Labour were signalling and later he conceded it would be 'very foolish' to rule it out. When Blair arrived in Blackpool for the conference dinner, he pointedly kept Labour's options open, while insisting that no one was talking yet about 'rushing into legislation'. In a rare public rebuke to a Labour leader, the TUC let it be known that the general secretary had complained to Blair before the dinner about the confusion created at the conference. Monks doubted whether tougher legislation would be required. He was clearly disturbed at the thought that a Labour government might enact what would in effect become the ninth round of employment law since the first Thatcher government began introducing curbs on union power.

That same evening, Blunkett, who by then had joined Blair in Blackpool, addressed a fringe meeting in the Renaissance Room at the Winter Gardens. He insisted that Labour were not proposing to attack the unions and said he had no idea why journalists were suggesting that a Labour government might impose 'compulsory arbitration and the withdrawal of the right to strike'. Blunkett could not imagine who it was who was 'spinning away', but he would offer a bottle of champagne to any reporter who could 'finger a spin doctor or politician who has committed Labour to compulsory arbitration'. Immediately after Blunkett's speech I was called across by the Labour MP Stephen Byers, another member of the party's employment team, who had been standing nearby. Taking me to one side, out of sight behind a curtain partitioning the room, he told me that while Blunkett's proposal at the moment was to hold consultations, if those discussions suggested that new legislation was necessary then Labour were not ruling that out. Later that evening Alastair Campbell briefed journalists. He said there was a clear difference of opinion between Blair and the TUC. Monks believed it was possible to say 'here and now' that there were no circumstances in which further legislation would be required; Blair was saying that the party 'could not possibly prejudge future circumstances'. When Blair was interviewed for BBC television next morning he appeared quite relaxed about his confrontation with the unions, but adopted an aggressive stance when defending Labour's search for better ways to resolve public sector disputes. 'If some people don't like that, I'm sorry. But that is the way it is going to be. We are not at war with the TUC. We disagree. But we will govern for the whole country.'

Within hours of Blair's departure from Blackpool later that morning, New Labour commenced the second act of what was beginning to look like a calculated attempt to upstage the TUC conference. Monks had no idea what was in store when he stopped to chat about the events of the previous twenty-four hours. He seemed to have been deeply offended by the way Blunkett had launched Labour's proposals without any warning or consultation in the middle of his conference. 'The first I knew about it was when we got a scrappy, faxed copy of Blunkett's article in the *Evening Standard*. Labour tried to cap the story that lunchtime and avert a row but it didn't work. I think Labour were trying to have a crack at the TUC, but they bungled it.' Monks' injured feelings were evidently of little concern to Stephen Byers, who had stayed on in Blackpool and was entertained that evening at the Seafood Restaurant by the political correspondents of four national newspapers. Their account of the conversation across the dinner table produced a spectacular finale to the week. The four journalists waited until the following day to file their stories, and did not name Byers as the source, but they all quoted a party insider speculating about the circumstances in which Blair would sever Labour's link with the unions. 'The End?' was the *Daily Mirror*'s headline above a report by the paper's political editor John Williams, who said the 'divorce scenario' was being actively canvassed by senior party figures. Roland Watson, chief political correspondent on the *Daily Express*, was equally categoric: 'Authoritative sources told the *Express* that a possible timetable for the parting of the ways is already being pieced together . . . it would involve a snap ballot of Labour members.' According to Jill Sherman of *The Times*, Blair would call for a ballot to break the link if the unions provoked 'a wave of strikes' during the first few months of a Labour government. Mounting concern within the party leadership about the 'summer of discontent' which had already engulfed the unions was cited by the *Daily Telegraph*'s John Hibbs as the reason why Blair was preparing contingency plans 'to cut New Labour free from its historical roots'.

Reporters who had not been privy to Byers' Wednesday evening engagement got wind of the story early the following evening. When challenged about the authenticity of what were still only garbled reports of Labour's intention to cut the link, Tim Allan, one of Blair's press officers, was unexpectedly forthcoming. Although he insisted the story had 'no foundation at all', because Blair had made 'no such proposal', he then volunteered a further statement on Byers' behalf, in which the party's employment spokesman acknowledged that he had spoken to the four correspondents but considered that he had said 'nothing to justify the ludicrous interpretation placed on the conversation'. In issuing the statement, Allan had blown Byers' cover. The four journalists had protected his identity in their stories, as they regarded the conversation as having been on lobby terms. By publicly identifying the source, Allan had given the story a whole new dimension: Byers was well known as a Labour moderniser and he ended up spending the next twenty-four hours being questioned on radio and television about the circumstances in which Labour might break the link with the unions. As the day progressed, trade union fears about what their leaders suspected was Blair's hidden agenda were amply justified. Instead of retreating, New Labour turned the story to the modernisers' advantage. In interview after interview Byers repeated the line that while there were 'no plans at the moment to dump the unions or have a ballot of individual members', the country would see a developing relationship between the party and the unions and that would be healthy for democracy. The week closed with Monks delivering yet another rebuke to Blair, this time from the conference platform. He said they had seen 'confusion, not clarity' in Blackpool, when millions in the country were desperate for a change of government and looking for a 'surer touch' from Labour.

Most union leaders seemed resigned to their fate. They realised that the TUC had to take second place if Labour were intent on playing an anti-union card in order to present themselves as tough in the newspapers and stave off attacks from the Conservatives, who were doing all they could to suggest that Blair would in the end have to succumb to union power. Consequently, despite the provocation offered at its conference, the TUC leadership did nothing to jeopardise months of behind-the-scenes negotiations over Labour's much discussed proposals for a national minimum wage and a 'positive framework of basic rights' for people at work. For many trade unionists the line in the sand for their future relationship with a Labour government would be the need for Blair to honour the party's pledge on union recognition. Labour had promised that where 'a majority of the relevant workforce' voted to be represented by a trade union, there should be a 'legal obligation on employers' to recognise that union. Without a change in the law and the restoration of negotiating rights on pay and conditions, the TUC feared there would be little chance of halting the steep decline in union membership.

In fact, far from the 1996 conference bequeathing a legacy of bitterness, it provided the spur for the publication the following February of a new, pre-election policy document, *Partners for Progress*, setting out ways in which the TUC hoped to minimise industrial disputes. In what the *Financial Times* described as a 'de facto manifesto', the TUC said it intended to create a partnership with industry and would seek 'far greater involvement of third parties in conciliation and arbitration' so as to avoid strikes. Monks acknowledged that two of the three previous Labour governments had encountered conflict with the unions. The TUC was looking for an arm's length relationship with Labour, and he hoped the unions could be 'part of the solution' to the problems which the country had to solve.

Blair entered the final straight of the election campaign in a far stronger position than any of his predecessors. No previous Labour leader had travelled so far and so fast along the arduous road of updating and reshaping the relationship between the party and the unions. Labour's modernisers reigned supreme: the union movement's compliance was not challenged publicly even by those presidents and general secretaries who in previous years had demanded the repeal of the Conservatives' employment laws. The contrast with the dissension in Tory ranks could not have been greater: for, whatever the doubts of left-wing trade unionists, they were at least keeping their opinions to themselves and avoiding publicity like the plague. The bitter divisions of the early 1980s over nationalisation and unilateral nuclear disarmament had become a distant memory; now it was Labour's turn to observe the damage which could be caused when a political party was wracked by dissension. The guerrilla war being waged against John Major by Conservative Euro-sceptics loomed as a constant reminder of the need for self-discipline and the importance of unity.

2

Manning the Barricades

John Major's decision to delay polling day until 1 May was born out of necessity. Only by hanging on, in the hope that voters might feel the benefits of an economic upturn, did the Conservatives think they stood a chance of rebuilding their popularity and eroding Labour's commanding lead in the opinion polls. Party strategists accepted that there were inherent tactical disadvantages in soldiering on for the full five years of the parliament: Major and his ministers would have no alternative but to brazen out any unexpected misfortunes, while trying, at the same time, to find ways to quell the Euro-sceptics' revolt over possible membership of a single European currency as well as repel the sustained pounding they were getting from Labour. Once the general election was called, the intention was to centre the Conservatives' campaign on the Prime Minister: Major was seen as the party's greatest asset. But this strategy implicitly recognised that the government was woefully short of new talent. All too often, Major's Cabinet colleagues had looked tired and dispirited. On the defensive ever since Britain's ignominious departure from the European exchange rate mechanism in 1992, they had seemed incapable of rejuvenating their appeal.

Major's decision to play it long not only perpetuated but deepened the antagonism within his party over the government's wait-and-see stance on the whole question of European monetary union. A painful dilemma for the party was that the Conservatives' two most accomplished media performers, the Deputy Prime Minister Michael Heseltine and the Chancellor of the Exchequer Kenneth Clarke, were both regarded by many Tory MPs as being far too divisive because of the way they pointedly paraded their pro-European beliefs. Nevertheless, when it came to defending the government's economic record or fighting off the latest onslaught from Labour, it was Heseltine and Clarke who were required to shoulder much of the burden; acting like lightning conductors, they helped deflect criticism from the Prime Minister. Their high-profile radio and television appearances became a regular fixture on the weekend political programmes. As the government continued to flounder amid a welter of ministerial gaffes, administrative mishaps and backbench rebellions, there was no option but to go on fielding these two authoritative voices, although all too often their attempts to quash dissent or calm the latest media frenzy were in vain.

Heseltine and Clarke were, without doubt, reliable, sure-footed performers. They were popular figures in the party and their long years of service as government ministers commanded respect. Interviewers rarely got the better of them. Even so, as the pre-election skirmishing dragged on and on, they were dreadfully over-used. The greater their familiarity with viewers and listeners became, the more threadbare their arguments justifying a fifth term in government for the Conservatives appeared. Being put continuously on the defensive is a considerable handicap for a politician. Opposition spokespersons can deflect critical questioning with comparative ease by simply using their next answer to open up a new line of attack on the government; but if an interviewer is determined, come what may, to pin responsibility directly on to a minister then the pressure can be relentless. Criticising the validity of the questions is a favourite tactic and can provide a useful diversion, but attacks on the integrity of programme presenters or reporters rarely go down well with the audience, and it can take real skill to escape unscathed. Sheer bravado was the trick deployed most frequently by Heseltine and Clarke. They would bluster and prevaricate or simply laugh off aggressive criticism; often, they would often poke fun at presenters for asking fanciful questions. By and large, they got away with it. Even if the interview ended up becoming an argument which went round and round in circles they just ploughed on, happy to go the distance.

Heseltine's nonchalance in the face of calamity became a sight to behold. One of his greatest fans was Charles Lewington, who after being appointed the Conservatives' communications director in December 1995 came to rely on the Deputy Prime Minister's ability to hold the line when all else seemed lost. Lewington gave every impression of dreading weekend duty, which all too frequently turned into a Tory spin doctor's nightmare. The combined efforts of the Sunday newspapers and the weekend political programmes usually succeeded in setting off several political bush fires, and Lewington told me he was always mightily relieved when he was able to wheel out Heseltine to douse the latest conflagration. 'He's such a smart operator. There's no one like him for being able to avoid elephant traps and turn it all round into an attack, either on Labour or the BBC. I can't tell you how pleased I am when he pops up wearing his cardigan on one of those Sunday television programmes. It's the only way to calm things down.'

Buffeted by a continuous fusillade of damaging headlines, the Conservatives seemed to have no alternative but to respond on a day-to-day footing, in spite of the political damage which endless firefighting could inflict on the party's image and reputation. While yet another knockabout performance by the Deputy Prime Minister might provide some temporary relief in terms of steadying the Conservatives' shattered nerves, the sight of a minister arguing the toss with seasoned broadcasters hardly inspired confidence in the electorate, nor could it be described as sensible crisis management for a government in dire need of an effective communications strategy. Nevertheless, far from rethinking his own approach, Heseltine gave every appearance of enjoying his Sunday jousts with television presenters. He clearly relished the chance to engage in a little point-scoring, whether it was with Sir David Frost on *Breakfast with Frost*, *On the Record*'s John Humphrys, ITV's Jonathan Dimbleby or Adam Boulton on Sky's Sunday programme. Heseltine realised that the presenters and their production teams were every bit as desperate as the government to get a favourable mention for themselves in Monday's newspapers; but he was equally well aware that the broadcasters could only achieve publicity for their programmes at his expense, either by extracting an unexpected answer or perhaps by tripping him up with an awkward question. As each programme tried it on, the Deputy Prime Minister could be seen revelling in the chase, teasing the presenters about their preoccupation with ministerial gaffes. Sometimes when an interviewer seemed on the point of enticing him into giving a newsworthy quote, Heseltine would put on a magisterial air and explain precisely why the answer he had just delivered was neither new nor contradictory and why it did not merit a press release from the programme's publicity department. To the uninitiated it must all have seemed rather like a political panel game: the in-jokes and interminable arguments over nuances were pretty impenetrable for most journalists, let alone the casual viewer.

To his great credit, Heseltine frequently managed to barge his way through what must have seemed like a web of interlocking questions to unleash a broadside against Labour. Whenever he thought that at last he had been allowed to let rip, only to be interrupted yet again, his indignation could make for compulsive viewing. John Humphrys triggered a memorable encounter during *On the Record* in December 1996, at the height of the conflict among Cabinet ministers over Major's declaration that the chances of Britain being in the first wave of countries to join the single currency had become 'very remote'. Heseltine, fulminating at his inability to complete a sentence, could take no more of Humphrys' interruptions: 'Do you want to keep jammering on or are you going to let me answer the question? . . . It is John Major who has given the lead . . . Tony Blair is like a gambolling poodle, lolloping along, saying "Me too" . . . You say Tony Blair has stolen John Major's clothes . . . This is a man who can never be relied on to stand firm on anything. He trembles and is then out there with a soundbite.' As Humphrys changed tack, and encouraged the Deputy Prime Minister to explain the reasons why Britain might benefit from joining a single currency, Heseltine immediately smelled a rat. He said he knew exactly what Humphrys was up to the moment he changed direction: 'I said to myself: "He's trying to get me to discuss the benefits of a single currency, so that once I have talked about the potential advantages he can then say this is a split." So here you are, John, suggesting that there is a stale, arid debate all about divisions. You are trying to take me to a position where you can trap me into a Tory party row.'

Heseltine expounded at greater length on the need for Cabinet ministers to be alert to the dangers of making gaffes when questioned on a Radio 5 Live phone-in some weeks later. He was asked about yet another Cabinet 'split' on monetary union. The Foreign Secretary, Malcolm Rifkind, interviewed on *Today* that morning by John Humphrys, appeared to have redefined the government's position by declaring that 'on balance, we are hostile to a single currency'. Heseltine blamed the confusion on Humphrys' line of questioning. He said Cabinet ministers had to be on their guard because of the way they were always being subjected to intense interrogation by interviewers. 'Don't forget there's an army of people out there ready to scrutinise what we have said to see if it differs by a millimetre. So obviously you will get alarums like this.'

Heseltine's own appearances on *Today* became something of an institution. One Monday in mid-January 1997 the *Guardian* published a report criticising the predictability of the programme's choice of politicians, saying 'if it's 8.10 a.m. it must be Michael Heseltine'. As luck would have it, the Deputy Prime Minister appeared precisely on cue: he was the first guest to be interviewed that Monday morning immediately after the main 8 a.m. news. His appearance prompted a letter to the *Guardian*'s

editor, congratulating the paper on its 'accurate reporting'. Heseltine
luxuriated in the attention. The previous month, during the Christmas
holiday, he had played host to both BBC and ITN. Camera crews had been
despatched to his country mansion at Thenford, near Banbury, on Boxing
Day in order to get his reaction to the news that John Major had been
voted personality of the year by listeners to the *Today* programme.
Heseltine was only too pleased to do the honours. On arriving to record
his interview the BBC's reporter, John McIntyre, was handed a glass of
champagne. The ITN crew did even better, persuading Heseltine to
cooperate with them in staging a seasonal set-up shot. On the main
evening news the Deputy Prime Minister, wearing his customary
cardigan, could be seen, armed with a carving knife, tackling the
Christmas Day left-overs.

Heseltine had every reason to be pleased with himself, because this
interview was something of a free hit for the Conservatives. Major had
been declared *Today*'s personality of the year after the first round of
voting was suspended when the programme's staff caught Labour
activists trying to boost Tony Blair's chances by urging party members to
vote for him. Helen Edwards, the Conservatives' broadcasting officer, was
pleased as punch with Heseltine's Boxing Day appearance. 'He looked
really composed doing that interview. Charles [Lewington] is right about
Heseltine. When he is filmed at home wearing his cardigan, he really does
give out oodles of reassurance and looks as if he's putting the nation at
ease.' On meeting Heseltine some weeks later, as he waited to enter a BBC
studio, I discovered that he had enjoyed his Boxing Day encounter with
the television crews and was quite happy to own up to a predilection for his
now characteristic form of casual attire. 'Yes, it was great fun that day . . .
and yes, I do have quite a range of cardigans.'

However, occasional rave reviews for Heseltine's deportment on
television were of little comfort to embattled colleagues in the Cabinet
who had been expecting a more substantive contribution from the man
who had been dubbed 'minister for presentation'. Heseltine had been
given the task of coordinating government publicity when he was
promoted from President of the Board of Trade to Deputy Prime
Minister in the July 1995 Cabinet reshuffle. Under the front-page
headline 'Enter Hezza The Enforcer' the *Daily Express* had listed the
'sweeping powers' he had been given to coordinate the Tory fight-back up
to the general election. Jon Craig, then the paper's political editor, said
Heseltine would have a 'licence to enforce and enthuse'; he would act as a

'firebrand spokesman', and become the 'sleazebuster general' for the government. According to the *Daily Telegraph*, Heseltine's move to the Cabinet Office had caused an 'earthquake' at the centre of government and was 'sending a frisson down every corridor' in Whitehall. He would be in control of the government's 'gaffe-busters' who were charged with the task of avoiding 'potential political banana skins'.

Few of Major's ministerial appointments had been given such a favourable build-up, and government information officers were soon enthusing privately about the effectiveness of the computerised link-up between departments which Heseltine hoped would avoid conflict and overlap in government briefings and announcements. A steady, controlled flow of ministerial news conferences and press releases was testament to the Deputy Prime Minister's application to the task of garnering favourable publicity for the government's achievements. There was certainly no shortage of what ministers were vainly hoping the news media might regard as 'good news' stories about their departments; but the heady predictions that the sheer force of Heseltine's personality would be enough to galvanise a fight-back proved woefully misplaced. Political correspondents were soon remarking that they could detect no real differ-ence: relations between the government and the news media were just as bad as before, and if Heseltine and his staff were picking up advance warnings of the pitfalls which lay ahead for ministers and their depart-ments, they were rarely, if ever, being acted upon.

Major's great mistake since becoming Prime Minister had been his failure to accept that he needed a forceful figure inside No. 10 to oversee government publicity. Not since the departure of Sir Bernard Ingham, whose name became synonymous with the firm grip of the Thatcher years, had there been a Downing Street press secretary who had understood the darker sides of journalism and gained the respect of the media profes-sionals at Conservative Central Office. If Major believed Heseltine would be a suitable substitute, he misunderstood both the man and the arena in which he would have to work. An administration engulfed in intractable problems like 'mad cow disease' and allegations of sleaze against Tory MPs needed a single, authoritative figure who could relate directly to journalists and who not only had the imagination to think of ways to close down troublesome stories but also had the flair to open up new lines of attack. By contrast, Labour's success in promoting Tony Blair was due in large part to the dedication of his indefatigable press secretary Alastair Campbell. No political correspondent was ever likely to be in any doubt as to what was being said on Blair's behalf – and if they were, Campbell soon put them right. But there was no one who seemed able to speak on Major's behalf with anything like the same verve or authority. In some respects the Prime Minister had been well served by his three chief press secretaries. Gus O'Donnell, who had been head of information at the Treasury when Major was Chancellor of the Exchequer, provided a welcome breath of fresh air when he took control of the No. 10 press office. After Ingham's bombastic tirades against the failure of political journalists to take due note of the achievements of the Thatcher years, a new approach was needed. In a move which reflected Major's desire to open up the machinery of govern-ment, O'Donnell decreed that political journalists could source his briefings directly to a 'Downing Street spokesman', thus allowing a degree of attribution in place of the anonymity which Ingham had preferred. Christopher Meyer's appointment in late 1993 was an inspired choice. His flamboyance belied a sharp appreciation of the pitfalls with which Major's path was strewn, and he established a workmanlike feel in the day-to-day contacts between the Prime Minister's press office and the lobby correspondents down the road in the House of Commons press gallery.

When Meyer left to become British ambassador in Bonn, he was replaced, in January 1996, by Jonathan Haslam – a move seen, at least by political correspondents, as something of a surprise. Haslam had been deputy press secretary at No. 10 under both O'Donnell and Meyer and had then spent ten months as head of information at the Ministry of Agriculture, but at no stage had he made any great impression on Westminster's journalistic fraternity. However, as far as Major was concerned he had recruited a safe if uninspiring spokesman: Haslam was rarely if ever indiscreet when in the company of political correspondents, and he worked so hard at playing down damaging news stories that his lobby briefings were often considered to be a tiresome irrelevance. Unfortunately for the government, this demeanour also conveyed the damaging impression of a lack of energy and enthusiasm. At times of crisis he had a tendency to display an air of indifference; perhaps he thought this would be interpreted as a sign of the Prime Minister's confidence, but in the event it only reinforced the impression of a government sliding slowly but surely to oblivion. Heseltine's own press secretary, Mike Horne, attended the morning lobby briefings but, at least in my presence, he was never heard to utter a word. In the final months of Major's government, there was an unmistakable feeling that the press departments in both Downing Street and the Cabinet Office were simply going through the motions: at no point did they seek to engage or excite what after all was a largely captive audience in the press gallery.

Heseltine's irritation at the government's inability to win what he considered to be suitable recognition from the news media for the stream of favourable economic indicators being released by Whitehall departments was understandable, indeed only to be expected. Nevertheless it was slightly surprising that he seemed unable to make any discernible impact on the procedures for promoting the government. He had demonstrated considerable flair in orchestrating his own personal publicity during his 1990 bid for the Conservative party leadership, but in subsequent years had often appeared somewhat aloof from the activities of government information departments, as though he were far happier taking responsibility himself for his relations with the media. While Bernard Ingham was, admittedly, an old adversary from the days of the 1986 Westland controversy and Heseltine's celebrated walkout from the Cabinet, the former Downing Street press secretary certainly had a point when he drew attention in February 1997 to the evident failings of the government's much trumpeted publicity coordinator. Ingham had become a successful newspaper columnist and television presenter on leaving Downing Street and he enjoyed exploiting his inside knowledge. In reviewing *Heseltine*, a newly published biography by Michael Crick, Ingham asserted that the Deputy Prime Minister had never been a man for detail. 'He is not exactly God's gift to administration or political management . . . He has not brought order, purpose or presentational flair to the government.' Sir Bernard was one of several media pundits who used their reviews of Crick's biography to assess Heseltine's likely effectiveness as cheerleader for the campaign to get the Conservatives re-elected. Writing in the *Guardian*, the former Labour deputy leader Roy Hattersley homed in on Heseltine's predilection for arguing with radio journalists and television interviewers, arguing that the Deputy Prime Minister's behaviour only antagonised an increasingly unpolitical electorate and that every appearance he made on the *Today* programme must lose the government votes.

As perhaps was only to be expected from a self-publicist of Heseltine's calibre, the hype surrounding the publication of the biography just happened to coincide with a headline-catching outburst from the man himself. Heseltine had decided to launch a one-man mission behind enemy lines in a desperate attempt to sabotage Tony Blair's increasingly successful charm offensive towards big business. His escapade not only ended in ignominy but was regarded by many political commentators as marking the moment when Major and his ministers took on the role of opposition spokesmen and Labour could truly be considered to have become the government-in-waiting.

Heseltine had invited himself along to the launch of a report entitled *Promoting Prosperity: A Business Agenda for Britain*. It had been produced by the Commission on Public Policy and British Business, which had in turn been funded by the Institute for Public Policy Research, a Labour-inclined think-tank. Several prominent businessmen were members of the Commission, including Bob Bauman, chairman of British Aerospace, George Simpson, managing director of GEC, and David Sainsbury, chairman of the Sainsbury's supermarket group. At the report's launch, Blair spoke first. On seeing Heseltine in the audience, he referred teasingly to the way the Deputy Prime Minister seemed to be 'stalking' him from one political event to the next, giving a new meaning to the title 'shadow minister'. Blair then developed his theme: New Labour had built a 'genuine, new partnership with business'. The basis of the new deal he was offering was that a Labour government would leave intact the main changes of the 1980s, as they affected industrial relations and enterprise, while addressing at the same time a new agenda for the twenty-first century in alliance with a new generation in business. Dave Longstaff, the BBC's cameraman, said Heseltine sat stony-faced while Blair was on his feet, but politely joined in the applause at the end of his speech. 'Blair was beaming at all the support he got, but he left almost straight away and didn't stay to listen to Heseltine. Heseltine also had some good jokes but he didn't go down very well.' The whole tenor of Heseltine's speech was that the businessmen who had lent their names to the report had been duped by Labour. He said they were guilty of perverse naïveté: the report's authors had used 'selective and out of date' facts and figures to bolster their case in support of key Labour policies, such as the introduction of a national minimum wage and British membership of the European social chapter. On his way out of the conference, Heseltine was stopped by a BBC producer, Philip Abrams, who sensed that if the Deputy Prime Minister was offered the chance he might well be tempted to harden up his criticism. Abrams was not disappointed: Heseltine promptly accused the Institute of Public Policy Research of being a 'front organisation for the Labour Party'.

Undaunted by any thought that he might be in danger of going over the top, Heseltine toured the television studios to give a further flourish to what was already being written up by journalists as a highly risky spoiling operation. He told *News at Ten* that the report had been drawn up to give the impression that Blair had a 'rapport with the business community'. Half an hour later, on *Newsnight*, he accused the organisers of staging an event which could be 'paraded as a great love-in' for Blair when in truth only twelve of the two hundred people attending the conference were genuine front-line businessmen.

Heseltine's outburst made front-page news next day. Boris Johnson, the *Daily Telegraph* columnist, who had attended the launch, said the Deputy Prime Minister's denunciations seemed 'somehow churlish', provoking 'little satirical chuckles' from his audience. 'Heseltine's voice soared and growled with his old sub-Churchillian rhythm. He spoke no more than the truth; and yet there are times when truths have been heard so often that they sound like cant.' Anthony Hilton, the *Evening Standard*'s City editor, said that as a businessman himself, Heseltine should have known better than to accuse other prominent businessmen of being 'Labour stooges' just because they were developing political contacts. 'Businessmen may choose to like or dislike a government, but business must always try to make the best of the government it has got, or is likely to get soon.' The following morning, by another odd coincidence, Major was guest at a business breakfast hosted by the public relations consultants Shandwick International, whose chairman Lord Chadlington, the newly ennobled Peter Gummer, was one of the Conservatives' long-standing advisers on publicity. Journalists attending the breakfast were anxious to get a reaction to Heseltine's tirade. I sat next to Simon de Zoete, vice-chairman of BZW, who was in no doubt that the Deputy Prime Minister should not have gatecrashed the IPPR's conference. 'It was counterproductive. Heseltine should not have attacked businessmen in that way.' Howell James, Major's political secretary, defended Heseltine. 'If he hadn't gone there, all we would have had was a news story about Labour's love-in with business.' Jonathan Haslam, the Downing Street press secretary, insisted that Major had given his deputy his full support for the action he had taken. The aim of Heseltine's intervention was to force the media to question whether the IPPR's gathering truly reflected the business community. Haslam said the idea that there was 'massive support' for a minimum wage and the European social chapter was 'out of kilter with small and medium-sized enterprises which are overwhelmingly negative about such proposals', and that this was a true distinction for the Deputy Prime Minister to have made.

That afternoon the Conservatives called a news conference at which journalists were handed a dossier of background information about the IPPR. This repeated the claim that the Institute was a 'front for New Labour' and suggested that by supplying material designed to underpin a political campaign, it might have contravened its charitable status. Heseltine announced that, as a result of their enquiries, the Conservatives could now confirm that Labour had tried to fake business support for Blair. Professor George Bain, chairman of the commission which prepared the report, had defended its findings in a letter published in that day's *Financial Times*, saying that its members were a group drawn from across the political spectrum, representing all sectors of British business, and had no party political agenda. But, Heseltine told the news conference, he had discovered that two of the businessmen whose names appeared beneath Bain's letter, Bob Bauman and George Simpson, had not in fact signed it. When asked by reporters whether or not he was in danger of digging himself into something of a hole, Heseltine retorted that the Conservatives intended to 'dig and dig deeper, because the deeper we dig, the more clearly the confidence trickery that is going on is revealed'.

Danny Finkelstein, head of research at Central Office, said the Tories had no alternative but to respond once Bain's letter appeared in the *Financial Times*. 'The story about Labour and their links with business is now getting so much credibility we've got to kill it. Labour are trying to imply they're signing up businessmen all the time. We know the way Labour's spin works. Somehow we've got to destroy the notion that Labour are the party of business, which is what the news media will run unless we challenge it.' Even so, Heseltine's action in keeping the story going for a second day seemed, on the face it, to be achieving the opposite effect to that aimed at. If Finkelstein imagined that the Deputy Prime Minister's barnstorming performances would strengthen the Conservatives' position, the following morning's newspapers must have been a grave disappointment. 'Why Tarzan lashed out like jilted lover' ran the banner headline across a two-page spread in the *Express*. Nick Wood, the paper's political editor, said Heseltine's raging against 'blue-chip treachery' was another 'grim omen of Tory mortality'. According to an unnamed but despairing minister quoted in the *Daily Telegraph*, the Deputy Prime Minister had lost the plot. Nevertheless, another minister believed he deserved full marks for having invited himself to the IPPR conference, and there was praise from some Tory MPs for his ability to create such a fuss. An unrepentant Heseltine was reported to have told colleagues that he was thrilled by the impact he had made in 'single-handedly sweeping Blair off the front pages after a week of favourable headlines for Labour'.

Philip Bassett, industrial editor of *The Times*, considered that the really curious fact about the whole episode was that Heseltine's own staff had not only been aware of the business commission's report for weeks but had taken part in its preparation. On being appointed Deputy Prime Minister, Heseltine had retained responsibility for the competitiveness unit which he had established four years earlier at the Department of Trade and Industry. Control over the unit had passed to the Cabinet Office and two of its officials, together with others from the Treasury and associated government departments, had given evidence to the commission. As a result it appeared the Cabinet Office was aware of the likely recommendations. At first Heseltine had declined an invitation to attend the IPPR's conference; but then, realising how much publicity it would generate for Labour, sought a last-minute invitation.

Heseltine's failure to take evasive action earlier, perhaps by encouraging Conservative Central Office to pre-empt the IPPR's conference with a business event or initiative of its own, came as no surprise to Hugh Colver, who had been the party's communications director for six months in 1995. Before joining Central Office, he had worked for the government's information service for sixteen years, rising to become head of public relations at the Ministry of Defence. Colver attributed his own hurried departure from the world of political publicity to his distaste for negative campaigning and the realisation that he lacked the 'missionary zeal' of a committed Conservative propagandist. He had witnessed at first hand the daily meetings which Heseltine held with the party chairman, Brian Mawhinney, in an attempt to get to grips with the task of promoting the government's achievements. In an article he wrote for the *Guardian* in November 1995, at the time of his resignation, Colver described in despairing tones how, with a well-oiled government machine at their fingertips, the Conservatives never quite succeeded in their efforts to track policy developments, identify the potential openings for positive presentation or spot the traps and banana skins: 'I have sat day after day in meetings of the party's high command where looming problems have been identified and endlessly discussed. Storm clouds are detected long before anyone else spots them on the horizon. But like Met Office weathermen, experienced ministers seemed helpless in the face of a pending crisis.' Colver detected two fundamental problems behind the government's failure to play what after all was the high-value card of being able to dictate the news agenda. First, too many ministers had lost their political instincts and were allowing themselves to be sucked into a civil service mentality, which, in turn, was taking them even further away from their own political agenda; second, Mawhinney's 'grit' as chairman was sadly lacking in many of his Cabinet colleagues and there had to be a 'ruthless imposition of the will' to gain political advantage from the government's day-to-day business.

One idea suggested by Colver was to provide every Cabinet minister with a political press secretary who could work alongside the officials running the departmental information machine, helping to identify promising opportunities or hidden pitfalls. Forward thinking of that kind would have been invaluable in tackling the insidious way in which sensitive information was being leaked to opposition parties and the news media. There was nothing new about government leaks: ministers had used them down the years to soften up public opinion before making unpopular announcements. But the final months of John Major's government were bedevilled by an unprecedented deluge of unwelcome disclosures and yet, even where it was known in advance that there were reports or findings over which ministers were highly vulnerable, there seemed to be little evidence of any contingency planning in case details were divulged prematurely. No government document appeared sacrosanct. Labour had become the leakers' friend, and one of the principal beneficiaries was the shadow Chancellor, Gordon Brown, whose press secretary Charlie Whelan dispensed the opposition's ill-gotten gains with deadly accuracy. There were many willing supplicants for Labour's largesse among Westminster's political correspondents, but there were preconditions attached to these gifts. Whelan's aim was to trip up the Chancellor, Kenneth Clarke, either by undermining his credibility or by sabotaging Treasury announcements, and no journalist was allowed to forget that when it came to the timing of a story it was Labour who were pulling the strings. In targeting Clarke, Labour had taken on the Cabinet's prize fighter, a political pugilist if ever there was one, who could absorb punch after punch and yet come back for more; and Whelan considered his greatest moment of glory in manipulating leaked documents was the afternoon in November 1996 when, after a Labour-inspired disclosure, Clarke was forced to make an emergency Commons statement at the despatch box on the eve of his last Budget as Chancellor.

The closer polling day came, and the greater the likelihood Labour would form the next government, the more shadow ministers put on an air of feigned responsibility, seeking to distance the party from what they had suddenly come to regard, at least publicly, as the rather reprehensible practice of exploiting secret or confidential Whitehall documents. But in the months before they began assuming their mantle of respectability, Labour's spokesmen used a succession of government leaks to distract attention from the Conservatives' achievements. Radio and television news bulletins inevitably played a part, however unwittingly, in the orchestration which went on behind the scenes as the opposition pursued its overriding objective of getting maximum political mileage out of the government's discomfort. I saw at first hand how the illicit information which Labour were deploying could be used with devastating effect. The preferred potential recipients were newspapers like the *Sunday Times*, *Observer* or *Independent on Sunday*. The advantage of using a Sunday paper was that it opened up opportunities for getting the leak trailed on Saturday evening television news bulletins, which often commanded the highest audiences of the week. All three participants benefited from the arrangement: pictures on television of a Sunday newspaper's front page, and the accompanying footage of the presses rolling, were like manna from heaven for the paper's circulation department; as Saturdays tended to be slow news days, television and radio newsrooms were delighted to be clambering aboard a moving story; and Labour's spin doctors, their mission accomplished, could start farming out shadow Cabinet ministers for interviews on the weekend political programmes to exploit the government's embarrassment.

My involvement in Kenneth Clarke's eve-of-Budget imbroglio began, as was so often the case in such episodes, with a request on my pager to telephone Charlie Whelan. The message came through mid-morning on Saturday while I was attending a Bruges Group conference which was being addressed by several Euro-sceptic Tory MPs. Gordon Brown had alerted me personally the previous Thursday evening to the likelihood of there being a 'significant development that weekend involving the Chancellor'. He told me to keep in touch. Whelan had reinforced that warning the following evening with a tip-off to the effect that a story about the European single currency would be emerging on Saturday evening, via the *Sunday Times*. 'This story is a blockbuster . . . It's dynamite. Obviously we want to get the BBC involved. You'll be able to interview Gordon in time for the main news.' On contacting Whelan after his

Saturday morning bleep, I learned that the *Sunday Times* had been given copies of four confidential documents which Labour believed had been withheld from MPs. He had arranged for BBC television to film the documents at 4.30 p.m. that day at News International's offices in Wapping, but neither the story nor the pictures could be used until the BBC's main news bulletin at 8.50 p.m. I was told Brown's adviser, Ed Balls, would personally give me a rundown as to what the documents contained. Balls said that one of the confidential papers, drawn up by the European Monetary Institute, showed that the pound would have to shadow the euro even if Britain opted out of the single currency, and an internal Treasury paper stated that the 'current proposals will not be acceptable to Parliament'. Labour were alleging a cover-up by the Chancellor.

Labour had a tendency to try bounce broadcasters into accepting their spin as to the likely purport or political implication of any leaked information. Because newspapers were more likely to reprint large sections of confidential documents, and put together a detailed interpretation of the contents, they were always given a head start. My worry, which was shared by my weekend television producer Julian Joyce, was that we would be presented late on Saturday afternoon with a heap of documents and end up having only a couple of hours in which to check out their authenticity and the validity of the story-line which Labour were pushing. We also knew that Brown and Whelan would be desperate to persuade the BBC to carry the story as a way of reinforcing its credibility.

On arriving at Wapping, we were shown the documents by the *Sunday Times*' political editor, Andrew Grice. He said Labour had given them to him on Friday and he had been up all night working out what they meant, researching the story, writing the front-page splash and preparing a feature for inside the paper. Grice showed me the story he had written. Under the headline 'Clarke in storm over cover-up', it said: 'Crucial documents about the preparations for a single currency have been withheld from MPs . . . Labour said they were "political dynamite" . . . The four documents, obtained by the *Sunday Times*, reveal that Brussels will interfere in Britain's economic policies even if the government opts out of the Euro.' Grice said Whelan had asked him to use the phrase 'leaked to the *Sunday Times*' so as not to reveal the source of the documents.

Once we got back to the BBC's offices at Millbank we began our own checks to establish whether the documents were genuine and, if they were, assess their significance. We attempted to get a reaction from both the Treasury's press office and Clarke's political adviser, Anthony Teesdale. Another priority was to arrange an interview with Gordon Brown because we needed a Labour spokesman to stand up the charge of a government 'cover-up'. Brown was only too happy to oblige. He arrived at Millbank together with Whelan, and immediately endorsed Labour's attack on Clarke, claiming that when documents were circulating freely in Brussels but were not available to MPs, it was clear Parliament had not been told the full truth. With less than half an hour to go to transmission time we finally got the confirmation we needed: although the government was denying a cover-up there was no attempt by the Treasury's spokesman to deny the authenticity of the documents. A statement, put out in Clarke's name, was short and to the point: 'No official document properly liable to Parliamentary scrutiny has been withheld.'

I discovered subsequently from a BBC producer, Martin Levene, that my initial call to the Treasury, seeking a statement, had caused something of a flap. Levene was working on the graphics for Clarke's Budget broadcast which was to be transmitted the following Tuesday, and at eight o'clock that Saturday evening he was at the London home of the Chancellor's press secretary, Jill Rutter, as Treasury officials were considering how to respond to the BBC's call about the leaked documents. Levene said he had to wait some time to show Rutter a video of the Budget graphics in order to get her approval. 'The room was full of cards for Jill's fortieth birthday but it was chaos because the phone wouldn't stop ringing. Finally a call came through with what must have been Clarke's statement to the effect that no documents had been withheld from Parliamentary scrutiny. Jill didn't like the wording but she said: "They're Ken's words . . . go with it." By then it was 8.15 p.m. and I could sense Jill was impatient. She just couldn't wait for the news bulletin at 8.50 p.m. She looked a bit relieved when Michael Buerk started reading the headlines. The leak wasn't the lead but the third story. When the documents were shown on the screen she sat there, just staring at the television.'

Events moved quickly next day. There had been pressure on the government for some weeks to allow an emergency debate on Britain's stance towards the single currency because of mounting unease among Conservative Euro-sceptic MPs. The leadership of the 1922 Committee, representing Tory backbenchers, had urged the Prime Minister to rearrange parliamentary business so as to provide time for MPs to vent their feelings. As soon as news emerged of the allegations of a cover-up, there were renewed calls for a full debate. Richard Shepherd, one of the former rebel MPs from whom the Conservative whip had been withdrawn, said the documents leaked to the *Sunday Times* indicated a lack of candour on the part of the Chancellor. When the President of the Board of Trade, Ian Lang, was interviewed on that Sunday's edition of *The World this Weekend*, he reiterated previous undertakings that no binding decisions would be taken by Britain at the European summit which was to be held in Dublin in mid-December. However, when pressed about the chances of an early debate, he said that 'anything is possible'. An hour later the Treasury sent a faxed message to the BBC and other news organisations announcing that the Chancellor would make a statement to the Commons on Monday afternoon to correct what he considered was a 'highly misleading and inaccurate' article in the *Sunday Times*. I was alerted to Clarke's announcement minutes before the shadow Chancellor was due to arrive at Millbank for a follow-up interview in which he was expected to repeat Labour's demand for a debate. On being shown the Treasury fax, Brown told the BBC he welcomed Clarke's 'climbdown' but felt the problem was entirely of the government's own making and resulted from the Prime Minister's unsuccessful attempt to 'patch over divisions in his party'. Whelan was ecstatic. Here was a Chancellor, he said, who should have spent the weekend going through his Budget, having instead to prepare for an emergency statement on the eve of his Budget speech. 'My job is to help Gordon wind up Ken. We never thought we'd get a direct hit like this. Our job is to try to derail the Budget and obscure the Chancellor's announcements. I can't believe we're forcing him to make a statement just because of our leaked documents.'

But Whelan's coup in 'winding up' the Chancellor turned into something of an anti-climax for Labour. Clarke thrived in the rough-house of politics. Whereas Michael Heseltine sometimes appeared to put on airs and graces and occasionally came across as rather grand, Clarke revelled in his image of the bloke next door. He was able effortlessly to pitch his despatch box appearances at a level which not only commanded the attention of his fellow MPs but could also be understood by the man or woman in the street. 'Clarke takes his greatest gamble' was the headline that morning in the *Express* over a report by the paper's chief political correspondent, Roland Watson, predicting an 'electrifying piece of Commons drama' as the Chancellor ended up 'in the firing line of mutinous Tory MPs'. The chamber was packed for the statement. Clarke told the House that he had ordered the immediate publication of all the documents relating to the draft legislation on monetary union. When MPs studied the correspondence in its entirety, rather than the misrepresentations of the *Sunday Times*, he believed they would see that he had shown proper regard for parliamentary procedures. One of the leaked papers was a briefing note prepared at the request of the British European Commissioners, Sir Leon Brittan and Neil Kinnock, and Clarke said he believed it was Gordon Brown who had 'seen fit to break that confidence and put the document in the public domain'.

Clarke's statement, and the subsequent questions and answers, lasted for an hour and twenty minutes. His parliamentary private secretary, Peter Butler, told me it was the best performance he had seen from the Chancellor in the eighteen months he had been working for him. 'Early that Monday afternoon the only question was: "Will the government fall?" But by late afternoon the row over the leaked documents and the euro was completely off the agenda. Ken can shrug off attacks like that because what he says fits completely with his philosophy and beliefs. Labour just can't rattle Ken. They try to punch him below the belt, but with a gut like his, he's cast iron all the way down.' Once the Chancellor had completed his statement, and journalists sensed that the crisis had passed, I could see the rival spin doctors eyeing each other up at the back of the press gallery, looking for all the world as menacing as a bunch of alley cats. Whelan and Blair's press secretary, Alastair Campbell, were obviously a bit miffed. Campbell growled at me something to the effect that all Clarke had done was 'buy a little time' with the Euro-sceptics. Charles Lewington could be seen a few paces away with an amused smile on his face, holding court with another group of journalists. He told me that 'candid Ken' had pulled it off yet again and Labour did not like it. Clarke's cheery countenance had made him a favourite with cartoonists but it seemed even they would have liked to have found some way to ring the changes. 'The trouble for us with Ken Clarke is that he never shows the pressure,' remarked Peter Brookes of *The Times*. 'A cartoonist can't show Clarke with raised eyebrows, looking anxious, because he never is.'

Labour's disappointment at the Chancellor's resilience was short-lived. Within an hour of Clarke leaving the chamber, Whelan received an urgent message on his pager asking him to contact Kevin Maguire, political editor of the *Mirror*. Labour were about to be given the sensational news that on the very eve of the Budget the *Mirror* had obtained leaked copies of the Treasury press releases explaining the background to the tax changes which Clarke intended to announce the following afternoon. Labour's spin doctors were delighted to get such a useful head start in working out how to make the most of a leak which would surpass all previous leaks under John Major's government. Not only would Labour be able to generate an air of mayhem surrounding what was supposed to be a key event in the Conservatives' pre-election build-up, but the party's frontbench spokesmen could also begin preparing their detailed responses to the Budget announcements. Whelan said it 'didn't half help' having twenty-four hours' notice of what Clarke would be announcing. 'I couldn't believe it when Kevin Maguire said on the phone: "I've got the Budget." Of course, the news of what the *Mirror* was up to was so sensational it spread round the press gallery like wildfire.' Maguire told me subsequently that walking round the House of Commons all afternoon with 'the Budget in his pocket' was the weirdest sensation he had experienced as a journalist. To the surprise of most political correspondents, the *Mirror*'s editor Piers Morgan decided not to publish details of what the press releases contained. After the government obtained an injunction from a judge in chambers, the *Mirror* returned the documents at 10.30 that evening. Maguire was dismayed by the decision; but by then the Budget secrets were being hawked round Westminster. Philip Webster, political editor of *The Times*, said that as the contents were effectively being 'touted about' to other news organisations, several political correspondents were able to piece together a credible story. Maguire was annoyed by, as he saw it, Labour's spin doctors using the *Mirror*'s information to 'give a steer' to other journalists.

Notwithstanding its decision to return the documents, the *Mirror* devoted four pages to what was headlined the 'Tory shambles of the decade'. Maguire's story made much of the fact that the ninety-four-page pack of press releases contained all the big announcements affecting income tax, petrol duty and prescription charges but, in compliance with the undertaking which his editor had given the government, he refrained from giving any of the details. Another *Mirror* journalist, Anthony Harwood, was photographed holding up copies of the leaked papers. His report described how he handed them back to the Prime Minister's press secretary, Jonathan Haslam, saying: 'Tell the Chancellor he'll be needing these tomorrow.' Other newspapers were only too happy to exploit the *Mirror*'s reticence. '1p off tax today' was the headline in the *Sun*, which correctly pre-empted several of Clarke's announcements. On an inside page, under the headline 'The Crusher', the paper's political editor, Trevor Kavanagh, reported the Chancellor's success in seeing off the threatened revolt the day before as the rebel MPs lost 'their Euro bottle'.

Clarke's first task on Budget day morning was to take his Cabinet colleagues through his proposals. While the meeting was still under way, Haslam was putting a brave face on the government's discomfort in the lobby briefing room situated in the basement of No. 10. He said the leak had occurred at some point during a massive printing operation which had been conducted on behalf of various government departments. All told, there were sixty-five separate news releases about the Budget and they had been bundled together at the Treasury into 2,800 press packs, ready for distribution that afternoon, once the Chancellor had completed his speech. The news releases leaked to the *Mirror* were from the Inland Revenue, Customs and Excise and Scottish Office. Haslam said that after Piers Morgan informed the Prime Minister's office of the leak at 7.20 the previous evening, the government had obtained an injunction against the *Mirror* by 8.05 p.m.; but in the event the matter was settled by negotiation between the paper and the Treasury Solicitor and the documents were returned to Downing Street at around 10.30 p.m.

On rising to the despatch box to deliver his Budget speech, Clarke immediately poked fun at the *Mirror*, cracking a joke at his own expense. Making capital out of his reputation for having a dishevelled appearance, he said that contrary to popular belief, he always 'looked at the mirror in the morning'. Nevertheless, some of the drama of the occasion had inevitably been dissipated. As he justified his decision to reduce the basic rate of income tax by 1p to 23p in the pound, Labour MPs chanted 'boring' and 'get on with it, Ken'. Clarke was at a further disadvantage because the leak had given Labour sufficient time to work out alternative financial projections with which to challenge the forecasts being given by Treasury officials at the news briefings that followed the Budget. Instead of having to wait until later that evening or next day to launch their counter-attack, Labour were able to mount an instant offensive. Gordon Brown had calculated that despite the 1p cut in income tax, there would still be a £300 million increase in the overall tax take. When this figure was quoted in teatime news broadcasts, Treasury officials protested to the BBC, insisting that the tax bill for the average family had in fact gone down. Labour's chief media spokesperson, David Hill, said the *Mirror*'s leak had been invaluable. 'Because we knew the figures in advance, we were able to start pushing the line that the Budget wouldn't leave the average family any better off. We knew if we could suggest the Budget wouldn't have any real effect, we could then say it wasn't worth waiting for and that it wouldn't change voters' minds at the election.' Hill said that although Piers Morgan was being vilified by other journalists for not publishing the details, the *Mirror* had shown its 'true colours as a Labour supporter and come up with a very effective Budget spoiler'. Had the *Mirror* actually printed each of the tax and revenue changes, Hill thought Labour MPs would probably have shouted them out themselves, one by one, in chorus with the Chancellor.

Next day's newspapers were full of detailed reports about the hunt for the source of the leaked documents. Andrew Pierce, political correspondent of *The Times*, described it as the 'worst government leak for fifty years'. The press releases had apparently been offered to the *Mirror* by a freelance investigative journalist, Peter Hounam, who had already been credited with several spectacular scoops. There were all sorts of theories about what lay behind the leak. The most popular suggestion was that it was connected with an announcement of job cuts at a south London printing plant owned by the newly privatised Stationery Office, but this was denied by the staff. At the height of the government's efforts to retrieve the press releases, one option which was considered was the possibility of the Chancellor having to make a late-night statement in the Commons to announce some of the price-sensitive tax changes in case the disclosures had caused alarm on international money markets. The seriousness of the position facing the Treasury was acknowledged by Gordon Brown on the morning of the Budget. He told the *Today* programme that if he had been offered the chance to see the leaked documents he would have refused. 'Nobody can condone the leak of sensitive Budget matters the day before the Budget . . . The most important thing to recognise is that the civil servant who did this is serving no public purpose.' Brown's condemnation of the leak failed to impress the Conservative MP, George Walden. Writing in the Budget day edition of the *Evening Standard*, he said Labour's 'shameless exploitation of every purloined document' which came their way was as cynical as it was short-sighted. 'As they will discover should they find themselves in office, this is a tawdry, self-defeating game that any fool can play.' Sir Bernard Ingham, writing in the *Express*, said the question he asked himself was 'which opposition spokesman had not handled stolen government documents'. A fortnight later at question time Michael Heseltine said that the whole basis on which documents were being leaked was severely prejudicial to the good government of the country and that it had been 'encouraged and abetted ruthlessly and remorselessly by Labour'.

Clarke's irrepressible good humour in the face of Labour's wrecking tactics was admired not only by his fellow Conservative MPs but also by many journalists. In a post-Budget profile in the *Financial Times*, Patrick Donovan said the Chancellor's ability to keep cool in a crisis had been tested to its limits during the preceding forty-eight hours. 'It is testimony to the resilience of his armour-plated image that he personally has yet to be publicly criticised over one of the biggest breaches in government security in recent years.' Janet Bush, who interviewed the Chancellor for *The Times*, concluded that he had a 'masterful knack of making Gordon Brown look inept'. The characteristic which I found most appealing was Clarke's readiness to take the excesses of the news media in good part. Although he must have been well aware that some correspondents and commentators were the beneficiaries of leaked documents, and were not only working in cahoots with Labour's Treasury team but also happily swallowing their media advisers' spin, he rarely retaliated personally. Nor was Clarke averse to facing awkward or embarrassing questions on radio or television. I knew of only one occasion when he had pulled rank and threatened at the last minute to withdraw from an interview. It happened two months before the Budget, during a finance ministers' meeting in Washington, and followed an interview he had given the day before to Alastair Stewart on GMTV. In response to a question, Clarke agreed that 'frothy tax cuts won't win a vote' for the Conservatives at the general election. When the Chancellor discovered that the Radio 4 news bulletin next morning was attributing this to him as a direct quote, rather than as a response to Stewart's question, he told *Today* he would pull out of the programme unless the news report was amended. Once the change was made he went ahead with the interview. Clarke remained affable throughout such encounters and his friendly demeanour made him popular with television crews. Mike Williams, a BBC cameraman who had spent many years at Westminster, said the Chancellor never avoided them. 'Whenever he sees cameramen he always waves, and he doesn't try to get out of the way or change his route. If he's smoking a cigar he never puts it out and whenever a reporter's questions get repetitive or too sensitive, he doesn't get nasty with them but just laughs and walks away.' Unlike some of the more hesitant members of the political fraternity, he was always keen to get his interviews wrapped up as quickly as possible and I knew of no occasion when he had demanded to retake an answer.

Even Peter Mandelson admired Clarke's panache when deflecting tricky questions or extricating himself from awkward situations. While

Labour's campaign manager was incisive when it came to determining the precise point which he considered Tony Blair or one of his colleagues needed to make in delivering a short, sharp response for a news bulletin, he lacked the fluency and quick-fire sentence construction of hardened frontbench performers like the Chancellor. As the election got closer Mandelson began making more frequent appearances on radio and television programmes. During live interviews he could be quick-witted and engaging; however, he still had a tendency to fluff his lines when asked to pre-record short answers for use in news bulletins. Sometimes he would stop the interview, pause for a moment and rehearse in his mind exactly what he wanted to say. On one occasion I recall him stumbling six times before he finally delivered a twenty-second answer. Gathering soundbites for use in news bulletins can be as frustrating for the broadcaster as it is for the politician. Time constraints rule out long replies or probing, follow-up questions. All that is required is one punchy, self-contained answer which ideally should be self-explanatory and capable of standing alone within a news report. Most politicians need firing up and it usually takes several attempts before they find a way of compressing what they want to say into the shortest possible utterance. Mandelson liked to take full advantage of repeated opportunities to hone his replies. Occasionally he would mock my questions while at the same time complimenting me for having persisted long enough to allow him to deliver what he considered was a 'quality' soundbite.

The trouble which Mandelson took in framing the one answer which he knew was most likely to be used in a news report reminded me of the meticulous attention to detail shown by the Home Secretary, Michael Howard, whenever he was interviewed on radio or television. Unlike the off-the-cuff responses of the happy-go-lucky Kenneth Clarke or the sometimes flamboyant tirades of Michael Heseltine, Howard's answers were measured and well targeted. Each word seemed to have been chosen with care and, when directed at his opponents in the Labour Party, his replies were clearly designed to cause them maximum discomfort. In my opinion Howard was the only member of John Major's Cabinet who had a clear grasp of broadcasting techniques and programme procedures. He also had the shrewdness and the resolve to protect himself against ambush by an unexpected question, and was rarely outwitted by a producer or presenter. If Howard was about to make a live appearance, nothing would be left to chance. He would insist on being told in advance about the content of any related report or item which was to be used to set up the subject under discussion. Producers would be asked to supply the names of any other guests who were to be interviewed on the same issue, together with details of their placing in the programme's running order. He invariably made a point of arriving in time to listen to any reports or interviews which preceded his interview; this enabled him to hit back immediately if he thought the programme had used dubious facts or figures, and it also reduced the chances of his being caught off guard. If Howard was not satisfied with the arrangements he would say so, and stipulate the conditions under which he would take part. Invariably there would have to be an undertaking that he would have the last word. If any attempt was made to change the arrangements which had been agreed, the Home Secretary would protest in the strongest possible terms; if he considered a programme had broken the undertakings which he had been given, he would make an immediate complaint.

Howard was equally methodical when giving interviews in his office or after news conferences. He would insist that only one television or radio reporter should be allowed into his room at any one time. The rest of them, together with their technicians, had to wait outside the door. By excluding all other broadcasters he made sure that they could not eavesdrop on their rivals' interviews. Consequently, if one reporter hit on a weak point in Howard's argument, or developed a line of questioning which caused him discomfort, there was less likelihood of this being picked up by the rest of the pack. Similarly, if he made a slip of the tongue, or sought to change an answer, knowledge of this would be limited to the one reporter present in the room. Occasionally, while waiting my turn in the queue, I would ruminate on the Conservatives' failure to recognise the Home Secretary's machiavellian talent for media management. To my mind he was their answer to Peter Mandelson. Indeed, Howard had demonstrated another of the Labour spin doctor's most menacing attributes: a deadly accuracy when making complaints. I knew from my discussions with programme editors that the Home Secretary was the minister they feared most: if he was dissatisfied with the way he had been treated, the production staff were told to make immediate amends. As perhaps was only to be expected, Howard succeeded in making mincemeat of me on the few occasions I had the misfortune to cross swords with him. My most bruising encounter occurred during the summer of 1991, during the build-up to the 1992 general election, when Howard was Secretary of State for Employment. I was tipped off by Barry Sutlieff, head of information at the department, that a complaint had been made about a report which I had compiled for the *Six o'Clock News* on Radio 4. Sutlieff said I should prepare myself for trouble: Howard was complaining directly to John Birt, the BBC's director-general, and the Secretary of State would not be satisfied until he had received an apology and I had been reprimanded.

My news report was based on a press release issued by Henry McLeish, the shadow employment minister, concerning leaked documents from the Department of Employment which had been obtained by the Labour Party. One of the documents, of which I was given a copy, was a two-page report written by Sir Geoffrey Holland, the department's permanent secretary. McLeish claimed they revealed that Howard favoured a 'laissez-faire' approach in the government's future relationship with the newly established training and enterprise councils. This was the fifth time within a fortnight that Labour said they had received leaked documents from Howard's department. Organisational changes affecting the training and enterprise councils had been under review for some time and the Civil Service unions feared they would involve redundancies. Labour had issued their press release under embargo and, as there was time that Sunday morning to check the validity of the story, I spoke at length to McLeish, to my contacts within the trade union movement, and to the duty information officer for the Department of Employment, Evelyn Smith. She rang back within half an hour to say the officials she had spoken to were unable to say whether McLeish's documents constituted a new leak. However, the department considered Labour's comments were pure speculation; there was no dissent between Howard and Sir Geoffrey; and there was no question of redundancies. I told her I would check again that afternoon, before my report was broadcast, to see if the department could throw any further light on the status of the documents. Despite the official denial, I considered Labour's latest allegations were newsworthy. There had been reports for some weeks in the *Financial Times* about 'conflict' between Howard and the training and enterprise councils, which had a £1.7 billion budget. Tony Blair, then shadow employment secretary, had been quoted at length in the *Independent* only the week before commenting on the other documents which Labour had obtained. He said the leaks had exposed Howard's 'wilful neglect of training needs'.

As this was clearly a sensitive issue, I was careful in my news report to attribute Labour's claims directly to McLeish and to give the department's denial in full. In his letter of complaint, Howard said the 'leaked' papers had 'simply been doctored' by Labour and could not 'remotely substantiate' Labour's allegations of a dispute between himself and his permanent secretary. He found it astonishing that my report had been broadcast without 'any apparent attempt to verify its accuracy' and that 'no other news medium had chosen to publicise the story'. Howard considered my conduct represented a 'severe lapse in reporting standards'. David Aaronovitch, head of BBC news at Westminster, asked me to account for my conduct. He said he was advising John Birt on the BBC's reply. I told him of the checks I had made and showed him the newspaper cuttings which explained the background to the story. They indicated that Blair and the rest of Labour's employment team believed the leaked documents were genuine. Among the cuttings was one from that Monday's *Guardian* which quoted McLeish at length under the headline 'Jobs fear in TECs change'. The following day Aaronovitch handed me a copy of the director-general's reply. Birt told Howard that he was not happy with the way the BBC ran the story. He took the view that allegations which were sometimes inaccurate and often, perhaps, unfair, were part of the cut and thrust of political life and the reporting of such allegations presented difficult issues. There were circumstances where the nature of an allegation, or the significance of the person making it, might require publication, but, he went on: 'I expect BBC journalists to be very cautious of reporting detailed and substantial allegations unless we have independent collaboration [*for* corroboration] of them. Having examined the circumstances in this case, I regret the terms in which the BBC reported this story and have informed those concerned that I do.'

Birt's letter was leaked to the *Daily Express*. In an exclusive headlined 'BBC says sorry', Michael Atchinson reported that the 'Tories had revealed' how a Radio 4 story about a leaked document, suggesting differences between Howard and his permanent secretary, had been 'invented' by the BBC. 'But there was no such leak, no such document, no such split – and no effort made to check the story.' Graham Riddick, a Conservative MP who specialised in employment affairs, said Birt's apology amounted to an 'outrageous' admission. 'Ordinary people are now asking questions about why the BBC seems so intent on undermining the party in power . . . The BBC seems to swallow every left-wing tale it hears and fails to repent, even when it is told the truth. Unlike newspapers, it forgets to check its facts.' Needless to say, from then on, after the publicity my reprimand had received, I approached Howard with a fair degree of trepidation.

Whenever I was asked to interview him I avoided getting drawn into small talk and I made no mention of his complaint. Nevertheless, I sensed he felt he had the upper hand and that he would not hesitate to complain again if he considered my reporting warranted it.

After the Conservatives won the 1992 election Howard was appointed Secretary of State for the Environment and then, following the sacking of Chancellor Norman Lamont, he was made Home Secretary in the Cabinet reshuffle of May 1993. Only the week before, Tony Blair, who by then was the shadow Home Secretary, had declared that Labour intended to be 'tough on crime, tough on the causes of crime'. At his first party conference as Home Secretary, Howard announced twenty-seven steps which he intended to take to protect 'people's freedom to walk safely on their streets and to sleep safely in their homes'; to strengthen the criminal justice system; and to show that 'prison works'. Within months of his speech there were newspaper stories suggesting policy disagreements between Howard and officials in both the Home Office and the Prison Service. By far the most spectacular of these confrontations culminated two years later in the sacking of the Prison Service director-general, Derek Lewis. The Home Secretary defended his action during a highly charged debate in the Commons which had opened with his opposite number on the Labour front bench, Jack Straw, deploring Howard's 'unwillingness to accept responsibility for serious operational failures of the Prison Service'. Despite being supported by a lengthy intervention from Blair, Straw failed to shake Howard's self-confidence. The Home Secretary was congratulated by Conservative MPs for withstanding Labour's attack and delivering what the *Daily Mail* described next morning as a 'bravura' Commons performance. Straw was said by the *Sun* to have been 'chopped to pieces' and Blair to have suffered his 'worst mauling' since becoming party leader. Labour tried to keep up the pressure on the Home Secretary that weekend. Donald Dewar, the Chief Whip, renewed their demand for his resignation. In an article for the *News of the World*, the Liberal Democrat leader, Paddy Ashdown, described Howard as the 'OJ Simpson of British politics'. He had concluded that the Home Secretary would probably 'get away with it'. My report on these developments for the Sunday morning news bulletin on Radio 4 provoked a complaint on Howard's behalf from Conservative Central Office. Brian Mawhinney, the party chairman, told me that the Home Secretary was incensed by my broadcast. 'He wiped the floor with Jack Straw, so why is the BBC reporting what Labour and the Liberal Democrats are saying . . . This is not news . . . Michael Howard won the argument and that should have been the end of it.'

A year later I was again in the Home Secretary's firing line following confusion over the early release of prisoners. Richard Tilt, who had succeeded Derek Lewis as director-general of the Prison Service, was recalled from his holiday in Italy in August 1996 after it emerged that eighty-six prisoners had been freed following a recalculation of their sentences. Because it was thought that as many as 4,000 inmates might be eligible for early release, Howard had asked to see Tilt that afternoon. My radio report that morning referred to concern within the Prison Service about possible disturbances because of the confusion over the unexpected releases. Robert Spink, who was parliamentary private secretary to the Home Office minister Ann Widdecombe, had told me the previous evening that some prisoners were obviously disappointed by Howard's decision to stop further releases pending a court ruling. 'Obviously we are having to watch this very carefully . . . Trouble in the prisons would be politically very embarrassing for Michael Howard.' After his meeting with Tilt, the Home Secretary held a news conference and surprised the assembled journalists by announcing that the Prison Service had discovered that it had in fact released 537 prisoners and not eighty-six as stated previously. Howard said he took a 'very serious view' of what had happened but was prepared to accept Tilt's personal apology.

Continuing to cover the story for BBC radio, I joined a group of broadcasters who lined up afterwards to interview Howard. The first hint I got that all was not well came from Mike Granatt, director of communications for the Home Office. He told me I would have to wait until last. On finally entering the room I told the Home Secretary that I only wanted a short interview. My final question, which I put to both Howard and Tilt, concerned the possibility of continuing uncertainty in the prisons while the Home Office waited for the courts to rule on the way sentences were being recalculated. I asked the Home Secretary if he could give the public any guarantee that the Prison Service would be able to cope with 4,000 disappointed inmates. Howard replied that he was confident the Prison Service would be taking steps to make sure that the circumstances surrounding the review of sentences were properly understood; then, the moment he saw me press the stop button on my tape recorder, he turned to me and said my question was the most irresponsible he had been asked by any journalist that day. He intended to seek an immediate assurance from the BBC that neither my question nor his answer was broadcast on the radio. Tilt and Granatt both looked on impassively as I was reprimanded by Howard. Granatt told me afterwards that he should perhaps have warned me that the Home Secretary was annoyed with my reports that morning, but I got the impression Howard had been waiting for the opportunity to rebuke me to my face and relished the occasion. I knew from bitter experience that the BBC was an easy target, so I made a point of never taking complaints personally and tried instead to concentrate on the way politicians behaved when remonstrating with a reporter. I had been fascinated to observe Howard's cunning. Even before he started criticising me I had sensed that he was watching me operate my tape machine; obviously he wanted to make sure it was switched off before he spoke. Howard was wily enough to have known that if I had managed to record his outburst I would probably have tried to get it broadcast and that might have caused him some embarrassment.

Howard's ability to withstand constant questioning without slipping up was widely admired. Peter Smith, a former BBC industrial correspondent who interviewed him regularly during his period as Secretary of State for Employment, had dubbed him the Cabinet's Geoffrey Boycott. 'No matter what question I threw at him each month about the unemployment figures, he just stonewalled. I could never catch him out.' Nevertheless, despite his technical brilliance in deflecting hostile questions, Howard did not come across to the public as a particularly appealing figure. Unfortunately for the Conservatives, too many of their ministers had spent too long stonewalling on radio and television. Being put continuously on the defensive was one of the handicaps of their fourth term in office. Heseltine, Clarke and Howard were without doubt the government's three most effective performers after John Major. The challenge they would face in the election campaign would be whether their expertise as broadcasters could be used to project a more positive image and win back popularity for their party.

3

The Dragon-Slayers

When an editorial in the *Sun* congratulated New Labour for 'slaying the high-tax dragon', Tony Blair's spin doctors had every justification for purring with delight as they spent the day preening themselves in the corridors of Westminster. 'It was one hell of an operation,' said Alastair Campbell. 'Tremendous' was the word which Peter Mandelson used to describe a publicity coup which had topped the news bulletins all day and provided the front-page splash for most national newspapers. The pledge by the shadow Chancellor, Gordon Brown, not to increase either the top or the basic rate of income tax for the full five years of a Labour parliament effectively marked the end of the phoney pre-election campaigning which had dragged on for so long.

In terms of its significance for Labour, and its impact on their opponents and political journalists, Brown's promise ranked alongside Blair's announcement at the 1994 party conference of his intention to rewrite Clause Four of Labour's constitution. The secrecy which surrounded the two decisions was comparable. So was the element of surprise. There was, nevertheless, one significant difference. At the 1994 conference, Campbell and his fellow press officers had not taken political correspondents into their confidence. By January 1997, when Brown announced his tax plans, Labour were so sure of their ability to manipulate the news media that they felt able to give some journalists advance notice and then go on, with almost clockwork precision, to orchestrate the day's coverage on television and radio and in the press. A week before the announcement, Campbell had told me that when Labour eventually unveiled their decisions on income tax, it would be 'a mega-story'. He gave me no inkling then of the timing of the revelations, but he was spot on with his prediction about their importance.

There could hardly have been a clearer example of a media-driven policy initiative. In preparing for the election, Blair had frequently been accused of putting presentation before policy: here were the two combined for maximum effect. A fraught debate had been going on for some months within the shadow Cabinet over whether it would be necessary to increase income tax, and the timing of the decision to rule it out was undoubtedly determined by a wish to wrong-foot the Conservatives. Charlie Whelan, Brown's dogged press aide, was the foot soldier who had to do most of the dirty work. As the plot unfolded, it was his job initially to throw reporters off the scent, even if this meant misleading them, and then, at the allotted time, to start giving political editors and correspondents the advance tip-offs which were designed to ensure maximum impact. There was no way that the Conservative Party could have pulled off such a coup: their publicity staff could not call on a similar network of friendly newspaper journalists, nor had they established anything like the same degree of trust among senior broadcasters. Brown's categoric pledge caught the Tories off guard. At a news conference in Central Office, organised on the mistaken assumption that the Conservatives would be responding to Labour's heavily trailed plans for a curb on public spending, the Chancellor of the Exchequer, Kenneth Clarke, had to fall back on bluster. He described the tax pledge as 'beyond belief': 'Hell will freeze over before Gordon Brown could control spending and keep tax down.'

'Slaying the high-tax dragon', as the *Sun* described it on 21 January, was always destined to be one of the peak points of Labour's campaign. The damage inflicted by the shadow Budget of the 1992 general election had left searing memories. In the opening days of that campaign, Labour had initially won plaudits for the honesty shown by the then shadow Chancellor, the late John Smith. Together with his frontbench team, Smith had posed on the steps of the Treasury for a cheeky photo-opportunity before announcing his plan to raise personal allowances and increase child benefit. He calculated that eight out of ten families would be better off. Only those on incomes above £22,000 would be hit by his proposals for higher national insurance contributions and a new top rate for income tax of 50p in the pound. The Conservatives could not believe their good fortune. Once the shadow Budget had been announced they immediately stepped up their offensive against Labour's 'tax bombshell'. Fear about having to pay more tax under Labour was subsequently judged by political strategists almost certainly to have clinched victory for John Major in 1992.

Blair was determined at all costs to avoid giving the Tories any repeat opportunity in the 1997 campaign to sustain their charge that Labour's instincts were always to put up taxes. However, members of the shadow Cabinet had been arguing for months as to whether an incoming Labour government should increase the top rate from 40p in the pound, perhaps by introducing a new rate of 50p in the pound for those earning £100,000 and above. Speculation about the possibility of Gordon Brown changing the tax rates was at its height during the summer of 1996. Despite repeated assurances that a future Labour government would not 'soak the rich', there was clearly a degree of conflict behind the scenes. Joy Johnson, who spent almost a year as the party's campaigns director and had worked closely with the shadow Chancellor during 1995, told me that Brown had always supported progressive taxation and she knew he believed that if fairness was to be achieved, a Labour government would have to introduce a higher top rate. As the months went by, in the face of opposition from Blair about the way tax increases would be exploited by the Conservatives, Brown shifted gradually from his initial starting point. Instead of seeking to apply a 50p rate on annual earnings of £60,000 and above, £80,000 a year was indicated as being the likely threshold and then £100,000 was mentioned. But in a move which confounded the Conservatives, and seemed to take even Brown and his advisers by surprise, Blair began the run-up to the October 1996 party conference by ruling out altogether any suggestion that Labour would put up income tax. 'We have no proposals to raise the top rate,' said Blair, when interviewed on *Today* a full month before the conference. He insisted that Labour's programme for government contained no plans requiring higher taxes, and stressed that the party's long-term objective was to introduce a lower starting rate of 10p in the pound.

Three weeks later, on the very eve of the conference, *The Times* reported that Brown was still considering a 50p top rate on earnings of over £100,000 a year. According to the paper's political editor, Philip Webster, Brown's announcement had divided the shadow Cabinet and he was continuing to meet resistance from Blair, whose 'personal inclination' was to leave the top rate unchanged at 40p. When I sought confirmation of this from Brown's press officer Charlie Whelan, he was quite emphatic about the authenticity of Webster's story, even giving me the impression that he had spoken personally to Webster about it. Whelan appeared quite prepared to contradict the briefings being given by the leader's office. 'Officially we are denying the £100,000 top rate, but of course the *Times* story is right. Gordon has never said on the record that he would go for a 50p rate but that is definitely what he would do if he was Chancellor.' The following week, in his speech to the party conference, Brown confirmed that his target was to achieve a 10p starting rate, in what he described as 'a people's tax cut for jobs', but he made no mention of a new higher rate. Undaunted, Webster repeated his line in the next morning's *Times*, now suggesting that Labour might raise some of the money it would need to compensate for the lower starting rate of 10p by introducing a new top rate of 50p. However, from then on Whelan seemed increasingly reluctant to speculate about the likelihood of a higher rate. He insisted that this was a decision for the shadow Chancellor and that Brown would, as promised, announce Labour's tax plans well before polling day. Subsequently there were suggestions that briefings given at the party conference were intended to lay a false trail, with the aim of building up expectations of a new top rate so that Labour's spin doctors, at a moment of their choosing, could knock it all down in a blaze of favourable publicity. The apparent cynicism was breathtaking: Labour, it seemed, were about to abandon, virtually without open debate, a belief long held by many in the party that high earners should be asked to pay more in income tax.

As in any political party, there must inevitably have been some tense moments and hurtful rebuffs as the Labour leadership thrashed out their tax policy in the latter half of 1996. Not unnaturally, the participants had no wish for the harsh reality of their discussions to be raked over by the news media, and they were highly self-disciplined. Unlike the government, with its many administrative layers and propensity for leaks, Blair presided over a tightly run shadow Cabinet and a close-knit support staff from whom, by comparison, little damaging information seeped out. Lurid newspaper accounts of a series of crisis summits, at which the shadow Chancellor's demand for a 50p top rate was repeatedly over-ruled by Blair, were hard to substantiate. When journalists face such an effective facade, there is no substitute for patience. I knew there would be other opportunities, later in the campaign, to dig away at the story. There was always the possibility that either Blair or Brown, or one of their advisers, would let slip clues as to what had gone behind the scenes.

Nevertheless, the build-up to the January announcement was not all plain sailing. The tension at the top kept resurfacing. A fortnight after the party conference, both the *Sun* and the *Express* carried exclusive reports saying Blair had definitely decided to go into the election promising no increases in income tax. Roland Watson in the *Express* was categoric: Blair was 'poised to veto' Brown's plans for a 50p top rate because the deputy leader John Prescott was now on-side and accepted that going for a higher rate would play into the Tories' hands. Although they did not challenge the tax prediction which the two papers had given, Blair's staff denied suggestions of a rift. 'This is fantasy land reporting,' said press officer Tim Allan. 'Blair and Brown have devised Labour's tax plans together ... and Brown is a brilliant tactician. We've stated on countless occasions that none of our policies involve extra taxation.' When I was interviewed on *Today* that morning I explained that although the leader's office was playing down the story of a split, Brown's aides had indicated previously that the shadow Chancellor favoured a 50p rate. Within minutes of my broadcast Whelan was on the phone, berating me for daring to suggest that 'Brown's aides' had briefed journalists about the possibility of a 50p top rate. 'Those split stories are complete fiction.' Whelan rang me again later to say my report had caused him a lot of trouble. 'Mandelson has been bollocking me all morning, accusing me of speaking to you and stoking up that story. He's doing everything he can to do me in. Don't you realise, Mandelson's permanently on the warpath against me.'

Despite strenuous efforts to play down their differences, arguments between Labour's spin doctors were a recurring feature of the tense months that led up to the election. News reports of a Blair–Brown split angered Peter Mandelson because they fuelled speculation that Labour were planning secretly to put up taxes and undermined the party's strategy of presenting the shadow Cabinet as a united team, with a decisive leader. The disarray among John Major's ministers was always being paraded by Labour as a sign of the Prime Minister's weakness, and consequently the slightest hint of dissension in Blair's team was always pounced on by the Conservatives. Any confirmation of Labour's underlying belief in higher taxes was also exploited by the government as it was said to indicate the kind of pressure for more public spending which would be put on Blair should he become Prime Minister. Mandelson's efforts to kill off follow-up reports were hampered by the fact that Labour's spin doctors were only too happy to plant favourable stories in newspapers like the *Daily Mail*, *Express* and *Sun*. Even though it had given a graphic, if unsourced, account of how Blair was 'locked in a battle' with his shadow Chancellor, the top line of a *Sun* exclusive, that Blair would go into the next election 'promising no income tax rises under Labour', looked to be entirely authentic and was exactly the kind of headline which would appeal to Mandelson. Nor would Alastair Campbell have been averse to the *Sun*'s leader that morning, which predicted Blair was about to make political history by being the first Labour leader who 'didn't threaten your pay packet'. Blair was keen to use any opportunity to strengthen the impression that Labour's high-spending days were over, but Brown could hardly make any firm promises until the Chancellor of the Exchequer, Kenneth Clarke, had revealed his hand in the November 1996 Budget.

Fearing a surprise attack, Labour's campaign team in Millbank Tower remained on constant alert, just in case the Conservatives mounted a surprise offensive and fired off the kind of 'tax bombshell' which had done so much damage in the 1992 campaign. Labour's success in convincing at least political journalists of the seriousness of their intent was causing increasing irritation at Central Office. What the Tories found particularly galling was the fact that Blair and Brown had achieved this without making any precise pre-election promises on taxation, and they were anxious to find some way of undermining the credibility which their opponents appeared to be establishing. Their retaliation came in mid-November 1996, much earlier than expected, and took the form of a 100-page document listing all Labour's known spending pledges. It identified eighty-nine separate policy proposals and costed them at £30 billion, the equivalent of an extra £1,200 a year in tax for the average family. *Newsnight* had the first report of the new 'tax bombshell', but the most detailed preview appeared in next morning's *Daily Telegraph*, which had obviously been supplied with an advance copy of the document. Boris Johnson, the paper's political columnist, claimed that even if 'keen Tory calculator artists have been chucking the noughts around' and were wrong by a factor of three, it still meant Labour would require an extra 5p on income tax and that should be 'enough to freeze the marrow of the floating voter'. Labour's spin doctors were incandescent: the sole consolation for them was that the party's much vaunted rebuttal unit finally had a real target to go for. In the ensuing day of drama, political correspondents were regaled with a dress rehearsal of the tactics promised for the general election. The costly computer software installed at both Millbank Tower and Central Office was finally put to the test.

Labour started accusing the Conservatives of smear tactics when they got wind the night before of the plan for an early morning news conference at Central Office where William Waldegrave, Chief Secretary to the Treasury, intended to substantiate his claim that a Blair government would have no alternative but to increase the basic rate of income tax to 33p in the pound and the top rate to 70p. His assertion that the spending commitments had been costed in accordance with guidance drawn up by Cabinet Secretary, Sir Robin Butler, was described by Labour as 'untrue' even before Waldegrave could present his figures to a rather sceptical

audience of political correspondents. The Chief Secretary attempted to
lighten the proceedings by pointing out that the £30 billion price tag on
Blair's programme was £7 billion less than the pledges which Neil
Kinnock had made in the 1992 election, so 'New Labour is not so much
cheaper than Old Labour after all'. By mid-morning newsrooms were
being bombarded with a constant flow of faxes as each side rebutted the
charges levelled by the other. Labour organised their own news conference early that afternoon. Gordon Brown declared that the Conservatives'
campaign had 'blown up in their faces' because no one could trust their
'politically loaded costings'. To back up Brown's denunciation of
Waldegrave's 'pack of lies', journalists were handed a thick document
produced by the Millbank Tower rebuttal unit. On the front page was the
headline 'Wheels coming off the Tory lie machine'. Within a matter of
hours reporters were called back to Central Office for a third news conference at which Waldegrave claimed Brown's rebuttal was 'riddled with
inaccuracies and distortions'. To demonstrate the effectiveness of the
Conservatives' capability for rapid response, journalists were handed yet
another weighty tome, this one entitled 'Labour's rebuttal rebutted',
which sought to demolish Brown's rubbishing of the way the eighty-nine
spending pledges had been costed in the first place. Waldegrave ended the
day claiming he had won round one but it seemed more like a messy draw.
Labour had shown considerable flair in repelling this latest assault, but the
Conservatives had achieved their aim of getting journalists to look more
closely at the cost of Labour's proposals.

Amid the fury of the rapid rebuttal cross-fire there was one amusing
interlude which made up for the tedium of what after all had been a day of
rather predictable claim and counter-claim. Journalists were eager to see
how Labour responded to an unexpected attack. Would Millbank Tower
live up to its advance billing of being quicker off the draw when it came to a
political shoot-out? How would Labour's famed election campaign
manager Peter Mandelson cope with the possible fall-out of a well-aimed
'tax bombshell'? Since taking over at Millbank Tower he had adopted a
rather low profile, certainly as far as political correspondents were
concerned, and I was longing to see him in action again so that I could
observe how he directed the proceedings. As the journalists took their
seats for the first act of Labour's rebuttal, he could be seen standing strategically positioned just inside the door. I was already seated at the rear when
my brother George Jones, political editor of the *Daily Telegraph*, entered
the room. Mandelson immediately started clapping. 'Stand back!' he

shouted. 'Applause, applause for George Jones. Applause, applause for George Jones, straight from the *Newsnight* programme and Central Office.' My brother's by-line had been on the *Daily Telegraph*'s front-page splash predicting Labour 'would cost families £1,200 a year' so he was hardly likely to have been Mandelson's pin-up that morning, but no one had expected the party's most eminent spin doctor to lash out publicly in this way and accuse a political editor of being a Tory stooge. Without responding to Mandelson's taunts, George promptly walked out, but not before Michael Brunson, ITN's political editor, had chipped in with his support, muttering something to the effect that he hoped 'George punches him on the nose'. Mandelson himself had disappeared within an instant, just as the television crews, alerted to the commotion, turned to see what was happening. Spin doctors have an aversion to being caught on camera, so his hasty retreat was only to be expected.

I was probably more hardened than my brother to Mandelson's jibes. He had made it his business to cast public aspersions on my work. I always took it in good part, in view of the maxim that all publicity was good publicity. However, if he had tried the same trick on me, and applauded my entrance, I hope I would have risen to the occasion and taken him for a ride. All it needed was a playful response which would have given the television crews and photographers a few extra moments in which to focus their cameras and put the spin doctor in a spin. Who knows, I might have taken Mandelson's cue, marched up to the platform, grabbed a red rose from the display on the table, and then attempted to take the microphone . . . Only the day before, at a conference on election campaigning organised by the Westminster Media Forum, Mandelson had tried to provoke me after he had spied me in the audience. He interrupted his speech to chide me for 'scribbling away madly in the corner, no doubt trying to fill up another book'. While I was happy enough to shrug off such nonsense, it did become a little tiring when Mandelson personalised his attacks on George and myself and sought to gain political capital from the fact that we were brothers. If he ever saw us chatting together in the corridors of Westminster, or at a party conference, he would immediately announce in a loud voice that this was the evidence he had been looking for of collusion between the BBC and the *Daily Telegraph*. Other taunts were more whimsical. He revelled in the chance to put us both in our place. On one occasion he delivered a critique of our respective performances on television and radio, delivering himself of the opinion that I was 'too animated' while George was 'not animated enough'.

By the time we filed out of the Millbank news conference after hearing Labour's rebuttal on the 'tax bombshell', Mandelson had resumed his position at the entrance and had clearly recovered his composure. On seeing me walk by, he leant over to remind me of what he had said the day before when he spotted me scribbling away in the corner. 'No one can understand why I gave your next book such a tremendous plug.' Donald Macintyre, political columnist of the *Independent*, got straight to the point: 'Peter, you should not have done that to George.' Tony Bevins, the *Independent*'s political editor, told him his conduct was 'awful'. But Mandelson was gloating over my brother's hurried retreat: 'Oh diddums, oh diddums, poor George Jones.' Afterwards Michael Brunson told me he thought Mandelson's conduct was disgraceful and he was only thankful he was not involved himself. 'If Mandelson had done that to me I'd have had a go at him.' ITN's political editor spoke from experience. At the 1990 Labour conference Brunson had lost his cool and grabbed Mandelson by the lapels after being accused by him of producing 'flag-waving' reports about Margaret Thatcher.

Later that day Mandelson regaled journalists in the lobby with a blow-by-blow account of his encounter with my brother. He had concluded that he had 'obviously touched a raw nerve with George'. He insisted he had no quarrel with the report which appeared in the *Daily Telegraph*, but he believed George had come across as a 'surrogate' Tory by revealing details of the Conservatives' attack in a *Newsnight* interview. 'I am sorry he is distressed. I shall apologise to him.' I was more interested in finding out how Mandelson rated the effectiveness of Labour's response to the 'tax bombshell'. He said that in fact his team had a lot to thank my brother for. 'It was very useful to get George's advance warning. But we had to run hard to knock it down. It was all hands to the pump and if George hadn't done his story we would have been hard done by to rebut it.'

My brother waited until next morning before producing his rebuttal. In a lengthy signed article in the *Daily Telegraph* he accused Mandelson of resorting to 'intimidation' in his efforts to prevent journalists writing stories which he did not like. George said he had walked out of the news conference because he was not prepared to accept the accusation that he had become a representative of Conservative Central Office. 'I ignored him the first time. But when Mandelson made the charge a second time, I decided such insults were unacceptable. Rather than make a scene I left the press conference . . . It may seem trivial. But it is another example of a campaign of intimidation by Mandelson against journalists who write

anything with which Labour does not agree . . . Mandelson seems to
believe that if he can embarrass people in front of their colleagues they will
be less likely to write anything that can be seen as anti-Labour.' That
afternoon, the accuser and accused appeared together on BBC2's
Westminster Live. Mandelson duly apologised on air, but as he walked off
the set he was seen to grab my brother's arm and say, in front of the studio
producers, that he had not realised George would be so sensitive to his
'teasing'. He had no idea the political editor of a national newspaper could
be 'so thin-skinned'.

There had been no shortage of advice to Mandelson as to how he
should make amends for his outburst. He had been urged to 'cool it' by the
Labour MP and former minister Gerald Kaufman, who had been a press
officer for the late Harold Wilson and therefore spoke with some
authority. In an article in that afternoon's *Evening Standard*, he urged the
'acknowledgedly brilliant' Mandelson not to fall into the trap of accusing
George Jones of 'peddling a Tory line'. Kaufman believed that broadsheet
newspapers like the *Daily Telegraph* were 'doing their best to report
honestly', and Tory newspapers were giving the Conservatives a harder
time than at any period since the dying months of the Macmillan government; so Mandelson should ring up George and admit that even the 'best
of us can get het up at testing moments'. Although Mandelson realised he
probably had no alternative but to apologise for going over the top, I
sensed that his attack on my brother would not be the last we would hear of
his criticism about the way the 'tax bombshell' had been reported. During
our conversations he had been particularly abusive about the way the BBC
had handled the story.

Mandelson chose his moment with care, waiting a full fortnight before
lodging his complaint. During the intervening period Kenneth Clarke
had delivered the Conservatives' last Budget of the parliament with its 1p
pre-election cut in income tax. The Chancellor claimed that the average
family was £1,000 a year better off than at the time of the 1992 general
election, a calculation hotly disputed by Labour who maintained that John
Major's 'twenty-two tax increases' had left families worse off. Statistics
were bandied back and forth all week and, as the *Daily Telegraph* observed
in an editorial, the public could be excused for 'finding the whole
argument bewildering'. One of the statistics seized on by Labour was an
admission by William Waldegrave on the Sunday *Dimbleby* programme
that the average income tax bill had risen by £50 a year since 1992. Gordon
Brown demanded the immediate withdrawal of the Conservatives' latest

poster which, superimposed over a close-up photograph of John Major's face, proclaimed: 'As promised – lower income tax'. Waldegrave was annoyed with himself afterwards for having failed to explain that people were paying more tax because earnings had risen. He was particularly aggrieved by the way Brown's staff had managed to 'spin this into a holy writ revelation'.

I was on duty that Sunday and had been bombarded with messages on my pager from two of Labour's press officers, Charlie Whelan and Tim Allan, demanding that the BBC report Waldegrave's 'gaffe'. It was a complex story, based entirely on statistics, and I felt it would require an interview with Brown himself if we were to broadcast a balanced report. Along with other political correspondents, I had been waiting for some time for the chance to ask the shadow Chancellor whether he still favoured imposing a new top rate of income tax, and the Waldegrave 'gaffe' appeared to provide an ideal opportunity. However, Whelan told me Brown was not available to do television or radio interviews that Sunday. Instead, Labour were fielding Dawn Primarolo, another member of the shadow Treasury team. I took this as indicating that Labour were more interested in scoring points against Waldegrave than in allowing journalists an opportunity to challenge the shadow Chancellor about his own tax plans. As Labour had ruled out any possibility of the BBC putting questions to Brown, the radio newsroom decided to stick with my lunchtime report about an earlier claim on *Breakfast with Frost* by the former Labour Cabinet minister, Lady Castle, that the party had reneged on a pledge to re-examine the possibility of linking increases in the state pension to rises in earnings rather than prices. Harriet Harman, the shadow social security secretary, had responded to Lady Castle's attack, disputing her version of events. The pensions issue had provided the only serious dissent at the 1996 party conference, and Lady Castle was vociferous in her charge that the undertakings then given to delegates had not been honoured.

The twists and turns of the previous two weeks had provided Mandelson with just the opportunity he was seeking to construct what he considered was a damning indictment of the BBC's news coverage. His letter of complaint to Tony Hall, the chief executive for BBC news and current affairs, harked back to the Conservatives' 'tax bombshell'. The BBC had given 'undue credibility' to this 'bogus "costing" exercise' and the coverage was 'excessive and unmerited'. Another illustration of the Corporation's 'uneven and partisan' treatment was the way the radio and television news bulletins 'chose completely to ignore' William Waldegrave's admission that 'direct taxes had risen by £50 a year' and instead reported 'a story without consequence or implication concerning Barbara Castle'. At no point in his letter did Mandelson challenge the accuracy of the BBC's reporting: his complaint was directed entirely at the news judgement of its journalists. He claimed the BBC had 'shifted gear' in its political coverage and would be 'guilty of a serious departure from its news programme guidelines if it carries on in this vein'. The letter was a typical Mandelson ploy. He had denigrated the reporting and judgement of a wide cross-section of the BBC's correspondents, producers and programme editors. I found his complaint about the news value of my own story on Labour's pensions dispute particularly illuminating. The level of public dissent within the Labour Party was minuscule when seen against the Conservative Party and their tumultuous split over Europe. Nevertheless Labour were not only tightening up on their own disciplinary procedures but also revealing, through Mandelson's letter, the lengths to which they were prepared to go to prevent such dissent as did exist being reported on radio or television.

Mandelson's letter to the BBC, like his brush with my brother, was part of a well-rehearsed repertoire. His ability to hit his target when making complaints explained why he was so feared by political correspondents. Although his clash with George Jones had necessitated an apology, Mandelson had nonetheless given a signal to the other journalists at that news conference that if they ever tried to mess with him in public, or answer back, then he could and would hit below the belt. With his letter to the BBC, Mandelson had gone direct to management, over the heads of the journalists who had no inkling that a complaint was on its way. The arrival, out of the blue, of a long catalogue of criticisms can have considerable impact, especially in an organisation like the BBC which is publicly accountable and has well-established procedures for examining complaints. Reporters, producers and editors are suddenly required to justify actions which they took days if not weeks ago. Mandelson took great delight in composing these catch-all letters of complaint, as though he was lighting a long fuse and wanted time to savour what might happen. Having been a regular target of such complaints in the past, I knew the warning signs. If there had been a run of news stories which happened to be unfavourable to Labour, Mandelson adopted a somewhat threatening pose as he patrolled the lobby, waving his finger at errant reporters or perhaps frowning at them as they passed by. Occasionally he could not resist letting slip that perhaps a particular journalist should think again about how a certain story had been reported. Mandelson invariably hurried away before he could be cross-questioned, leaving the reporter undecided as whether it was all just bluster or perhaps the prelude to a serious complaint.

Even if his intervention had hurt feelings, or generated other unpleasant repercussions for newsroom or programme staff, such was Mandelson's self-confidence that he expected journalists to continue to respond with the same enthusiasm to Labour's constant flow of publicity initiatives, as though nothing had happened which might in any way have damaged the relationship between the news media and the party. Whenever I managed to discuss with the rest of Labour's spin doctors Mandelson's tactic of making so many belligerent complaints it was clear they were being advised to adopt the same strategy. Fault-finding was regarded as part and parcel of the everyday cut and thrust of political journalism, and while it was intended to make life as uncomfortable as possible for the individuals involved, it was not aimed at jeopardising day-to-day relations. Therefore, as far as Mandelson was concerned, it should always be business as usual with the BBC or any other news organisation. Mandelson liked to cultivate an impression of being hard to please, as if urging journalists to go one step further to win his favour. As he was so rarely prepared to be complimentary about the extensive coverage and favourable treatment which Labour had succeeded in achieving, I was struck by his effusive praise for the way the BBC, along with all other news outlets, reported Gordon Brown's pledges on income tax in January 1997.

Labour's New Year tax offensive took off earlier than the spin doctors had planned. The intention was that Brown should give a series of speeches to business audiences at which he would progressively outline his plans for Labour's first Budget. However, Blair effectively upstaged the first speech with the launch of his draft of Labour's pre-election manifesto, entitled *Leading Britain into the Future*. The Union flag, which was displayed prominently on the front cover, provided the backdrop for a news conference at which Blair was joined on the platform by his deputy John Prescott, Brown and two other members of the shadow Cabinet, Robin Cook and Margaret Beckett. Most of the questions were directed towards probing what the document described as the 'truth' about the funding of Labour's programme. 'There are no uncosted or unfunded spending proposals, no concealed tax increases . . . There is no evasion, no double-dealing, no hidden agenda.' When asked if Labour still intended to bring in a 50p top rate of income tax, Blair could hardly have been any clearer. 'If there are to be any changes to the top rate of tax we will make them clear . . . nothing will be concealed . . . but there is not a single spending commitment which requires an increase in personal tax.'

After the news conference it soon became apparent Campbell was irritated at the way journalists had concentrated on asking about a 50p top rate and appeared to have ignored the rest of the pre-election manifesto. As correspondents gathered round to hear his assessment of the proceedings, Campbell scolded journalists with whom he had previously worked, before becoming Blair's press officer. 'The trouble with you lot is that you're all higher rate taxpayers yourselves. You're just obsessed about the top rate because you'd all have to pay it. How many times do we have to say this is a programme for government? It's fully costed and funded.' A few paces away another group of journalists was clustered around Charlie Whelan and the shadow Chancellor's adviser Ed Balls. The spin they were offering was not quite so emphatic. They said Brown would not be revealing his hand for some weeks, until he gave his planned series of speeches. When asked if journalists were correct in their assessment that the 50p rate had been ruled out, Balls said that was not 'necessarily so'. He felt the public were more concerned about whether Labour would push up spending than about possible tax increases under Blair. 'Hitting Labour on tax is the only shot left in the Conservative locker, but the Tories know their attacks aren't credible after the twenty-two tax rises there've been under Major. So if they're not landing punches on us, why should we announce our tax plans now?' If Brown had harboured any thoughts of keeping the media guessing about a new top rate, next morning's newspapers effectively closed off that option. The front-page headlines were almost uniform, saying Blair 'backs away' or 'retreats' from a 50p tax rate. Most of the reports said that the shadow Chancellor had lost the argument with Blair because the Labour leader feared that talk of an increased top rate would allow the Conservatives to brand Labour as a high-tax party. When I challenged Whelan next day about why he thought the newspapers had been unanimous in taking the line that Blair had personally ruled out the higher rate, he sounded a bit miffed. 'That's just what the papers say. It's for Gordon to decide. You'll have to wait for his speeches.'

I was puzzled by Labour's tactics. Brown's staff still seemed to be leaving the door slightly ajar over possible tax increases, and although Campbell had sounded pretty emphatic there had been a degree of coat-

trailing in his briefing. According to a report by Jill Sherman, chief
political correspondent of *The Times*, Labour's intention was to get 'as
much mileage as possible' out of Brown's announcements on tax by
staging them over several weeks in order to 'maximise favourable
headlines'. But Michael Jones, writing in the *Sunday Times*, thought Blair
had given a 'smoke-screen performance' on Labour's tax plans and
accused the party's spin doctors of laying 'maze-like adventures for
seekers after truth'. After Blair had been interviewed that Sunday
morning on *Breakfast with Frost*, I finally succeeded in persuading
Campbell to come clean. He said Blair was not 'leaving the door open' to
higher taxes. 'We are definitely going to say, in black and white, that
Labour won't be putting up your taxes. However, as Jill Sherman said in
The Times, we can't get enough of that kind of publicity. So when it finally
comes out, it will be a mega-story which will definitely break through to
the public. But Blair isn't going to say it until Gordon decides to and has
said it himself.'

During the prolonged political jousting over tax, Labour took delight
in taunting the Conservatives for having no alternative but to resort to
negative advertising campaigns, like the 'tax bombshell'. Underlying
these jibes was the fear of the party's spin doctors that it remained vulnerable to a surprise attack. But, despite having given the impression that
Blair had no intention of descending to such depths and intended to
campaign solely on a positive platform, Labour were about to play what
they thought was their own trump card. In the event, their first sally into
unashamedly negative campaigning produced something of a damp
squib. If a 'tax bombshell' is to have any hope of succeeding, it must not
only create a big bang on impact, so as to attract attention, but also send a
credible and lasting message. Therefore the target of an attack has to be
chosen with care in order to give it at least some chance of inflicting
permanent damage. Labour believed that one of the Conservatives'
significant weak points was their record on value added tax. John Major's
pledge in the 1992 election, that the government had 'no plans and no
need to extend the scope of VAT', was broken within a year by the then
Chancellor, Norman Lamont, who applied the tax to domestic power and
fuel in his 1993 Budget. His successor, Kenneth Clarke, was seen as being
especially vulnerable to the accusation that a future Major government
might be tempted to extend VAT even further, perhaps by levying it on
food. Labour thought that if they could get the charge to stick, this would
be a worthwhile scare tactic. In a move which had all the makings of

another dress rehearsal for the general election campaign, Labour launched a synchronised propaganda offensive which featured an elaborate photo-opportunity, a big-hitting news conference, a new poster campaign and a specially commissioned party political broadcast.

In order to make sure that the Conservatives had as little advance notice as possible of the attack, Labour's chief media spokesperson, David Hill, waited until 10 p.m. on the eve of the launch before briefing the Press Association news agency with a story timed for release at 4.30 the next morning. But although Hill seemed unaware of it, one of the new posters was already on display on a hoarding in Ebury Bridge Road, less than a mile away from Conservative Central Office. Apparently it had been put up a day early by mistake, giving the Tories just enough time to organise their rebuttal and pre-empt the carefully primed Labour 'tax bombshell' which warned that the Conservatives might put VAT on food. Even before the Press Association's chief political correspondent Amanda Brown had time to file her embargoed story from David Hill she was being advised by Sheila Gunn, one of the Conservatives' senior press officers, of an unexpected late-night intervention by the Chancellor. After being tipped off that evening about Labour's campaign, Clarke saw John Major and immediately issued a statement accusing Labour of trying to promote a 'deliberate lie'. 'Neither the Prime Minister nor I have any intention of imposing VAT on food so long as we are in government.' Clarke's statement was released by the Press Association at 11 p.m., in plenty of time for the next morning's newspapers, which carried photographs of the new poster. It showed a large clenched fist crushing an egg. Alongside was the message: 'Next Tory tax? £10.50 a week VAT on food.' Most papers took the line that Major and Clarke were so angry at what the *Sun* described as Labour's 'dirty tricks' advertising blitz that they decided to issue an 'unprecedented' statement promising not to extend VAT to food. On that morning's *Today* programme the Chancellor sallied forth as a one-man rapid rebuttal unit, lambasting 'Blair's tawdry PR men' for depriving the British public of a grown-up debate about the economy. Although Labour had produced a list of quotations derived from Clarke's speeches, in which he had in the past gone through the various options for extending VAT, there was no specific reference to his ever having suggested that it should be levied on food. Clarke could not be shaken in his rebuttal. 'I have been four years as Chancellor. It has never crossed my mind to put VAT on food ... and I don't expect to live to see the day when any government puts VAT on food in this country.'

Labour had lost both the element of surprise and any serious credibility in their message. The whole basis of their campaign was becoming less plausible by the minute, and the news coverage was rapidly turning into a farce. A photo-opportunity at a Sainsbury's store just across the Thames from Westminster, intended to be the opening salvo, degenerated into the battle of the supermarket trolley. Two Labour frontbenchers, Alistair Darling and Margaret Beckett, were lined up to pose as a happily married couple buying their weekly groceries. Before they even had time to consult their shopping list, the attention of the photographers and television crews was diverted by the animated arrival of the Conservative MP Alan Duncan, who had been assisting the party chairman, Brian Mawhinney, with the Tory campaign. Duncan dived between the shelves and emerged triumphant with a large bunch of bananas. After paying at the check-out, he held them aloft for the cameras and said the bananas were for the shadow Chancellor Gordon Brown, who had made 'a complete monkey of himself with his disgraceful lie and smear' about the Conservatives putting VAT on food. When the commotion had subsided, Darling and Beckett walked sedately up and down the shelves, emerging at the check-out with a trolley load of groceries costing £37.90. If there had been VAT on food, they said, the bill would have been £44.53.

By now Labour's attack had definitely been blunted by the Conservatives' counter-measures. When Darling and Beckett joined other shadow Cabinet members at a news conference in Millbank Tower, where the new poster was on display, the reporters' questions illustrated the effectiveness of the Conservatives' rebuttal. Darling, the shadow chief secretary, who was representing Labour's Treasury team in Brown's absence, was asked repeatedly if he could do any better than the Conservatives and give a firm election pledge that a future Labour government would not levy VAT on food. The platform party seemed caught off guard. Darling clearly had no inkling that Labour's VAT 'bombshell' could be thrown back in his face. Like most cautious Treasury spokesmen, he had been programmed to avoid using the words 'pledge' or 'promise' when speaking about his party's tax plans. On trying once more to get Darling to explain why Labour would go no further than the Conservatives, in saying they had 'no intention' of extending VAT, I eventually elicited this heated response: 'Don't be daft. It is abundantly clear we have no intention of putting VAT on food. Do you think we would be mounting a campaign like this if we had that intention? Come on!' Robin Cook sprang to Darling's defence, quoting an earlier promise by

Gordon Brown that Labour 'stands by and repeats its pledge not to extend VAT to food and children's clothes'. Margaret Beckett said it was not Labour's fault that words like 'promise' and 'pledge' had been devalued by the Conservatives.

Labour's spin doctors were annoyed at the way journalists had turned the news conference on its head. Charlie Whelan told me to my face that my question to Darling had been 'ridiculous'. Alastair Campbell denied Labour had resorted to negative campaigning. 'What we are doing is reminding people that the Tories lie on tax . . . that is different from a negative campaign.' A few hundred yards away at Central Office, the Conservatives' spin doctors were chortling with delight, claiming their first successful 'prebuttal' of 1997. By getting in first with Clarke's denial, they had knocked down Labour's news story even before it was up and running. To press home their advantage and provide balancing television film and pictures, the Conservatives laid on their own photo–opportunity in Smith Square. Mawhinney walked out of Central Office to unveil yet another new poster. Pasted on to the side of a mobile hoarding, it claimed a Blair government would cost the 'average family £23 a week extra in tax'. Danny Finkelstein, the Conservatives' research director, insisted that this counter–attack had far more credibility than Labour's initial assault because it was part of a carefully costed exercise, and dismissed the tactic of trying to frighten voters by suggesting Clarke might put VAT on food as the least substantiated claim of the pre–election campaign. 'If this is Labour's first attempt at negative advertising, it's pretty useless. To attack us for putting VAT on domestic fuel is one thing, but to suggest we would put it on food is ludicrous and unprovable. All Labour have got are some Ken Clarke quotes about him keeping his options open. If a negative campaign is going to work it has to make a genuine point and at least be believable.'

Clarke's robust denial of the charge was regarded as having been a critical factor. David Ruffley, one of the party's campaign officers, who had previously been the Chancellor's political adviser, said Clarke's great strength was that the 'punters think he tells it to them straight'. 'Ken wasn't messing about on *Today* this morning. You could tell there was a whiff of campaigning in his nostrils and he loved it. That's why he's such an electoral asset.' Sheila Gunn, who had telephoned lobby journalists the night before with Clarke's rebuttal statement, was ecstatic. 'Although I shouldn't be saying it, we were pretty cute. Our timing was brilliant. We found out about the Labour poster and then beat them to it.' The party's head of broadcasting, Anthony Gordon Lennox, hoped it would be a sign of things to come. 'It meant being up all night, but Labour should realise we've got our act together at last.' By mid-afternoon there was a grudging acknowledgement of the effectiveness of the Conservatives' rebuttal from Labour's campaigns spokesman, Brian Wilson. He said that while Clarke's 'prebuttal' did raise the profile of the story and put VAT on the agenda, the news coverage had 'just about evened itself out'. By teatime, the story had been written off as a one-day wonder, having been overtaken by news of the death of the Conservative MP Ian Mills which had dealt the Tories another unexpected blow, leaving John Major heading a minority government.

Although the VAT debacle had revealed the Labour spin doctors' inexperience in the black art of negative campaigning, their pre-eminence in puffing up positive stories was beyond question. Now, instead of retreating to lick their wounds, they set to work immediately to prepare the ground for Gordon Brown's unprecedented promise not to increase either the basic or the top rate of income tax for the full five years of a parliament. Delivering a pledge of that magnitude would be a key moment in the pre-election campaign: it had to be milked for all it was worth and this time there would be no slip-up or advance warning to Central Office. In retrospect, one could not but admire the sheer effrontery with which Labour eventually succeeded in marshalling the news media into greeting Brown's promise with such uncritical acclaim.

The intention was to make the announcement during the first of the shadow Chancellor's set speeches to business audiences, which had been arranged for the following Monday afternoon. Charlie Whelan wasted no time in building up interest in what Brown might say. His aim was to raise expectations without stealing Brown's thunder. He did all he could to cajole journalists into writing weekend preview stories which hammered home the line that Labour would be tough on public spending while making no mention of the possibility that Brown would also be announcing his proposals on personal taxation. In order to throw the Conservatives off the scent, Whelan tipped off the *Independent on Sunday* that Labour intended to double its windfall levy on the privatised utilities to at least £10 billion. This provided the paper's political correspondent, Paul Routledge, with the front-page splash.

Whelan's hardest task was to ensure that Monday morning's newspapers and news bulletins gave Brown's speech top billing but again gave no hint of the punch-line.

Instead of talking to individual papers on the telephone, Whelan, and Brown's adviser Ed Balls, took the unusual step for a Sunday of going personally to the House of Commons to brief political correspondents in the press gallery. They went armed with a strong message: Brown would announce that Labour intended to accept the spending targets which Clarke had already declared for the next two financial years. By going along with the government's squeeze on public spending, Labour were acknowledging that they too would be unable to provide any extra money for pay increases for workers in the public sector. Correspondents who asked whether Brown would also be mentioning his tax plans in the speech were told that this was not his intention. Whelan need not have had any fears about next morning's headlines. News of the two-year freeze on public pay was the front-page lead in *The Times*, *Daily Telegraph*, *Financial Times*, *Guardian* and *Independent*. Radio and television news bulletins were also previewing Brown's speech. On *Today*, the BBC's political correspondent John Pienaar led the 7 a.m. and 8 a.m. news bulletins with his pre-recorded report on Labour's undertaking to keep to the government's spending targets. *Business Breakfast*, which like Pienaar had been briefed by Whelan the night before, had taken the same line at 6 a.m. They had been assured Brown intended to make no mention of income tax. However, once Whelan had finished briefing the correspondents who were at work that Sunday evening, he began a discreet ring-round of broadcasters and other journalists who would be on early duty the following morning. Gordon Brown's intention all along was to trail his promise on tax during a prime-time interview which had already been arranged with *Today* for that Monday morning, just after the 8 a.m. news. Whelan's tactic throughout the weekend was to make sure that the story turned into a blockbuster once Brown had revealed the importance of the announcement which he would be making that afternoon. Labour's covert orchestration of the news coverage was risky, but worked like a charm.

Taking the precaution of ensuring that the *Today* programme asked the shadow Chancellor the right question and tackled Brown on income tax as well as public spending, Whelan primed the presenter, James Naughtie, that Sunday evening. Then both the BBC's early-morning political correspondent Carolyn Quinn and the Press Association's political editor Phil Murphy were alerted as to what would happen and told to make a point of listening to *Today* at 8.10 a.m. Whelan was particu-larly anxious that Brown's tax pledge should be reported prominently by the London *Evening Standard*, in view of the impact its coverage had on newsrooms throughout the capital. Patrick Hennessy, the paper's duty political correspondent, said he would have to be given a firm steer earlier than other reporters because the first edition went to press before 8.10 a.m. Whelan took a chance and revealed the details to the *Evening Standard*. At 7.30 a.m. Whelan also alerted Michael Brunson of ITN and the BBC's political editor Robin Oakley to Brown's imminent proclamation.

Once the interview had started, Naughtie seemed in no hurry to get to the point. He asked Brown several questions before referring rather obliquely to the fact that Labour were making no public expenditure commitments which required 'additional tax'. The moment the shadow Chancellor had been given his cue he leapt in with his answer:

Brown: Tax should encourage employment and work, savings and invest-
    ment. I want tax rates to be fair. I will leave the basic and top rates
    unchanged . . . and, to create an even fairer tax system, I want to
    introduce a 10p starting rate, but I will only do that when resources are
    available.
Naughtie: So this is the Brown statement on tax? You will leave the top rate
    unchanged?
Brown: I will be making commitments for our manifesto. They are
    commitments for a parliament. The basic rate and top rate will remain
    unchanged.
Naughtie: Throughout the parliament? That's a very important
    announcement.
Brown: Yes, throughout the parliament.

The moment Brown had delivered his tax promise on air, Phil Murphy released his newsflash. It was timed at 8.17 a.m. and said: 'Gordon Brown will later today rule out introducing a higher level of income tax.' Carolyn Quinn's report for the 9 a.m. news on Radio 4 went hard on Brown's announcement, saying that 'for the first time, categoric-ally, he'll rule out raising the basic rate or introducing a new top rate of income tax'. The *Evening Standard*'s first edition came up trumps: 'Labour: No income tax rises for five years' read the front-page splash under Hennessy's by-line. Alongside was a comment column saying Brown's words of reassurance were 'wholly welcome'. The headline on later editions was even more supportive: 'Labour fires tax Exocet'. The comment column had also been revamped, declaring that Brown's promise 'could prove to have provided the knock-out blow to Major'. Brown had repeated his tax promise for television crews which had been waiting for him outside Broadcasting House. His statement led the television news summaries all morning.

When political correspondents assembled in Downing Street for the 11 a.m. lobby briefing, the one talking point was Labour's audacity in making what Hennessy had described as 'the most far-reaching promise ever made by a would-be incoming Chancellor'. Some of them, including Martin Bentham of the *Sun*, felt they had been misled by Labour the night before. In his report that morning Bentham had topped his story with the spending freeze, and now was somewhat disgruntled. 'We made a point of asking whether Brown would mention income tax but we were assured it would be in a later speech.' Charles Reiss, the *Evening Standard*'s political editor, admired Whelan's tactics. 'We were told in advance that Naughtie had been tipped off to ask the tax question although we knew all the morning papers were going hard on the steer about spending. But the Tories are gobsmacked by it. We've been on to them all morning but so far got no response. All we get is spluttering down the phone.' ITN's political editor Michael Brunson could barely conceal his excitement: 'We're on to the big one now . . . the big boys fighting over the big issue.' Brunson was spot on with his assessment. Three-quarters of an hour later Kenneth Clarke took the platform at a hurriedly arranged news conference in Smith Square.

Conservative Central Office had been refurbished some weeks earlier in readiness for the election campaign. New lighting, microphones and state-of-the-art visual display equipment had been installed in the room set aside for news conferences. On show for the first time on the walls of the new waiting area were the Conservatives' latest 'New Labour, New Danger' posters, including the 'demon eyes' advertisement of Tony Blair which proved so controversial. Against the background of so many threatening images, the Conservatives' publicity staff seemed particularly ill at ease that morning. Sheila Gunn looked agitated as she handed an advance copy of Clarke's statement to the *Evening Standard*'s reporter. The Chancellor's former adviser David Ruffley muttered something to the effect that Brown's pledges on tax were too incredible to be believed. There was an evident sigh of relief from the spin doctors as Clarke finally emerged and began reading his prepared statement. 'Gordon Brown's claim that he could control public spending is beyond belief . . . Labour say one thing and do another. They talk tough but act feeble.' Clarke was clearly taken aback by the obvious impact Brown's promise had made on the assembled political correspondents. 'No one with anyone common sense can possibly believe him. He's not trustworthy. He's just making bland assertions. I have reduced the standard rate. I have raised thresholds. I want a 20p standard rate. I think that is a credible aim. The election shouldn't consist of Gordon Brown getting into a game with the electorate and matching the most attractive things that we have done.'

Clarke's passionate denunciation of Brown's evolving tax policy cheered up party workers. Ruffley said the Chancellor had got rather animated because he took pledges on tax 'very seriously' and thought Brown's promises were just a gimmick. Anthony Teesdale, who had taken over from Ruffley as Clarke's political adviser, thought the Chancellor had struck the right note. 'Clarke's heart was really in that attack this morning. He thinks Brown and his Treasury team are a load of wankers.' Danny Finkelstein said Brown's pledges were implausible because Labour had never come up with any 'credible' ways of cutting tax. 'I can't understand why Labour are doing this. We'll go all the way to the election fighting them on tax and spending. They'll lose the election because of this. People know Labour put up taxes.'

But at the Queen Elizabeth conference centre that afternoon congratulations all round were the order of the day as representatives of City firms began arriving to hear the shadow Chancellor speak. Whelan was already taking bids for radio and television interviews with Brown once the speech had been delivered. I had been reporting for the television news summaries all morning and Whelan was chuffed with my script line to the effect that Labour had delivered a 'double whammy' on the Conservatives by promising to control public spending and keep down income tax. Here was a rare sight: a Labour spin doctor waxing lyrical about the BBC's reporting. 'You're right, Nick, we have hit the Tories with a double whammy. The coverage has been tremendous. It all worked liked a dream. The great thing was the secrecy. We flung out that £10 billion windfall tax story to the *Independent on Sunday* just to confuse the Tories. Obviously I had to tip off Jim Naughtie. I briefed him on what the papers would be saying and then told him to put a question to Gordon on tax once they'd discussed spending. We were relying on Naughtie. He did leave it a bit late to pop the tax question. You could tell Naughtie was really surprised the pledge was so hard. But now John Pienaar is complaining to me, saying I'm "evil" for lying to him when I said tax wouldn't be in the speech – but I've apologised. I couldn't tell him. I had to do it.' Whelan said they had decided to press the button and push the tax story because the papers had already gone so hard in reporting that Labour was backing away from a new top rate. 'It would have been silly to hang around.'

While I was still trying to absorb Whelan's brazen account of the way he claimed to have manipulated so many journalists, he let slip that the very event we were attending, which had been organised by Labour's finance and industry group, was itself a sham. 'It's not a real conference at all. We've stage-managed the whole thing to build up the drama. It's costing us £5,000 to hire the Queen Elizabeth centre this afternoon and could you believe it, there are people at party headquarters who are complaining about the expense. But look at the effect. We've got the television political editors here for the speech and they're all lining up as good as gold to interview Gordon.' Labour's investment paid off handsomely next morning with some highly flattering editorials. The top leader in *The Times* said Brown's promise to bind himself on tax 'more tightly' than any previous Labour Chancellor had 'burnished his party's electoral image with boldness and vim'. The *Daily Mail* was equally complimentary: Brown's speech 'was as significant an act of exorcism as we have witnessed in the post-war history of British politics'. Of even greater concern to the Conservatives must have been the *Mail* leader writer's conclusion that as the Tories had 'destroyed their own credibility as tax-cutters' and had rendered themselves 'most ill-qualified to mock New Labour's new-found fiscal restraint'. The *Sun* welcomed the prospect that Brown would be 'the first Labour Chancellor in history vowing to reward rather than penalise success' and gave this assessment of the problem now facing John Major: 'With New Labour slaying the high-tax dragon, he needs a new monster to fight from his soap box.' Brown's pledge also provided the front-page lead for most of the nationals. Sheila Gunn admitted the morning's papers made grim reading for Conservative MPs. 'Labour did catch us on the hop. They had flagged up public spending so comprehensively that we really thought that was what they'd go on. But already people are asking, where is the money going to come from? Labour might get away with it now but our job is to stop them once the election is called.'

In contrast to Ms Gunn's rather forlorn demeanour, Peter Mandelson was beaming as he chatted to journalists in the lobby. When I congratulated him on the coverage Labour had secured he reacted rather suspiciously. 'Yes, it was tremendous. And don't forget we gave the story first to the BBC. I do hope we will get some reward in the future, perhaps rather more balanced coverage and a little less favourable to John Major. He only has to get out of bed and he leads the BBC news.' Alastair Campbell thought Labour could hardly have had a better day. 'It was one hell of an operation.' Whelan's audacious behaviour had certainly left some journalists pondering on the way they had been used. Tucked away in Brown's speech was the caveat that his promise related only to income tax. He told his City audience that he was not giving 'blanket commitments on each and every one of more than 200 tax exemptions, reliefs and allowances'. Michael Brunson believed the lobby had been swept along by the story. 'We were too kind to Brown. I should have hammered the fact that he could find other ways of raising tax.' But Kevin Maguire, political editor of the *Mirror*, said Labour had played it brilliantly. 'It would have been very hard for any journalist to go against the flow.' In a subsequent interview in *The Times*, Kenneth Clarke admitted that Brown's pledge to leave income tax unchanged for five years had come at him 'out of the blue', but he still thought the public would be wary of a shadow Chancellor who made 'policy on the hoof' and threw out 'populist pledges' in what he dismissed as sheer electioneering.

Several newspapers tried to piece together what had gone on behind the scenes. Philip Webster, political editor of *The Times*, said 'military planning' and 'a measure of subterfuge' had been essential in order to surprise the Tories. A fortnight before the speech Brown had met Blair at the Labour leader's home in Islington and, although he had 'for months flirted' with the idea of a 50p top rate, had finally agreed it would give the 'wrong signal' to voters. According to Webster, in the days before the announcement, only seven people in the party knew of the pledge on income tax. On the Sunday night before the speech Brown telephoned members of the shadow Cabinet, 'swearing them to secrecy'. Ewen MacAskill, chief political correspondent of the *Guardian*, reported that Labour's press officers knew they had 'spun it beautifully' after deliberately building up speculation at the October party conference that Brown wanted to impose a new top rate on those earning more than £100,000 a year. 'Having floated the idea, Labour had only to decide on when to knock it down . . . Three days of headlines and the Tory campaign on tax was neutralised.' Patrick Wintour, the *Observer*'s political editor, pursued the same point the following Sunday, asserting that the shadow Chancellor's staff had 'planted' the story about Brown wanting a 50p rate to create 'deliberate confusion' and keep the Tories guessing. Wintour agreed that Labour had achieved the maximum possible 'media hit'. Depending on one's point of view, it either represented the 'culmination of Labour's four-year battle to bury its tax and spend image, or alternatively, spelt not simply the end of socialism, but of social democracy and the whole Croslandite commitment to use public spending and tax to reduce inequality'.

Brown was decidedly enigmatic when I tried to pin him down about what had been his true intention over the possibility of introducing a higher top rate of income tax. I spoke to him the week after he had given his speech, when the media spotlight was less intense. Brown went some way towards confirming my own suspicions that in the months leading up to his announcement, Labour had been playing fast and loose with the news media. I asked him directly if he had ever favoured a rate of 50p in the pound. Brown smiled somewhat mischievously and insisted that there had never been any real likelihood of Labour bringing in a new top rate. 'We always thought that the fair range for income tax should be between 10p and 40p. So yes, trails were being set for journalists at the party conference over the possibility of a 50p rate. As that suited our purpose, we were happy with the way it was being reported.' As was only to be expected, Whelan took exactly the same line. Nevertheless his spin was a complete contradiction of what he had said the previous summer. 'Look, don't you understand, a 50p rate was never a serious option. We were always against it because it would never have raised a lot of money and we knew it would be a tremendous story when we ruled it out.' While this seemed entirely plausible as a strategy for manipulating the news media, there was more than one weak link in Whelan's attempt to distance Brown from the reports that he was originally in favour of a 50p rate above a £100,000 threshold. In the months leading up to the 1996 party conference, the shadow Treasury team had gone to great lengths to exploit the enormous salary increases which had been handed out to the 'fat cat' directors of the privatised utilities. Brown's underlying message had always seemed pretty clear: Labour did believe in fairness and they were therefore preparing the ground for some kind of assault on people taking home vastly inflated salaries. Another discrepancy in Brown's version of events was that he had left open the option of increasing other taxes and allowances, suggesting that once in government, Labour might find alternative ways of taxing high earners.

But by far the greatest flaw in Brown's assertion that the leadership had been in agreement on their tax strategy as far back as the 1996 conference was that party officials had been desperately worried for months by polling evidence which indicated that voters still did not trust Labour on tax. Although the gap had narrowed, opinion surveys and focus groups continued to show that voters thought taxes were more likely to go up under Labour than under the Conservatives. Against this background, for Labour to adopt, as a deliberate strategy, a tactic of teasing voters about the possibility of a new top rate, just to amuse the news media and confuse the Tories, was a political nonsense: the only conceivable explanation for the delay in ruling out the possibility was that it resulted from an underlying disagreement between Blair and Brown. If there had been a settled policy there is no doubt it would have been announced much earlier. Once the Conservatives launched their 'tax bombshell' in November 1996, claiming Labour had hidden spending plans of £30 billion, the pressure on Brown became intense. If Labour were to have any chance of destroying the Conservatives' continued credibility on tax they would have to do more than just remind voters of John Major's twenty-two tax increases. The promises on income tax were therefore regarded as the cornerstone of a concerted pre-election push to eliminate Labour's high-tax image. Even after Brown had delivered his pledge, there was to be no let-up in the drive to din into voters Labour's determination to keep a tight rein on spending. Charlie Whelan worked away feverishly with friendly journalists, conjuring up a succession of stories which he thought would help foster Brown's advance billing as the 'iron Chancellor' of a future Labour government. Buoyed up by his undoubted triumph over the tax speech, Whelan began taking ever greater risks on Brown's behalf.

Spin doctors can easily get carried away when caught up in fast-moving political developments. Journalists love nothing more than to keep a good story going and their enthusiasm can prove infectious. The temptation for a political propagandist is to nudge a story in the direction that looks like helping their party. As Whelan was to discover to his cost, there are dangers in putting the demands of presentation before policy. A week which had opened with the Labour leadership congratulating themselves on the breathtaking reception they had secured for Brown's speech ended in disarray with the party's spin doctors tripping over each other in a flurry of contradictory briefings. The event which unsettled them was the surprise announcement on Wednesday of that week by the Secretary of State for Defence, Michael Portillo, that the government intended to spend £60 million on building a replacement for the royal yacht *Britannia*. The aim was to have the new vessel ready in time for the Queen's golden jubilee in 2002, and it would be paid for out of the

Treasury's contingency funds. Replying to Portillo's statement in the Commons, the shadow defence secretary, David Clark, said that while there were benefits to the country in having a new royal yacht, Labour were not satisfied the government had chosen the most cost-effective method of financing the project and a future Labour government would look at ways of attracting private money to help fund the construction.

After this exchange, Whelan gave journalists a far harder steer: Brown would not be tricked into giving a 'blank cheque' in advance for such an important public spending decision. Whelan told me the priority was to ensure the shadow Chancellor looked tough on spending even if there was a danger it might lead to a 'class-envy backlash' against Labour. However, because of concern in the leader's office at the way Labour's reluctance to fund the new yacht was being firmed up in the teatime news bulletins, Alastair Campbell told BBC correspondents not to go as far as suggesting that the party was against building a new *Britannia*. He said Blair remained a 'staunch monarchist' and the emphasis should be on the efforts Labour would make to bring in private finance. Press reaction to the government's decision was largely hostile. That Friday two of the tabloids published the results of telephone polls of their readers. The largest vote against was reported by the *Mirror*, which said 'a massive 95 per cent' of its readers were critical of the Tories for 'lavishing so much on a new floating palace for the Queen'. Readers of the *Sun* voted by 'a stunning five to one to give the thumbs-down' to the scheme.

Friday is always a busy day for the spin doctors who patrol the press gallery because it is the last parliamentary day of the week for the lobby journalists who work for the Sunday newspapers. Each Friday the Prime Minister's press secretary holds a briefing attended exclusively by the Sunday lobby. Spokespeople for the opposition parties frequently pitch in as well, holding their own off-the-record sessions. When I saw Whelan chatting away that Friday to Paul Routledge, political correspondent of the *Independent on Sunday*, he told me immediately that he felt Brown's refusal to give a blank cheque for the funding of a new *Britannia* had been entirely vindicated by the opinion polls in the *Sun* and the *Mirror*. I heard Routledge mention to Whelan that he was still looking for a lead political story. I had an inkling that Labour's position on the funding of a new royal yacht might well be on the move but Whelan gave nothing away. Political journalists for the Sundays are only too ready to exercise their consider-able collective strength if they feel they need to guard their exclusive briefings, and will go to almost any lengths to make sure that the anonymity of their sources is preserved and that the information which they are given is not compromised or published in advance through being overheard by journalists employed by daily papers, radio or television. Therefore it was not until the first editions of the Sundays were published that Saturday evening that the BBC's television newsroom was alerted to Whelan's handiwork by a fax from Routledge, who sent through his story in the hope the main evening news might give the *Independent on Sunday* a plug. His report stated that 'the Queen has been told a Labour government will not pay for a £60 million replacement for the royal yacht *Britannia*'.

Jeremy Vine, the duty political correspondent, and his producer Julian Joyce set to work to see if they could stand up the story. Whelan was bleeped and responded instantly. He confirmed Routledge's report and said the BBC should telephone one of Labour's defence spokesmen, John Reid, who would supply an on-the-record quote. Luckily, Reid answered the phone immediately – but, unaware that the policy had changed, was still sticking to the line that Labour were keeping their options open. However, after agreeing to speak to Whelan himself, Reid subsequently gave a telephone interview. He could hardly have been more definite about Labour's intentions: 'We are saying that we will not fund out of public expenditure £60 million for a royal yacht when there are demands such as hospitals, the heath service and education which a Labour government will be expected to meet.' Reid's answer catapulted the report to lead item in the main evening bulletin. Next morning the Sunday papers all gave considerable prominence to the story. The angle which generated most interest in the *Sunday Times* was that the Queen had been 'formally notified' of the decision.

Labour's refusal to pay the £60 million was featured heavily in the newspaper review on *Breakfast with Frost*, but David Frost's first interviewee, the shadow Treasury chief secretary Alistair Darling, was unaware of any hard-and-fast decision. He said provision for the funding of a new royal yacht had not been included in the government's last Budget and therefore an incoming Labour administration would have to judge it alongside other projects. When Frost pointed out that the *Independent on Sunday*'s front-page headline was emphatic in saying Labour 'won't pay for *Britannia*', Darling, unwisely in retrospect, decided to attack the messengers: 'I do wish people who write these stories would actually come and ask, rather than rely on leaks and so on. We've made it clear, of course, that in principle the royal yacht would be an asset for the country and that to rule out private finance could be short-sighted.' When Frost pointed out that the journalists were all quoting 'a top source in the party', Darling was just as withering, saying that's what journalists 'always do'.

To be fair to Darling, he was in good company in refusing to go along with the story. Tim Allan, a press officer in the party leader's office, had been telling reporters all morning that Blair rather liked the idea of a new royal yacht, and that public money might be used if enough private finance could not be arranged. Jeremy Vine, who by then was preparing his report for the Sunday lunchtime television news bulletin, said that all of a sudden Labour's spin doctors stopped answering their phones. 'It was obvious they were trying to sort themselves out in order to see if they could all agree to go along with the line being put out in Brown's name. It was a moment to savour. This time they couldn't browbeat the BBC. They had only themselves to blame.' In his report for the main news bulletin that evening Vine remarked, with a degree of understatement, that the on-off saga had not been Labour's 'clearest hour'. Monday morning's newspapers were full of nautical puns at Labour's expense. The *Daily Mail*'s leader writer said the country had been given a 'revealing glimpse of the tension on New Labour's bridge' over what was, relatively, a 'ha'p'orth of tar' in a £300 billion budget. 'While Brown attempted to steer a straight course, Blair tried to tack.' The *Guardian* concluded that the 'zig zag' on the royal yacht meant Labour had failed to score 'an undisputed political bull's eye'.

Several days later, Labour's chief media spokesperson, David Hill, told me there was no excuse for their 'cock-up' that weekend. If Alistair Darling had been in any doubt about the party's position he could have rung in to the media monitoring unit at Millbank Tower before appearing on *Breakfast with Frost* and been briefed on what the news bulletins were saying. Hill said he was always ready himself to brief members of the shadow Cabinet before they did live interviews. 'Political reporting nowadays is all about gaffes and nuances and there can be a real problem about the different emphasis which members of the front bench put on the same story, so we have to get this right.' Darling had apparently taken the blame himself. Mistakenly, there was an assumption within the shadow Treasury team that he had been alerted. Darling told me that he did check out the position himself before doing his interview but the conversation ended up at cross-purposes. 'I accept I've had to pay the price for having had a Saturday off. I didn't watch the television news on

Saturday evening or keep up with the news on Sunday morning.' Whelan, by contrast, was proud of his weekend's work despite the hiccup over Darling's interview. 'We did think it through very carefully and we decided on Friday afternoon to harden up Labour's position. We realised that the row over *Britannia* was the one story which people were still talking about. The newspaper telephone polls were in line with what Labour's focus groups were saying. So we had to think of a way of cranking it up for the Sunday newspapers. I knew that if we could get that line in about Labour telling the Queen then the story would take off again and Gordon would look tough on spending.'

Whelan's glowing account of what happened was disputed the following weekend by Andrew Grice, political editor of the *Sunday Times*. He reported that Labour's confusion the previous weekend was another sign of the 'simmering tensions' between the party leader and the shadow Chancellor. 'Blair was taken aback by banner headlines saying Labour would not provide a penny of public money for a new *Britannia*. His staff "went nuclear" because Brown's aides had kept them in the dark . . . A compromise was eventually found: a Labour government would provide no money for two years.' Grice believed that differences between Blair and Brown over income tax, culminating in the leader's 'veto' of his shadow Chancellor's proposal for a 50p top rate, had left 'a legacy of bitterness' between the two men. The claim that Brown had shown his independence by 'seizing command' of the *Britannia* controversy was backed by the *Mail on Sunday*. Its columnist 'Black Dog' said Blair's office had been caught 'on the hop' and Alastair Campbell had 'confessed later that, unusually, he knew nothing about what was going on. Campbell, who likes to be regarded as the keeper of all Labour knowledge, had to undergo the humiliation of phoning Brown's office for a briefing. "I was off that day," was his implausible excuse to Black Dog.'

Undaunted by the confusion over his briefings on a possible replacement for *Britannia*, Whelan had no hesitation in telling the *Sunday Telegraph* the following month that a future Labour government would consider selling off the Tote, the state-owned betting organisation. Monday's national newspapers went hard on the story, predicting that Labour's first privatisation could bring in up to £500 million as an alternative way of raising cash for education and training. Ewen MacAskill, the *Guardian*'s chief political correspondent, quoted a 'Labour source' as saying there had already been discussions about selling the Tote as a money-raising option. However, the following day MacAskill reported that Robin Cook, who had overall responsibility for Labour policy, had stepped in to 'kill off' the proposal. Cook, who was a passionate supporter of horse racing and wrote a weekly tipster column for the *Herald* newspaper in Scotland, told the *Guardian* that the idea had never even been discussed by the shadow Cabinet. 'This is not a U-turn because there never was a policy. It all began as a hare that got running before we had the chance to stop it.' John Prescott, Labour's deputy leader, told *Today* that Cook was right to point out that the party had no policy towards the Tote. Prescott used his interview to issue an extraordinary rebuke to Labour's spin doctors. He accused the party's 'press guys' of 'running around with their little stories for the Sunday papers' and urged them to remember that while they might seek to brief the media on possible options, that did not mean their ideas were party policy.

Two days later the *Guardian* returned to the story, attempting to unravel what MacAskill described as the 'personal acrimony' between Brown and Cook which had developed into 'one of the most bitter feuds in British politics'. The 'rivalry had burst into public view again' when Cook intervened to 'stamp on a proposal touted' by Whelan for privatising the Tote. MacAskill believed the feud had the potential to cause problems during the election because although Brown had been appointed the election campaign coordinator, Cook remained in control of policy. Cook was said to resent the way he had been leapfrogged by Brown in shadow Cabinet seniority. Another reason for their 'war' was that Brown was popular with journalists and had become the 'King of Leaks, a good source of exclusive stories'. MacAskill said Cook's supporters believed Whelan was to blame for much of the subsequent trouble between the two men. Whelan himself was unusually subdued when I tackled him about the way he had been reprimanded publicly by both Prescott and Cook. He confirmed that he stood the story up for the *Sunday Telegraph* but believed he had been pilloried unfairly. 'I could just as easily have put out a statement in Gordon's name but I let them quote me instead as one of Brown's aides and that gave Cook the chance to say it wasn't policy and to take a pot shot at me.'

Conservative Central Office took immediate advantage of Labour's internal spat. In a trenchant press release, the Chief Secretary to the Treasury, William Waldegrave, said the 'shambles' over the Tote was part of the 'continuing battle being waged by Gordon Brown against the laws of arithmetic'. Just when the shadow Chancellor thought he had 'plugged at least £500 million of the missing £1.5 billion privatisation proceeds', he was vetoed by the shadow Foreign Secretary. The following week Waldegrave joined the Chancellor, Kenneth Clarke, at a Central Office news conference where they tried again to suggest that Labour would have to make tax increases. They outlined what they claimed was a '£12 billion black hole' in Brown's spending plans, a shortfall that had, they said, opened up because Labour were opposed to the government's money-saving measures and would miss out on any further proceeds from privatisation. Clarke insisted that right up to polling day he intended to 'ask and ask and ask again' until Labour told him where the money would come from. 'If Gordon Brown were an accountant he'd be sued for professional malpractice. New Labour's public finances have been drawn up by the Bob Maxwell school of accounting.' Danny Finkelstein told me the news conference was designed to exploit Labour's mix-up over the Tote. 'Labour will have to find some way of replacing the loss of the privatisation receipts. We think Brown sent Whelan out to test the water for privatising the Tote. Now that Cook has ruled it out presumably that goes for any other sell-off as well.' Later that day Whelan acknowledged that the Conservatives' allegations about a '£12 billion black hole' were potentially more troublesome to Labour than the earlier '£30 billion tax bombshell'. 'We are going to be exposed to difficult questions about how to fill that black hole. That's why it was a huge mistake of Cook to rubbish the idea of privatising the Tote. Anyway, Cook was talking bollocks. Is he saying we can't do anything? Tony Blair wouldn't be where he is now if he'd had to make sure everything he said was party policy, nor would Labour be where it is in the opinion polls.'

It was little wonder Whelan was so sore: he was still recovering from an equally fraught dust-up with Peter Mandelson. Whelan's difficulty all week was that Brown was in the United States and he clearly felt vulnerable without his boss there to back him up. The main purpose of the trip was for the shadow Chancellor to meet the US Treasury Secretary, Robert Rubin, to explain Labour's approach towards a single European currency. Brown intended to set out the five tests which he thought Britain should apply when considering monetary union. Carefully prepared plans had been made for Whelan to promote the shadow Chancellor's speech and contrast it with the turmoil within the Cabinet which had followed the assertion by the Foreign Secretary, Malcolm Rifkind, that the British government was 'on balance hostile to a single currency'. Whelan's intention was to get the story written up overnight by the newspapers, radio and television. Therefore he had arranged to brief political correspondents late in the afternoon. However, his plans were thrown into confusion when he was beaten to it by Mandelson, who gave an early-morning briefing to the BBC. 'Senior Labour sources' were quoted in news summaries as having confirmed that Brown would harden Labour's stance on a single currency while maintaining the 'negotiate and decide' approach which had been adopted by the government. Whelan told me that he had been caught entirely by surprise. 'Mandelson ruined our story . . . he doesn't have the authority to speak for the shadow Chancellor and he knows it.' To spike Mandelson's guns, Whelan said, he took out of Brown's speech the words from the text which Mandelson had released to the BBC. He was ready to admit that it was a case of 'too many spin doctors spoiling the broth'. He also let slip that both he and Brown had gone out of their way to keep Mandelson in the dark about the shadow Chancellor's pledge on income tax. 'We never told Mandelson about it because we realised he would have been unable to resist telling one of the journalists he's friendly with.' Rarely had Whelan been so indiscreet; but I knew that when provoked he could give a graphic account of the tensions that existed at the top of the party.

Many of the disagreements between Brown and Mandelson revolved around the timing and presentation of policy announcements. Territorial disputes of this kind were commonplace among Labour politicians, just as they were in other political parties, but the feuding seemed to have been getting worse by the month, which seemed surprising in view of the leadership's success in winning support so quickly for the concept of New Labour. Blair, Brown and Mandelson were the trio who had paved the way for the transformation which had taken place in the party's organisation and policies since May 1994, when John Smith's death and the election of Blair as the new leader had given the modernisers their chance to take control. Brown withdrew from the leadership contest even before it had officially started, in order to give Blair a clear run. Mandelson sided with Blair, covertly advising him on publicity, and it was his precipitate action, in telling broadcasters to expect a statement from Brown announcing his withdrawal from the contest, which soured relations with the shadow Chancellor's newly appointed press officer. Whelan had been taken on five months earlier and had established a close working relationship with Brown. He was furious that, without even having had the courtesy to inform him, Mandelson had undermined his position as Brown's spokesman and revealed the shadow Chancellor's intentions to the political editors on radio and television. Although Brown was subsequently forthright in applauding Blair's overwhelming victory in the leadership election, Mandelson's conduct left a legacy of ill-feeling.

The chain of events which led to Brown's decision to stand aside remained something of a mystery. Whelan told me at the time that Brown was surprised and upset by the way Blair went for the leadership 'from the word go', and that the shadow Chancellor's decision to stand down followed a series of strained meetings between the two men and was not settled over one meal in a restaurant as was widely reported. Mandelson gave me a different version. He said Brown had been ready to put party above personal ambition and stood aside because he knew that was the best way to preserve unity. 'Gordon and Tony are close friends . . . they have been friendly throughout. Both of them recognise the strength of the partnership they have built up together. They understand the longing of the party to work as a team and to use all its talents.' A fortnight after Brown's withdrawal, Whelan told me that he still had not exchanged a word with Mandelson. As the leadership campaign progressed there were further differences over the interpretation being put on the declaration in Blair's election statement that he supported a 'fair tax system'. Whelan said Mandelson had deliberately sought to challenge the shadow Chancellor's authority by telling journalists that Blair believed a Labour government should introduce a starting rate for income tax of 15p in the pound.

Blair's victory party for his campaign team gave Whelan the opportunity to retaliate. In thanking those who had helped him, Blair paid special tribute to 'Bobby'. Whelan, who had gone to the party with Brown, inquired as to whom Blair was referring to. He was told by the campaign team that 'Bobby' was the codename for Mandelson, whose work promoting Blair had been kept secret because it was thought it might damage Blair's chances and annoy those members of the shadow Cabinet who had been assured that Mandelson was not taking part. The first public reference to Blair's use of the name 'Bobby' to describe Mandelson appeared in the Peterborough column of the *Daily Telegraph*. Later, when I asked Whelan if he thought this report was correct, he said he was the source of the diary story and had given it to Kevin Maguire, then the *Daily Telegraph*'s industrial correspondent. 'I don't care who knows what I did after the way Mandelson abused me in the leadership election.'

Brown and Whelan were a surprising pair of political soulmates. The shadow Chancellor was dour and thoughtful whereas his press officer, who had previously been on the public relations staff of the Amalgamated

Engineering and Electrical Union, could have been mistaken for a garrulous market trader. What they had in common was a passion for manipulating journalists, and their hard man/soft man routine was highly effective. Whelan went to inordinate lengths to get the best possible coverage for his boss. He would pester journalists on the telephone and bamboozle his way into newsrooms when promoting Brown's speeches or trying to talk up the news value of what he considered was the latest gaffe by Kenneth Clarke. Frequently the shadow Chancellor's speeches or soundbites did not match their advance billing, but more often than not Whelan's hard sell proved effective in gaining publicity. Brown would look on with wry amusement as Whelan berated reporters for failing to recognise the significance of the latest story he was touting or for their reluctance to give it sufficient prominence. Brown had certainly been in sore need of a forceful press officer. He had always been known as a workaholic and was constantly sending out news releases or offering himself for interviews on radio and television. Whelan halved the shadow Chancellor's broadcasts and stopped him writing press statements which stood little chance of being published. By pruning the number of Brown's press conferences and interviews and targeting them carefully, Whelan ensured they were given greater weight by the news media. While he could be injudicious when talking about his own activities, he was always the soul of discretion when asked probing questions about Brown's true feelings or his relations with Blair.

Because the sense of self-discipline within the party was so strong, underlying differences of opinion, such as those between Brown and Mandelson, were rarely paraded in public. When they did surface it was usually because Brown had discovered what he believed were attempts to encroach on his economic brief. When Mandelson joined up with Roger Liddle to write *The Blair Revolution*, the book published in spring 1996 which set out the modernisers' vision for New Labour, Whelan said Brown made sure that their ideas on tax and spending were properly vetted so as to avoid any conflict with party policy. Whelan told me that Brown had effectively 'filleted' the book, taking out all Mandelson's controversial proposals on the economy. 'Gordon put his foot down and said to Mandelson: "Take it all out or the game's off."' One suggestion which did appear in the book was Mandelson's idea for ensuring a stronger political presence in the Prime Minister's press office should Blair reach No. 10. At the time I took this as confirmation that, should Labour win the election, Alastair Campbell would be appointed Blair's press secretary. I asked Whelan if he feared that Campbell or Mandelson might succeed in influencing appointments in the Treasury press office were Brown to become Chancellor. 'Don't worry,' said Whelan. 'Gordon will have the set-up that he wants in the Treasury and I'll be running it.'

Joy Johnson, who had worked closely with the shadow Chancellor during 1995, thought the real trial of strength between Brown and Mandelson would not take place until the election was declared. As Brown was campaign coordinator there was an assumption that he would automatically get the job of chairing the daily news conferences; but Ms Johnson told me that this task was seen as 'quite a prize', because of the media exposure it entailed, and that it had been the source of a tremendous argument behind the scenes. 'Prescott wanted to do it but Mandelson wouldn't have him. I still think Gordon will be given the job of chairing the news conferences because he's Labour's safest pair of hands. Whenever radio and television interviewers try to catch him out, he just grinds them down. Yes, Gordon might be cautious and repetitive but journalists can't trip him up.' Ms Johnson's fears that Mandelson might make a successful bid for the role proved unfounded: two months before polling day Blair confirmed that Brown would chair the daily news conferences and be Labour's front man for the election campaign.

My fascination with the machinations of the spin doctors, and my temerity in daring to write down what they said about the intricacies of their own work, was a constant source of friction in my dealings with Mandelson and Campbell. They regretted, they said, the way other journalists were following my example and taking a growing interest in political presentation rather than the content of each party's policies. Campbell considered the danger for a correspondent like myself in becoming 'obsessed' with the day-to-day role of the spin doctors was that I would end up being mesmerised by their trials and tribulations and ignore the long-term effect of their efforts to promote the changes which had taken place in Labour's policies. He took the shift in public opinion in the month since Brown had delivered his tax pledge as an example of what could be achieved. Despite what for months had been an unshakeable overall lead in the opinion polls, Labour had continued to trail behind the Conservatives on questions about economic competence. Campbell was on firm ground: a clutch of opinion surveys during February showed that Labour were gradually shedding their high-tax image. An ICM poll in the *Guardian* found that although Labour had failed to persuade voters that they would hold down public spending to existing levels, 74 per cent of those questioned thought taxation as a whole would increase under the Conservatives while a slightly lower proportion, 67 per cent, believed there was a danger of this happening under Labour. Campbell was delighted by the findings. 'We're now in a position where more people trust Labour on tax than the Conservatives. Given all the history over tax between the two parties you couldn't have a better result.' Two subsequent polls reinforced Campbell's prediction that Labour were at last turning the corner and eroding the Conservatives' long-standing advantage on tax and spending. A survey conducted by the *Financial Times* and the FCB advertising agency showed that most undecided voters believed the Conservatives no longer deserved to be a seen as a low-tax party and that Labour would raise the overall burden of tax 'only slightly more' than the Tories. Readers of the *Express*, usually regarded as loyal Conservatives, had a similarly dismal message for Central Office. Of those questioned, 53 per cent felt betrayed by Tory tax promises. An opinion poll conducted for the Reuters news agency, however, contained better news for the Conservatives: out of 1,000 voters, 32 per cent thought taxes would be higher under Labour, compared with 19 per cent for the Tories.

Not unexpectedly, the Conservatives' communications director, Charles Lewington, took comfort from the Reuters poll. 'We know Labour are peddling the line that they are making inroads on tax, and that they claim to have neutralised the Tories' lead on the economy, but once you start talking to people they always say they think Labour will spend more and therefore tax more. What we have got to sort out is people's dislike of the Conservatives. We know we've a fight on our hands: it's so unfashionable now to even admit you vote Tory. But our focus groups show people are concerned about Labour and their tax plans – and don't forget, no government has lost a general election when most people say they trust it to run the economy. What we've got to do is extend our lead on tax and spending between now and polling day.'

Lewington gave me this pep talk just forty-eight hours before the Wirral South by-election delivered another hammer blow to John Major. A true blue Conservative seat, held by the late Barry Porter with a majority of 8,183 votes in the 1992 election, fell to Labour with a massive 17 per cent swing. The majority of 7,888 secured by the new MP Ben Chapman was described by Tony Blair as representing 'nothing short of a political uprising against the Tories, deep in their heartlands'. The Conservatives' fight to retain the seat was an unmitigated disaster. On the day the campaign opened, the Deputy Prime Minister, Michael Heseltine, was accused by Labour of having 'thrown in the towel' in saying that he expected the voters of Wirral South to 'kick the government'. Major greeted the result with a similarly bleak admission. He acknowledged in an interview for ITN that the long pre-election campaign had reached a defining moment: 'If opinion doesn't change, then we are going to have a Labour government.' According to the *Guardian*, the Prime Minister had 'pressed the panic button' and his response had been to try to frighten the voters by attacking what he called Labour's 'secret Budget plans' to raise taxes within weeks of winning power. Major went some way towards recognising Labour's success in reassuring the electorate about their economic competence. He told Elinor Goodman of *Channel Four News* that Blair had achieved this by going round the country telling people what they wanted to hear. 'Labour have done it brilliantly, as a marketing exercise, but I still believe the British people will see through it.' Labour believed it was their ability to put over a positive message which had done so much to convince the electorate. As the political parties reviewed their tactics for the final two months before polling day, the only option left open to the election strategists at Conservative Central Office seemed to be another round of negative campaigning. In the event, however, they seemed more adept at undermining themselves than their opponents.

4

Firefighting

After so many tiresome months had been frittered away, waiting for the government to go to the country, the general assumption was that once the Prime Minister named the day there would be a short, sharp campaign up to the poll. As the timing of the election was in John Major's gift, there appeared to be no reason why he would not be able to clear the decks at a moment of his choosing and, despite their poor showing in the opinion polls, still find a way to engineer the best possible send-off for the Conservatives. But, by hanging on for so long, Major lost the element of surprise; and then, in what turned out to be another grave tactical mistake, he decided to drag out the election campaign itself for as long as possible. His calculation seemed to be that the longer he allowed for electioneering, the greater would be the Conservatives' chances of exposing what his ministers believed were weaknesses in Tony Blair's policies and the inherent dangers of electing a Labour government. The fatal flaw in Major's strategy was that it was based on an insufficient foundation: if the Conservatives were to stand any chance of mounting an effective attack against Blair, they had first to raise morale in their own battered parliamentary party and then see if they could find some way of maintaining the kind of self-discipline which New Labour had drilled into their MPs. Major's other miscalculation was to disregard the damage which might be inflicted by the heightened exposure of ministers who were seen to be out of touch with public opinion and whose regular appearances on radio and television had become constant reminders of the Conservatives' unpopularity. A long campaign, instead of strengthening their own appeal, might only end up hardening support for Labour and the Liberal Democrats.

Major's inability to influence, let alone control, the news agenda had already left the Conservatives at the mercy of Labour's ruthless publicity machine. No opportunity was being missed to provoke fresh outbursts from dissident Tory Euro-sceptics or to inflame news coverage of alleged cases of financial impropriety or other misconduct among Conservative MPs. Labour had a ready supply of material on which to work: the

Conservatives gave every impression of being on a helter-skelter to disaster, and each new setback was pounced on by political journalists with ever greater enthusiasm. Blair's spin doctors had spent years perfecting their routines for generating unwelcome publicity for Major and his ministers. Their dual strategy, of exploiting the Conservatives' disarray while at the same time orchestrating the promotion of New Labour's positive policies, was aimed at depriving the government of opportunities to promote a run of healthy economic indicators which were expected in the months leading up to polling day.

Nevertheless, some Conservative MPs were looking forward to the campaign. They believed that once the party's star performers were relieved of their time-consuming ministerial duties, they would be able to force Labour on to the defensive. But behind the bravado of even the most sanguine there was a sense of foreboding and a recognition that perhaps catastrophe lay ahead. In mid-February, at a Lancaster House reception given by the Secretary of State for Defence, Michael Portillo, I was struck by the way he had personally come to terms with the fact that his ministerial career might be over within weeks. He told me he hoped Major would do all he could to hang on until on 1 May before holding the election. 'I've enjoyed being defence secretary more than any other job . . . I just hope it can go on for as long as possible.'

Once gathered together at social occasions such as this, Tory MPs would do their best to enliven the proceedings by trying out their latest line in gallows humour. At the same reception, James Arbuthnot, the Minister of State for Defence Procurement, cracked a joke about the possibility that they might suffer a repeat of the meltdown which the Canadian Conservatives experienced in 1993 when they lost all but two of their 154 seats. Arbuthnot's previous constituency of Wanstead and Woodford had disappeared under boundary changes and he was standing in the new seat of Hampshire North East, which had a notional Conservative majority of 20,000. He said that if they did experience a Canadian-style wipeout, he had calculated that on the basis of what were supposed to be the Tories' safest seats there would be just three of them left: himself in Hampshire North East, John Major in Huntingdon and Alan Clark in Kensington and Chelsea. The defence chief, who was standing alongside us, must have heard the joke before because he did not seem particularly impressed; and when Arbuthnot had walked away, he turned to me and said that he was personally predicting a Labour majority of thirty. Moreover, he welcomed the prospect of a change of government:

Tony Blair had impressed members of the Defence Council by offering stability to the armed forces and that had gone down well.

The same air of grim reality pervaded a party the following week, laid on by journalists in the House of Commons press gallery dining room for retiring MPs. John Carlisle, the outgoing Conservative in Luton North and a harsh critic of John Major, told me he was convinced a severe defeat was in prospect. He thought Labour would get a sixty-seat majority. 'What my colleagues don't understand is that once we're in opposition the news media just won't be interested in what the Conservatives are saying.' Carlisle said he had been struck by the way the constituencies were intent on getting their own back against MPs like himself and the Reigate MP, Sir George Gardiner, who had been deselected after his outspoken attacks on the Prime Minister. 'I think this explains why so few of the retiring MPs who were hit by the boundary changes have managed to get new seats. I do detect a real sense of the constituencies wanting to punish us. Although they like Major out there on the doorsteps they still think he is a wally.' Gloomy predictions poured out whenever one stopped to chat to Conservative MPs. David Wilshire, who was defending the ultra-safe seat of Spelthorne, thought they could be out of office for the next fifteen years. Graham Riddick, fighting to retain marginal Colne Valley in West Yorkshire, did not think the government up to the job of winning. He had supported John Redwood's 1995 challenge for the party leadership. 'If we had elected a new leader two years ago we could have transformed our position. We won't win under Major. He and his Cabinet are a load of deadbeats and has-beens.' Sir Sydney Chapman, who told me he was preparing to fight his safe seat of Chipping Barnet as though it were a Tory marginal, was equally despondent. 'Ninety-nine per cent of Tory MPs know we are going to lose. The only person who doesn't say so is John Major.'

Standing outside the lobby as MPs trooped by on their way to vote in one of the last divisions of the session, I managed to exchange a few words with John Patten, who was standing down as MP for Oxford West and Abingdon. Secretary of State for Education until sacked by Major in the 1994 Cabinet reshuffle, Patten had remained loyal to the government and, unlike some former ministers, had refrained from voicing his opinions on the party's troubles. As he rarely spoke to political correspondents, I was keen to engage him in conversation and I was immediately struck by his downcast demeanour. 'Look at the Conservative MPs who're walking past us. There's no banter, no joshing, no camaraderie. Can't you feel the terrible hatred that there is in this place? They're endlessly forming and re-forming into leadership cliques. Our trouble is Tory MPs have no tune to march to. I haven't said anything myself since I left office but once the election is over I shall be rejoining the debate, trying to help create a credo for the Conservative Party.' Patten's sombre assessment summed up the air of resignation and finality which pervaded much of the parliamentary party. Tory MPs seemed incapable of rising above their own despondency.

If they thought they were about to go down with all hands, the Conservatives' disastrous performance in the Wirral South by-election demonstrated the accuracy of their intuition and the pitiful inadequacy of their campaign strategy. Labour treated the contest as a dry run for the general election and an opportunity to test out their procedures for identifying undecided voters and persuading disenchanted Conservatives to switch their votes. As it seemed increasingly likely that Major would wait until 1 May to hold the general election, Labour's tactic was to portray the Conservatives as desperately trying to hang on to power. Journalists who covered the by-election noted the rigid control which Labour maintained over the campaign and the tightly managed media appearances of their candidate, Ben Chapman. He was put forward to answer questions at only two news conferences; as had been observed at other by-elections, Labour concentrated much of their publicity effort on photo-opportunities, thus restricting the chances for reporters to challenge the candidate. Chapman, a local businessman and former diplomat, was selected to fight the seat at the end of November 1996, within a few weeks of Barry Porter's death and the unexpected resignation of the previous Labour candidate, Ian Wingfield, who stood down because he feared 'untrue allegations' against him were being circulated which could damage Labour's prospects. There was speculation that the contest might be delayed and the seat left empty until the general election, but Major stuck by the parliamentary convention that the date should be announced within three months of the incumbent's death and the by-election was called for 27 February.

Labour mounted what was in effect a three-month campaign. Rory Scanlan, one of the party workers despatched to the Wirral, told me they estimated that by the day of the poll Chapman had met or been seen by 15,000 people in the constituency, through knocking on doors, visiting supermarkets and leisure centres and even by calling out numbers at the local bingo hall. Ever since taking South East Staffordshire on a 22 per cent swing in a by-election in April 1996, a victory Blair had described as one of symbolic importance because it was a classic Conservative seat in middle England, the party had been waiting for another opportunity to demonstrate the electoral appeal of New Labour. John Williams, the *Mirror*'s political columnist, described Wirral South as the 'capital of Blair country . . . a prosperous stretch of Merseyside commuterland, with more golf courses than any metropolitan borough in the country . . . more people who own their own houses, more two-car families, more members of the managerial classes, less unemployment and less council houses than the national average'.

Labour MPs who went to the Wirral to help out on polling day were impressed by the efficiency of the campaign and amazed by the support they were getting. Barry Jones, a former shadow Welsh secretary, who knew the area well, having represented the adjoining constituency of Alyn and Deeside since 1970, was told to knock up voters in the wealthy Heswall area which, he said, was as prosperous as the Surrey commuter belt. 'As I walked up the drives of expensive detached houses, where I was told the families had switched to Labour, I just couldn't believe what was happening to me. I'd never seen anything like it. Don't forget I'd campaigned in that area during Labour's massive victory in 1966 and the switch to Labour was nowhere near as big then as it was in the by-election.' Although support for the Conservatives had just 'fallen away', there was one consolation for them: their core vote stabilised at around 30 per cent and remained solid throughout the by-election campaign. Tim Collins, a former director of communications at Central Office, who was drafted in to advise on publicity, said Wirral South was unlike other by-election defeats. Tory canvassers at both Newbury in May 1993 and Christchurch two months later had found that people who promised to vote Conservative at the start of the campaign had switched to the Liberal Democrats by polling day. 'Our estimate at Wirral South was that we'd get between 28 and 32 per cent. On the day we told Major it would be between 32 and 33 per cent and in fact we got 34 per cent. So it was the first by-election where people weren't lying to us: those who said they were Conservative stayed with us and for the first time we could predict accurately what was going to happen.' Collins agreed that the 17 per cent swing to Labour was a frightening portent for the Conservatives so close to a general election. So too, I thought, was his acknowledgement that support for the Conservatives had levelled off at around 30 per cent, as the opinion polls had been saying for months, and that despite all their efforts in what was previously a safe seat they had found it impossible to rebuild Tory support beyond this level.

Labour had left nothing to chance, so determined were they to secure the largest possible share of the vote. If canvassers met trade unionists or other potential Labour supporters from the left who sounded disenchanted with Blair, or who said they might not bother to vote, they were asked if they would like to talk their doubts over with the veteran MP Dennis Skinner. For the last week and a half of the campaign, he was given a list each evening of potential waverers. 'I'd ring about six of them a night. I'd be frank with them and say we could argue all evening about Blair. But I'd warn them that if the Conservatives got back in, then another Tory government would have a licence to do what they liked with the health service and the old age pension. I'd explain also things like Labour's promise to allow recognition for trade unions. I think I pulled most of them round.' Skinner's support and his involvement in the campaigning techniques of New Labour was a graphic demonstration of his party's unity. The gulf between John Major and Tory mavericks was, to all intents and purposes, unbridgeable and the likelihood that Conservative Central Office would have been able to persuade a leading Euro-sceptic to make a similar gesture was remote. Skinner's discreet contribution stood in marked contrast to an insensitive outburst by David Evans, the Conservative MP for Welwyn and Hatfield, whose behaviour in the wake of the by-election defeat illustrated both the extent to which Major's control over his party had broken down and the insuperable difficulties he faced in trying to regain the initiative.

In order to recharge their pre-election offensive after the anticipated loss of Wirral South, the Conservatives had planned a fresh advertising campaign, to be followed by a significant policy announcement. The new poster was unveiled on 5 March by Brian Mawhinney, the party chairman, and William Waldegrave, the Chief Secretary to the Treasury. In the centre of it was a photograph of Blair with a wide grin on his face and above it the words 'Tony & Bill' in large capital letters. Beside Blair's picture it said: '£30 billion spending promises' and beneath that was the question: 'Who pays?' Some journalists attending the launch of the poster were bemused by it and thought voters would not understand the reference to 'Tony & Bill', but Waldegrave insisted that middle England was waking up to the danger which lurked behind Blair's spending promises. 'Tony's £30 billion bill would have to be paid by every ordinary taxpayer in the country.' The Conservatives' attempt to revive media interest in their claim of the previous November that Labour had made eighty-nine uncosted spending pledges was already being overtaken by a comment which Major had made during a phone-in on Radio 5 Live. He had acknowledged that the argument that it was 'time for a change' was the biggest challenge facing the Conservatives. 'When you have been in government for eighteen years, you are fighting in a sense a phantom enemy and I think that is a bigger problem for us than any other.'

There was worse to come. Major had been challenged in an editorial in that morning's *Daily Mail* to put a stop to the 'anarchy' which threatened to consume the Conservatives. 'Do the Tories have a death wish? . . . With only eight weeks to go to polling day, they seem intent on destroying themselves . . . What they lack is leadership.' Later that same day, these words took on an air of prescience as the combined efforts of Major and Mawhinney to revitalise the Conservatives' campaign were obliterated by reports in the teatime news bulletins of David Evans' outspoken attack on Melanie Johnson. Referring to the Labour candidate in Welwyn and Hatfield in an interview which he gave during a current affairs lesson at Stanborough College, Evans had told sixth-formers that Johnson had 'three bastard children' and had 'never done a proper job'. Hugh Pym, an ITN political corespondent, broke the story on the early evening news. He said that ITN and Anglia Television had obtained a tape recording of the conversation and he knew that a transcript had subsequently been acquired by the Labour Party. Within half an hour of Pym's report, fax machines at the BBC's studios in Westminster were printing off copies of Labour's press release in which Ms Johnson called on Evans to 'get out of the gutter and fight a proper campaign'. Minutes later the full transcript arrived. It had been sent out on plain paper with no marking or heading, but the source was unmistakable: Labour's media centre at Millbank was demonstrating yet again the speed with which it could respond when exploiting the constant setbacks to the Prime Minister's campaign.

Evans' tirade against Ms Johnson was given front-page treatment in next morning's newspapers, all of which devoted considerable space to the rest of the MP's remarks. He had described the Secretary of State for National Heritage, Virginia Bottomley, as being 'dead from the neck upwards', and said he found Major 'vindictive and not forgiving'. Downing Street and Central Office were desperate to play down the story and made no comment. According to *The Times*, urgent talks were held to ensure there was an 'official wall of silence', although the *Guardian* claimed the Conservatives had accused Labour of 'dirty tricks' in distributing transcripts of the interview.

Tory party officials were distraught, fearing that Labour's demand for Evans to be deselected as a parliamentary candidate would distract attention from the launch later that morning of the government's plans to restructure the old age pension. The importance attached by the government to what journalists were encouraged to describe as the 'big idea' for the Conservatives' manifesto was all too apparent. In order to avoid leaks and ensure secrecy until the official launch, the news conference was organised by the Prime Minister's press office and held inside No. 10. The new scheme it intended to introduce was to be known as 'Basic Pension Plus'. In future everyone entering the workforce would make contributions into their own privately managed pension fund which, when the scheme was fully in place by 2040, would provide the average earner with a pension worth the equivalent of £175 a week. Most newspapers had predicted that morning that the state earnings-related pension would be privatised, but political correspondents were taken aback when they discovered that it was in fact the funding of the basic state pension which was to be to be radically transformed. With Peter Lilley, the Secretary of State for Social Security, beside him, Major said that Basic Pension Plus would enable every young person to accumulate an investment fund yielding considerably more than the basic state pension.

Once the presentation had been completed, Major invited questions. His face visibly tightened when he was asked by ITN's political editor, Michael Brunson, if he would 'unreservedly condemn the remarks by David Evans, in their totality'. In a clear, firm voice Major answered 'Yes', and then immediately invited another question. Labour kept up their own efforts to exploit Major's embarrassment and the Tory party's failure to discipline Evans. A delegation of thirteen of Labour's women MPs, led by Janet Anderson, who had frontbench responsibility for women's affairs, walked into Downing Street with a letter to the Prime Minister renewing their demand for the MP to be deselected. Ms Anderson said that if Major failed to order Evans' removal, every Tory MP would be tainted by the 'blatant sexism of this vulgar and uncouth little man'. However, although the repercussions of Evans' outburst, and his subsequent apology to the Prime Minister, continued to attract attention, Conservative fears that the government's announcement on pensions policy would be eclipsed were unfounded: the unveiling of Basic Pension Plus secured widespread coverage. Much of the editorial comment was highly favourable. In contrast to its highly critical tone earlier in the week, the *Daily Mail* said nobody could accuse the Conservatives of running out of steam: Major and

Lilley had taken the Tory agenda where New Labour had not dared to go and, with an 'almighty eruption', had lit up the election landscape. 'Within a generation, the elderly should enjoy a far more prosperous retirement and the Treasury should be saved tens of billions of pounds. That's the big idea. And they don't come much bigger.' There was praise too from the *Sun* which called on the shadow social security secretary, Harriet Harman, to stop 'carping and spreading ill-informed doom and gloom' when she should have been welcoming a long-overdue reform that would make people better off and save taxpayers' money. Nevertheless, there was a word of caution from the *Express*, which questioned the timing of what ministers clearly hoped would be a vote-winner. It feared that 'in the frenzy of an election campaign the risk of misrepresentation must be great'. In announcing Basic Pension Plus so close to polling day, and without the prior consultation which usually accompanied significant social security changes, ministers ran the danger of finding that their proposals might be rejected out of hand by their opponents and then be portrayed as a threat to the very principle of a state pension. While there had been arguments in previous years about calculating the size of the basic pension, the way it was funded had not been widely debated. The Conservatives also ran the risk of being criticised for having used a government news conference for party political purposes. Major spoke in front of a blue backdrop which had been erected inside No. 10 and the news releases were issued on the headed paper of Downing Street and the Department of Social Security rather than that of Conservative Central Office.

Jonathan Haslam, the Prime Minister's press secretary, was in charge of the proceedings and, while waiting for the news conference to begin, I asked him to comment on a press release which Labour had distributed to journalists outside the gates to Downing Street. Under the heading 'You can't trust a word the Tories say' it contained details of a parliamentary answer which Lilley had given when asked by Ms Harman to deny reports that he intended to do away with the basic state pension. Haslam looked at the press release and was clearly angered by it. 'She's got it all wrong, the silly thing. She shouldn't be commenting on something she doesn't know anything about.' At the end of the news conference reporters were briefed by Danny Finkelstein, head of the Conservatives' research department, and David Willetts, the former Paymaster-General. Willetts had joined the election team at Central Office following his resignation from the government in December 1996 after being criticised for misleading the House of Commons Standards and Privileges Committee during its inquiry into the allegations that several Conservative MPs took cash in return for asking parliamentary questions. When asked by reporters about the presence of Central Office staff at a Downing Street news conference, Haslam denied having seen them and insisted he would have been 'annoyed' if they had been in attendance. He said Basic Pension Plus had been launched in No. 10 because it was government business: only civil servants had worked on the details and if the government were re-elected their proposals would be published as a Green Paper.

Whatever their long-term intentions, the Conservatives were making reform of the state pension a manifesto commitment and there was no doubt that Major had taken full advantage of the opportunity to launch their plans in Downing Street. Haslam would undoubtedly have been anxious to comply with Major's wishes. Operational considerations, such as the need to ensure secrecy, could have been said to outweigh concerns over the dividing line between government and party work and, to be fair to Haslam, some information had leaked out despite all the precautions which No. 10 had taken. A report in the *Evening Standard* by the paper's political editor, Charles Reiss, said Lilley was disappointed by the 'garbled' reports about his pensions package which had appeared in the morning newspapers and which had concentrated on the negative side of the story. Reiss said that to prevent details leaking out, information had been restricted to the 'need-to-know circle' of those directly involved. Despite the difficulties which Haslam had encountered, the news conference had gone well and the use of No. 10 to launch a Conservative manifesto commitment had undoubtedly given the story added weight. Nevertheless, I could not help thinking back to the highly politicised years of Margaret Thatcher, when notwithstanding the undoubted ability of her press secretary Bernard Ingham to orchestrate favourable publicity for her government, he had always sought to reassure journalists that he either returned to his office or went off home if he thought there was any danger that, as a civil servant, he might get caught up in Conservative Party business.

Labour wasted no time in attacking Basic Pension Plus. At a hurriedly called news conference that afternoon the shadow Chancellor, Gordon Brown, said there would be huge front-end costs and taxpayers would finish up having to find billions of pounds to finance it. Major had given an assurance that morning that whatever the level of contributions made by young people entering the scheme, the state would continue to guarantee that everyone received 'at least their basic state pension, uprated at least for inflation'. Brown challenged the undertakings which the government had given: 'There will, first of all, no longer be a basic state pension covering everyone. So this is privatisation of the basic state pension, starting with those in their early twenties.' Brown's response was described by Peter Riddell, political columnist of *The Times*, as a 'depressing example of kneejerk opposition politics at its worst'. Brown's claims were either 'wrong or alarmist' because the state would still guarantee an inflation-proofed pension. The shadow Chancellor's blanket criticism was not, however, shared by the Labour MP Frank Field, who had gained a considerable reputation for his ideas on reforming social security. In an article in the *Daily Telegraph*, Field praised the 'careful way' Peter Lilley had begun his reforms and promised that Labour would be responding positively. Field said he personally could support the idea that people should contribute to their pension through savings from taxed income and in return gain a pension free of tax. Nonetheless he considered the Conservatives were going to the country with a scheme to 'wind up the state retirement pension' and Labour's immediate task was to stress the risks involved now that Lilley had thrown caution to the winds.

Having so frequently seen their campaign strategy derailed by the indiscipline of their own MPs, the Conservatives were heartened by their success in steering the news agenda towards what they considered was a positive policy issue for them. Alan Duncan, parliamentary private secretary to Brian Mawhinney, thought their pensions proposals were as far-reaching as the Beveridge report of 1942, which had paved the way for the welfare state. 'Basic Pension Plus does everything which is required of social policy reform. We move from unfunded to funded, from state to personal, from short-term to long-term and we jump a generation.' Duncan said the presentation of the announcement had been brilliant except for the way an 'arsehole of a junior minister had half leaked the story'. Among those praised by newspaper columnists for assisting Peter Lilley in preparing the Conservatives' most ambitious manifesto idea were the party's leading policy researchers: Danny Finkelstein, director of the research department; its chairman, David Willetts; and Norman Blackwell, head of the Downing Street policy unit. In fact, the blueprint for privatising the state pension system was said by Robert Peston, political editor of the *Financial Times*, to be the product of a strand of Tory thinking which he had christened 'Finkwellism' and which was searching for 'technocratic market solutions to the crisis of confidence in the welfare state'.

Finkelstein was regularly described by journalists as a 'thoroughly modern policy wonk'. His appointment was one of the first to be made by Brian Mawhinney on becoming party chairman after the Cabinet reshuffle of July 1995, and his arrival heralded the start of a reorganisation at Central Office which was intended to prepare the party for the general election. Finkelstein was well known in the world of political think-tanks: he was previously director of the Social Market Foundation and before defecting to the Conservatives in 1992 had been political adviser to Dr David Owen when he led the Social Democratic Party. His switch of allegiance was described by the *Observer*'s columnist, Sarah Baxter, as an 'interesting case of political transvestism' and she said he had consciously adopted the label 'Tory moderniser'.

David Willetts, like Finkelstein, had a well-established track record as a political guru and had been given the nickname 'two brains' by newspaper journalists. He was appointed chairman of the research department in January 1997, a month after his resignation from the government following criticism of the evidence which he gave to the Standards and Privileges Committee about a memo he had written in 1994, when serving as a government whip, concerning the cash-for-questions investigation. The committee all but accused him of lying, stating in its report that it was 'very concerned that any member should dissemble in his account to the committee'. Willetts had made a speedy comeback, his rehabilitation having been assisted by his prompt resignation within minutes of the committee publishing its report. Before being elected MP for Havant in 1992, Willetts had been director of the Centre for Policy Studies and had worked for two years in the No. 10 policy unit. His commitment to Basic Pension Plus was reinforced by his appearance on Channel Four's political comment programme, *The Slot*, predicting that it would trigger the 'biggest spread of personal ownership since the spread of home ownership'.

Willetts and Finkelstein were a powerful double act. After policy launches they would immediately set to work briefing journalists and answering their questions. As part of the reorganisation of Central Office, the work of the research department had been integrated far more closely with the activities of the press and public relations staff, under their director, Charles Lewington, who was another of Dr Mawhinney's appointments and had directed much of his effort towards repairing relations with Tory-minded newspapers. Lewington, a former political editor at the *Sunday Express*, was nowhere near as combative as Blair's press secretary, Alastair Campbell. Rather than get involved in aggressive confrontations with hostile journalists about issues which he felt damaged the government, he tried to promote stories which he considered would help the Conservatives, and he preferred to cooperate with reporters he thought were prepared to put both sides of the argument.

Lewington was seen as an astute defender of Conservative interests and Charles Hendry, the party vice-chairman responsible for communications, believed that his success in this role was due in part to improved cooperation between the research and public relations staff. The two departments had been brought together in one 'war room' and were regarded as being far more focused than in the 1992 election when trying to expose Labour's weaknesses or counter their attacks. Labour's emphasis on rapid rebuttal, and the speed with which Millbank Tower could respond, had clearly been a source of considerable discussion at Central Office. However, Labour's tactics were not seen as a severe threat. In my conversations with Tory spin doctors, I got the distinct impression that they believed Labour had gone overboard in copying the American Democrats' techniques and had overlooked the fact that newspapers and broadcasting organisations in Britain were more varied and in many cases more sophisticated than their US counterparts. Tim Collins, who had remained a media adviser to the party chairman after his stint as director of communications, believed there was a fundamental weakness in Labour's rebuttal strategy. If Millbank Tower responded to every attack which Central Office made, the Conservatives could decide, for example, to concentrate their offensive on the economy and so encourage Labour to campaign on an issue on which the Conservatives thought they were strongest. 'Labour have been so influenced by Clinton's techniques, they don't realise that rapid rebuttal can become a weakness rather than a strength. That's certainly how we intend to play it in the general election.' Danny Finkelstein was just as dubious about the effectiveness of the rebuttal strategy and the torrent of press statements which poured out of Millbank Tower. He thought most of Labour's news releases were ignored by journalists.

In fact, political correspondents felt that many of the Conservatives' press releases were equally unfocused, while Labour were far sharper, and much faster, when it came to exploiting differences of opinion between ministers or the divisive outbursts of the Euro-sceptics. Among Tory MPs, Alan Duncan was one of the few to sense the danger posed by the superiority of Labour's rebuttal techniques. 'Labour know that for every one word of effective propaganda which is said against them, it can take five words to neutralise, so they're right to kick hard to counteract it.' David Willetts also seemed far readier than his colleagues at Central Office to acknowledge the damage which Labour were inflicting on the government through the speed of their response and their skill in exploiting ministerial gaffes. The expansion in broadcasting had led to a significant increase in the number of political interviews, widening what Willetts described as the 'quotes gap' which could open up when several ministers were interviewed within a few hours of each other across a range of radio and television channels. Yet he thought there was no practical way of keeping every minister instantly informed of potentially damaging nuances in answers given by their colleagues, while Labour's chief spokesperson, David Hill, who shared Willetts' assessment of the potential danger of gaffes, had tried to bring in effective counter-measures. Before setting off for the studio, or starting an interview, shadow ministers were urged to telephone the media monitoring unit at Millbank Tower so that they could be briefed on topics which might be contentious and warned of possible pitfalls. Willetts seemed to me to have come closer than any of his colleagues to admitting the Conservatives' vulnerability in the face of Millbank Tower's formidable firepower. There seemed to be no limit to Labour's ingenuity and resourcefulness in highlighting inconsistencies in what ministers had said, and the fruits of their efforts were regularly being broadcast on radio or television or published in the newspapers.

Political journalists had expected Central Office to take full advantage of the heightened pre-election atmosphere by providing advance information about the Conservatives' manifesto and by publicising what they considered to be damaging revelations about Labour's policies. For weeks Tory spin doctors had been promising a 'drip feed' of stories – but very few emerged. David Hughes, political editor of the *Daily Mail*, was mystified by the Conservatives' failure to respond. 'We just aren't getting any stories from them, but Labour come up with something every night. No wonder Labour are having such an easy time: the government are a sitting target for whatever Labour think up, it's like shooting fish in a barrel.' David Mellor, the former Secretary of State for National Heritage, believed the root of the problem was the government's inability to hold the party together for long enough to mount a sustained offensive. Every time the Conservatives managed to seize the advantage another of their MPs would come along and 'blow it apart'. Mellor used an interview

on *Today* to deliver a celebrated put-down to Tory dissidents. He congratulated Labour on the tightness of their media operation and the steadfast
refusal of Labour MPs to display their divisions. 'They clam their jaws
together with Araldite. They know just how dangerous it is to appear
divided. I think our divisions will cost us the election.' Mellor's strictures
on the need for Conservatives to ingest large quantities of glue could have
been directed just as forcibly at his former colleagues in the Cabinet,
whose contortions over Britain's approach to possible membership of a
single European currency became even more labyrinthine after the
Secretary of State for Health, Stephen Dorrell, added his name to the list
of ministers who were prepared to depart from the government's carefully
crafted stance of 'wait and see'.

As the party picked up the pieces after their humiliating defeat in
Wirral South, Charles Lewington and the rest of the election team hoped
that an interview by the Deputy Prime Minister, Michael Heseltine, on
that Sunday's *On the Record*, would calm the party and encourage
Conservative MPs to close ranks. What looked like a newly decorated
room at Heseltine's country house had been set aside for the occasion.
Programme staff told me that the Deputy Prime Minister's wife Anne sat
in for the interview, which was conducted live from London by John
Humphrys. Heseltine was in fighting form and, when challenged about
his prediction during the Wirral South campaign that the Conservatives
would win the general election with a sixty-seat majority, he stuck to his
guns: 'We are going to win the election by sixty seats, nudging up to sixty
seats . . . That is an attitude of mind, a manifestation of determination . . .
We are determined to win, we deserve to win.' When harried by
Humphrys about the precise figure, Heseltine bridled and said that before
On the Record sent out a 'phoney press release' he would repeat his prediction that it would be 'nudging up to a sixty-seat majority'. He insisted that
the Conservatives' manifesto would express the government's 'clear,
united view' on the prospects for a single currency and their decision to
negotiate and then decide. 'The fact is that in today's media world, you
journalists spend your entire time trying to find a phrase or word on which
to base a story . . . It is preposterous to suggest that the Cabinet are at each
other's throat . . . Blair is putting sticking plaster over his MPs. We don't
believe in putting sticking plaster across our party members. You can't live
just by soundbites. You have to take decisions.' As it turned out, a strip of
sticking plaster might just have come in handy for Stephen Dorrell who,
while Heseltine was being interviewed on BBC1, was preparing for his

appearance on LWT's *Dimbleby* programme. Dorrell was about to shatter the 'clear, united view' which Heseltine had so confidently predicted.

When asked by Jonathan Dimbleby about the prospects for British membership of a single currency, Dorrell seemed to be totally unaware of the line agreed by John Major and Kenneth Clarke that it was 'very unlikely, though not impossible' for Britain to join in the first wave in 1999. Dorrell was emphatic about the Cabinet's position: 'First of all, no single currency without a referendum and, secondly, we shan't be joining a single currency on January 1, 1999.' When Dimbleby queried this, Dorrell went further: 'I said we shall not be joining on January 1, 1999, because we shan't be putting the legislation through on the timescale that makes that possible.' On being told that he appeared to be going further than any other minister, Dorrell said he thought it was right to say there was a 'vanishingly small possibility' of Britain joining on the first possible date. Within two and a half hours of the interview, he issued an abject retraction through Central Office, stating that he entirely agreed with the government's position that Britain had 'not ruled out' joining the single currency in January 1999. Dorrell tried to limit the damage by suggesting that he had simply used the wrong form of words. 'My thought process was blurred at that particular moment. I had the government line. The truth is I couldn't remember precisely at the right moment precisely what the formula was.' Dorrell's explanation failed initially to impress political correspondents. Under the front-page headline 'Dorrell does the splits', the *Daily Mail*'s David Hughes said some party insiders believed it was a 'clear pitch for the Euro-sceptic vote' in any leadership contest, should Major lose the election.

Dorrell telephoned Kenneth Clarke to apologise, and the Chancellor, interviewed on *Today* next morning, described their conversation as a 'very relaxed chat'. Indeed, despite a barrage of newspaper headlines about Dorrell's gaffe having wrecked Tory unity, Clarke was in a bullish mood as I showed him into one of the BBC's radio studios at Westminster for his interview. As I pulled open the door, he smiled and said: 'Don't worry, I'm not going to do a Stephen Dorrell and give you a story.' Clarke's joke went down well with his political adviser, Anthony Teesdale, who reminded me of an earlier occasion when he had described the Chancellor as having the 'hide of a rhinocerous' and an unfailing sense of humour in the face of media pressure.

Clarke was by far the most vociferous of the Cabinet's pro-Europeans and had been equally robust the previous month in defending the

John Prescott and 'the two faces of John Major'.

Martin Bell ambushed by Christine and Neil Hamilton
at the Battle of Knutsford Heath.

Spinning for Labour:
above Alastair Campbell minding Tony Blair;
below Peter Mandelson minding Fitz the bulldog.

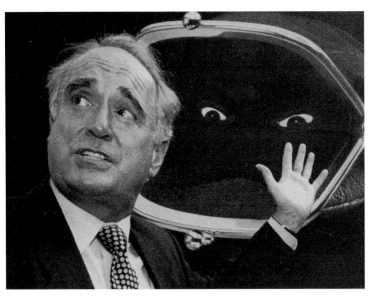

Spinning for the Tories:
above Brian Mawhinney proclaiming 'New Labour, New Taxes';
below Charles Lewington, director of communications for the
Conservatives, monitoring John Major.

'Don't bind my hands.'

LABOUR'S POSITION ON EUROPE.

Helmut Kohl (Chancellor of Germany) pictured with Tony Blair (leader of the Labour Party.)

Britain faces the most momentous decisions for generations. Do we want a Federal Europe? Do we want a Single European Currency? Or European laws governing British jobs, pay and border controls? The key question is: Who can best negotiate these issues to Britain's advantage across the table from the immensely experienced leaders of Germany, France and the rest of Europe? Labour were once blindly anti-Europe. Now they're equally blindly pro-Europe. The next few weeks and months are going to call for the most skilled negotiators Britain can muster. Don't send a boy to do a man's job. You can only be sure with the Conservatives.

Published by Conservative Central Office, 32 Smith Square London SW1P 3HH

The carefully choreographed 'spontaneous outpouring
from offices and factories to greet the new Prime Minister'.

Cabinet's wait-and-see stance on monetary union after the Foreign Secretary, Malcolm Rifkind, appeared to have hardened the government's position. Rifkind was interviewed on *Today* by John Humphrys and declared that the government had not adopted a neutral stance: 'No, we are not neutral. We are actually, on balance, we are hostile to a single currency.' Brian Mawhinney, campaigning in the Wirral South by-election, stood by Rifkind's remarks, insisting that the Foreign Secretary was speaking for the 'whole Cabinet'; but two hours later Clarke told *Sky News* that he had been listening closely to the interview on *Today* and was confident Rifkind had not changed the government's policy. 'It was obviously a slip of the tongue under pressure from a very skilful interviewer.' Undaunted, Rifkind appeared on *The World at One* an hour later and told Nick Clarke that he did not regret using the word hostile. 'No, I don't regret it because, in the context in which I was using it, it made sense and it was consistent with what the government's policy is.' Labour's media monitoring unit at Millbank Tower must have been hard pressed to keep pace, but by early afternoon the table in the press gallery was piled high with a complete set of transcripts of the various conflicting interviews. 'Rifkind v Ken: Now it's War' was the splash headline in the London *Evening Standard*, which said the Cabinet's hard-won agreement on monetary union had dissolved into chaos.

In an attempt to sort out their differences, Clarke went to Rifkind's official residence in Carlton Gardens at 10.30 p.m. After a glass or two of whisky, they issued a joint statement in the early hours of the morning to the effect that the government was 'only hostile to a fudged single currency'. Trevor Kavanagh, the *Sun*'s political editor, said that both Major and Mawhinney were backing Rifkind, with the result that the government had 'sensationally declared war' on the single currency and even the Euro-fanatic Kenneth Clarke had given up his battle to 'dump the pound'. Kavanagh claimed that Mawhinney had to be 'restrained from dancing in public' and party officials were cracking open the champagne because the Conservatives at last had a united policy of hostility to monetary union. The Tory backbencher Jerry Hayes said Clarke had been 'popping mad' with Rifkind and was 'like a volcano waiting to explode'. 'Eventually Ken rowed back but we have planted the word "hostile" in the public's mind and that's no bad thing.'

After a Cabinet meeting that morning, the Prime Minister's press secretary, Jonathan Haslam, said ministers viewed the confusion between Clarke and Rifkind as caused by 'press misrepresentation', which was 'very often the case'. Even so, Clarke acknowledged later that he was taken aback when he heard Rifkind say on air that the government was 'hostile' to a single currency. 'I was out in the kitchen at the time and whenever I hear a familiar voice I do try to listen in. I went into the other room to hear what Malcolm was saying and I just couldn't believe it.' During his *Today* interview Clarke told John Humphrys that he did not watch the *Dimbleby* programme so he had not heard Stephen Dorrell's assertion that Britain would not join the single currency in January 1999. 'I never watch any of those Sunday political programmes. People only hear about what you have said if you have said something wrong.' Humphrys asked Clarke if he thought it was a 'rum old business' that a minister could say something was not government policy and then say he did not mean it. The Chancellor refused to be put off his stride: 'Yes, it is a rum old business when you get political correspondents putting everything under close textual analysis.'

Once Clarke had finished in the *Today* studio I had to interview him for BBC television. He had been hoping to publicise a speech he was making that evening to the annual dinner of the British Retail Consortium in which he intended to paint an optimistic picture of the British economy, declaring that the country was 'fighting fit and raring to face the challenge of the future'. When it became clear I was only interested in asking him questions about his reaction to Dorrell's remarks, he sighed good-naturedly and said philosophically: 'Bang goes another speech.' His press secretary, Jill Rutter, sensing the Chancellor's disappointment, complimented him on the way he had rubbished the Sunday political programmes. 'They really are only of any interest to political anoraks, the real sad cases.' Nevertheless I could not help thinking that Clarke was right in his conclusion that politicians knew full well that they only made news on the Sunday programmes if they said something which was 'off message', and I sensed that he perhaps suspected as much of Dorrell. All the same, after a day's heavy briefing by Dorrell and his political adviser, Tim Ryecroft, most political correspondents accepted that it was a genuine mistake. As he walked off the set with Jonathan Dimbleby at LWT's studios Dorrell was said to have realised that he had slipped up, and while he spoke on the phone to the Chancellor at Dorney Wood, Ryecroft alerted Downing Street and Central Office. Ryecroft told journalists that the headlines in the morning newspapers 'hadn't done the government any good, the party any good or Dorrell any good'. When he was asked at the morning lobby briefing if the Prime Minister thought the

Secretary of State for Health had been 'chipping away' at the wait-and-see position on monetary union, Jonathan Haslam insisted there was no question of the Cabinet changing their position and Major was satisfied that Dorrell supported government policy.

Sir Bernard Ingham told me he was amazed at the incompetent way Downing Street had handled the affair. If he had still been press secretary he would have briefed hard that Dorrell had made a mistake and he would have advised the Chancellor and other ministers to have refrained from giving further interviews. 'Ken Clarke really is the problem. He should leave it alone when something like this happens and stop giving further mileage to a story like that.' When Major was asked for his comment on a Radio 5 Live phone-in, he said he accepted that Dorrell had made a mistake. 'He's human, as we all are, and he made it clear that afternoon that he supports the policy.' Dorrell seemed encouraged by Major's readiness to accept his explanation and he looked rather more relaxed later that day as he chatted with political journalists in the lobby. His wife was expecting a baby within a matter of weeks and it emerged subsequently, in published extracts from a diary kept by the junior Treasury minister, Phillip Oppenheim, that the health secretary had faced a punishing timetable in the days leading up to his *Dimbleby* appearance. Oppenheim concluded that Dorrell's slip was 'far too crass' to have been an attempt to position himself for a leadership election and, as he noted in his diary in the *Sunday Times*, put it down to a busy weekend: 'He looks shattered. Bags under the eyes. No doubt he's been on a ridiculous schedule. Department of Health from 8.30 a.m. to 6 p.m. during the week, followed by a balls-aching dinner and a box or two, then up to the constituency through Friday traffic, a couple of evening functions, Saturday surgery and then an early rush to London to the studio. It looked like a genuine slip.'

Although the Chancellor's upbeat speech to the British Retail Consortium was overshadowed by Dorrell's remarks on the single currency, his attendance at the annual dinner succeeded in generating widespread publicity the following week. After completing his address to the Consortium's 550 guests, Clarke was asked by Yvette Murphy, a journalist on *The Grocer* magazine, to comment on Labour's claim that if the Conservatives were re-elected they would put value added tax on food. He told her 'categorically' that was not his intention. But when challenged about the way the government had imposed VAT on domestic fuel, she said Clarke responded by saying the 'challenge now is to get the rate up to

17.5 per cent'. Ms Murphy's exclusive report was published in that Saturday's edition of her magazine, but it was not until the following Monday that it came to the attention of political correspondents. I was one of those alerted to the story soon after 6 p.m. Charlie Whelan, press officer to the shadow Chancellor, told me he was tipping off the BBC and the Press Association news agency that next morning's *Mirror* was publishing a 'sensational' quote from Clarke admitting that he wanted to double the VAT rate on fuel, and said the source of the story was *The Grocer*.

BBC correspondents set to work to see if Clarke's quote was correct. The headline over Ms Murphy's report was that Clarke had said 'No way' to VAT on food. The reference to the challenge to increase VAT on fuel to 17.5 per cent was given no special prominence and was not mentioned until a third of the way into the story. Clive Beddall, the magazine's editor, said he stood by their report. When Ms Murphy, who was having a workout at her gym that evening, was finally tracked down by the BBC correspondent Jon Sopel, she too stood by her story. Although she had no shorthand note or tape recording of the conversation she said it was an accurate recollection of her conversation with the Chancellor. However, Lesley McLeod, the Treasury press officer who was present during Ms Murphy's conversation with the Chancellor, told me she had no recollection of his making any comment about the future rate of VAT on fuel. Ms McLeod said attempts were being made to get clarification from the Chancellor himself but this was taking time as he was on an official visit to China. After much deliberation in the newsroom it was decided the story should not be mentioned on the *Nine o'Clock News* because there were too many unanswered questions about exactly what had taken place, and that decision was considered to have been vindicated when, at 8.15 p.m., Clarke issued a statement in Beijing categorically denying that he had made any statement to *The Grocer* about an intention to increase VAT on fuel.

After the *Nine o'Clock News* failed to run the story, Whelan phoned to complain. I told him of the checks which had been made and the strength of the Chancellor's denial, but he took a dim view of the BBC's news judgement. 'You're a load of wankers for not running what Clarke said.' However, Whelan's efforts to talk up the story, and his attempts to persuade the BBC to run it, annoyed Kevin Maguire, the *Mirror*'s political editor. He said a reader had alerted their newsdesk to Clarke's quoted remark on VAT, and although the *Mirror*'s political correspondent Nigel Morris had discussed their story with Whelan and Labour's chief media spokesperson, David Hill, they were annoyed their exclusive had been touted around to other journalists at Westminster even before their first edition had been printed. 'We're angry with Labour. They really are too greedy using the *Mirror*'s stories like that.'

In the event, Whelan's hard sell so early in the evening was counter-productive, because it gave the Treasury the chance to get out a categoric denial in time for the main evening news bulletins and well before the deadline for the next morning's newspapers. Clarke's press officer, Jill Rutter, said it was 3 a.m. in Beijing when she was woken and told of the story. 'I had to wake up Ken just before 4 a.m. but we were really grateful to have found out about the story when we did because it meant we could kill it off in time for all the main editions of the papers.' When Clarke was interviewed later that morning on *Today* he insisted that the possibility of increasing VAT on fuel had never crossed his mind. He had always accepted the House of Commons vote in December 1994 to keep the VAT rate at 8 per cent and to reject the staged increase to 17.5 per cent. He thought it was obvious Ms Murphy knew she had not obtained a sensational new remark from him because her reference to his supposed comment was buried in the middle of her report on an inside page in *The Grocer*.

Although the Treasury's damage limitation had been effective, most newspapers still ran the story, together with Clarke's denial. Whelan had not caused the Chancellor as much trouble as on previous occasions, but the Conservatives had been put on the defensive and Labour had succeeded in raising fresh doubts about the government's intentions on possible VAT increases. Time and again during early March, Labour succeeded in generating stories which resurrected the news media's interest in the government's long-standing problems and diverted the attention of Major and his ministers as they prepared for the election. By far the most successful of these spoiling operations was Labour's orches-tration of a succession of damaging revelations about the failure to enforce adequate safety precautions in abattoirs in the wake of the spread of BSE in beef cattle. Admittedly the Ministry of Agriculture's incompetent handling of the crisis caused by 'mad cow disease', and the unsympathetic manner of the Minister of Agriculture, Douglas Hogg, provided an easy target, but Labour's prowess in piling on the agony for the government was breathtaking.

Nigel Griffiths, Labour's consumer affairs spokesman, told me that he seized the opportunity to revive interest in the BSE story when he discovered that Labour's agriculture spokesman, Gavin Strang, had done nothing to publicise a report entitled *Red Meat*, prepared for the Meat Hygiene Service, which warned of 'major contamination' because of chronic lapses of hygiene in some abattoirs. Bill Swann, the editor of the report, who had since become the RSPCA's assistant chief veterinary officer, was annoyed that the ministry had first tried to tone down their findings and then suppressed their report when they had been promised it would be published in March 1996. Griffiths said Swann felt so aggrieved by what had happened that he had sent a copy of the report to Elliot Morley, Strang's deputy. 'Swann was hopping mad that Gavin and Elliot had just been sitting on the report for a fortnight and had done nothing about it. They said they were keeping it for Tony Blair to use in the election campaign, but I told them you can't leave it as long as that and that we must get the report out to the news media immediately.' Next morning both the *Financial Times* and the *Mirror* ran 'exclusive' stories which included extensive extracts from Swann's findings. Griffiths said that before releasing the report to the press he had taken the precaution of supplying a copy to Professor Sir Hugh Pennington, chairman of the group investigating the Lanarkshire outbreak of *E. coli* food poisoning. 'Pennington told us he didn't even know the Swann report existed and that he was most grateful for a copy of it. We wanted to make sure that if Pennington was contacted by journalists he'd know all about it.' Labour's advance planning paid off handsomely. When Sir Hugh was approached that morning by reporters who were following up the revelations in the *Mirror* and the *Financial Times*, he was highly critical of the ministry's conduct and said he would have liked to have seen the Swann report as soon as he started his investigation into the Lanarkshire food poisoning outbreak.

Labour's charge that the report had been purposely suppressed gained considerable credence as the morning progressed because of Sir Hugh's intervention, and the government's discomfort at being caught off guard was evident at the 11 a.m. briefing for lobby correspondents. Jonathan Haslam denied there had been a cover-up. He said the report had been commissioned by the Meat Hygiene Service to recommend best practice for abattoir inspectors. It was an internal management report and had not been sent to ministers. Nevertheless he announced that Douglas Hogg would be making an emergency statement that Thursday afternoon. Once more Labour had put the government firmly on the defensive and gained a tailor-made opportunity for Blair to attack Major at Prime Minister's questions, which preceded Hogg's statement. Waving a copy of the unpublished report across the despatch box, Blair said that if it was a working document on improving best practice in slaughterhouses that was all the more reason why it should have been provided to the Pennington inquiry. Major accused Labour of exaggerating the problem to the detriment of the meat trade. The Prime Minister was taunted by shouts of 'stay, stay' when he walked out of the chamber without waiting for the statement. Hogg said that Swann's first draft of his report was regarded as 'rather unsatisfactory' by the editorial board of the Meat Hygiene Service, and when he refused to recast his contribution, the section on red meat was redrafted. The final report reflected the majority judgement of the veterinary staff who carried out the review and the most important recommendations had been acted upon. Hogg gave his statement standing on one foot: he had broken his ankle the previous weekend and the papers had been full of photographs of the minister negotiating his way round Whitehall on crutches. Hogg had a reputation for being accident-prone, and his current predicament made him the butt of MPs' jibes. There were shouts of 'peg leg' and references to the minister who had 'shot himself in the foot'. Parliamentary sketch writers were withering about Hogg's performance: Edward Pearce, writing in the *Glasgow Herald*, said he had addressed MPs as if they were halfwits.

Labour waited until the Tuesday of the following week before releasing another batch of leaked documents in the hope of keeping the media spotlight trained firmly on the hapless minister. Again, their publication was timed to give Blair every opportunity to embarrass Major at Prime Minister's questions. An hour before the *One o'Clock News*, Blair's office faxed the BBC copies of correspondence between the Association of Meat Inspectors and the Parliamentary Secretary for Agriculture, Angela Browning. One of the Association's letters, dated January 1996, told the Meat Hygiene Service that standards in slaughter-houses were steadily declining and that problems caused by faecal contamination in beef were a 'potential time bomb'. At question time, Blair demanded a full account of the steps the government had taken to prevent contamination because the letters contradicted the assurances which Hogg had given the previous week. Major was again on the back foot, having first to acknowledge that the correspondence which had 'attained some notoriety on the lunchtime media' was a matter of concern. He assured MPs that abattoir owners and managers who flouted the regulations would face prosecution and inspectors who failed to enforce the rules would be disciplined. Immediately after questions, said Nigel Griffiths, there was a meeting in Blair's office to plan the next move.

Labour's aim was to try to humiliate the government by forcing Hogg to make a second statement. Griffiths had further correspondence to release, including letters from trading standards officers in Northumberland who had warned the Ministry of Agriculture the previous year that they did not have enough resources to police the anti-BSE controls. 'We decided to fax the letters to *Today* so that they could refer to them in their programme next morning. We'd purposely held some back, rather than release them all at once, so as to cause maximum trouble for the government.' In a speech that evening Blair called on Hogg to make a full statement; and the next morning, Griffiths told *Today* that the leaked letters from Northumberland's trading standards officers revealed serious breaches in the regulations: ten per cent of meat samples were being falsely described as BSE-free.

Even for Hogg, grown used to unfavourable publicity, the morning papers cannot have been pleasant reading, plastered as they were with yet more uncomplimentary accounts of his ministerial conduct. Under the headline 'Hogg's head on block in meat row', the *Daily Mail* published a diary of the 'Six days in the humbling of Hogg'. It showed how the progressive leaking of the various confidential reports and correspondence had highlighted Hogg's 'cack-handed incompetence' and left him isolated within the Cabinet. Speculation continued throughout the lunchtime programmes about the possibility that Hogg would be forced to the despatch box that afternoon. In his report for *The World at One*, the BBC correspondent Jeremy Vine quoted a Central Office source as saying that Hogg needed to be 'locked in a fridge until polling day'. Finally confirmation came that the minister would make a further statement. He told MPs that he accepted there was scope for further improvement in meat hygiene but he considered much recent reporting by the news media had been misleading and had failed to take account of the important progress which had been made in the previous eighteen months. Hogg's statement was a comprehensive account of the action being taken by the Ministry of Agriculture. The guidance given to political correspondents was that Major had ordered him to make the fullest possible report to the House so as to ensure there could be no further damaging disclosures before polling day. Journalists were left in no doubt that Major expected Hogg to keep the lowest possible profile during the election campaign. Tory party managers feared that if he were seen on television he would remind voters of the whole sorry saga of BSE. Nevertheless, Labour had achieved their objective: reports exposing the government's repeated failings over 'mad cow disease' and Hogg's insensitive handling of the crisis had been high up in the news bulletins for nearly a week.

Labour's supremacy in directing the news agenda towards issues which were troublesome for the government owed much to their persistence. Unlike their counterparts at Conservative Central Office, the duty press officers in Blair's office and at Millbank Tower always made a point of discovering which BBC correspondents were compiling overnight reports for radio and television or were broadcasting first thing next morning. Once armed with the names of those worth contacting, Labour's spin doctors became as assiduous and as brazen as double-glazing salesmen. They would think nothing of making several unsolicited calls to the same correspondent and would not relent until they considered they had convinced the journalist concerned of the newsworthiness of their latest story or alternatively until they had discovered whether the BBC was working on something which might be of interest to the Labour Party. As the election campaign got closer, Labour tried to synchronise the coverage so as to ensure that exclusive stories which had been fed to the newspapers were featured prominently in the morning news bulletins and programmes. The calls usually started coming through once the *Nine o'Clock News* and *News at Ten* were off the air, when Labour knew that newsrooms had switched their emphasis towards preparing material for next morning's output. The leaking in mid-March of a report critical of the government's nursery voucher scheme illustrated the potency of Labour's strategy. Shortly before 10 p.m. I was notified by Labour's chief spokesperson, David Hill, that both the *Independent* and the *Mirror* were going to publish leaked copies of a report by the House of Commons Select Committee on Education and Employment which stated that parental choice would not be enhanced by the nursery voucher scheme. Hill said he could confirm that the extracts from the report which the two newspapers were publishing were accurate and had been verified by Labour members on the committee. Within the hour the BBC had managed to contact several of the Labour MPs involved and they too confirmed the accuracy of the story.

Labour knew that their advance warnings were appreciated by broadcasting organisations. Sometimes it was nearly midnight before all the first editions of next morning's newspapers were delivered to the BBC's studios, by which time it was almost too late to film pre-recorded interviews, so giving the earliest possible notification was one way of ensuring widespread coverage. In this case, Hill's telephone call to the

BBC about the leak of the select committee's report had the desired effect: I was able to verify the story for myself and by the time the papers arrived I was already well advanced in preparing my radio and television reports for next morning's bulletins. I made a point of including reaction from Conservative MPs on the committee who blamed the leaks on blatant electioneering by Labour. At Prime Minister's questions, Major described the leaking of the select committee's findings a week before their official publication as 'an abuse of the procedures of the House'. As political correspondents and party spin doctors milled about on leaving the chamber, Hill said he hoped his telephone call the previous night had been of value. He seemed pleased with his handiwork. 'I suppose you heard me being suitably admonished by the Prime Minister.' At this point Alastair Campbell leant over, as if to head-butt me, and chipped in with his halfpenn'orth: 'I suppose you were involved in that sordid scam the Prime Minister was complaining about.'

Major's irritation at finding himself constantly on the ropes was shared by his Cabinet colleagues. Gillian Shephard, the Secretary of State for Education, told me she could not wait for the campaign to start. 'I know it doesn't look good for us, and there has been a run of bad news for the government, but what makes an election so exciting is that the outcome is unknown. Anything can still happen.' Party workers at Central Office were as anxious as government business managers to get the parliamentary session completed so that they could launch the Conservatives' campaign and concentrate their efforts on retaliating against Labour's attacks. Charles Hendry, the party vice-chairman responsible for communications, conceded that it had been a difficult week for the government because of the way Labour had forced a statement out of Douglas Hogg on beef and then surprised ministers by the premature leak about nursery vouchers. 'The trouble for us at the moment is that we just don't know where the next damaging story is going to come from, so we are having to spend a lot of time on firefighting. We are managing to neutralise some of Labour's scares, like that VAT story from *The Grocer*, but ministers are so tied down on government business they haven't got time to do anything else or think about the election. We just can't wait until the campaign gets going so that at last we'll get a level playing field against Labour.' Hendry said speculation in the press about dissension at the top of the party over election tactics was misplaced. He was confident that once the campaign got under way there would be a clear command structure: when John Major was out electioneering around the country, Michael Heseltine would remain in London and be available to give instant responses to radio and television, while Brian Mawhinney would be running the campaign at Central Office. 'Michael is tremendous when we need someone instantly to go round the studios and face down the broadcasters. Brian doesn't like doing a lot of media work. He's not so happy with the instant interview and he far prefers to be running the office.'

Heseltine had certainly done what he could to dispel persistent newspaper reports of animosity between himself and Dr Mawhinney. On the first Sunday in March they were both questioned at length about who would take responsibility for the election campaign when the Prime Minister was out of London. When asked on *Breakfast with Frost* what would happen if Heseltine disagreed with him in Major's absence, Mawhinney was adamant about the division of responsibility: 'I am in charge of the Conservatives' election strategy and performance. I am happy to have that responsibility. I think Michael Heseltine is an asset.' Four hours later, *On the Record* tried to put the Deputy Prime Minister on the spot, but Heseltine told John Humphrys that Major had made the position abundantly clear: 'The Prime Minister is the leader of the Conservative Party. He is therefore totally in charge and determined to win. Brian Mawhinney is chairman of the party. He has responsibility for the campaign. There is not the sliver of a cigarette paper between us. We know what each other's jobs are and we respect each other's positions.'

As the election drew closer, Mawhinney impressed me by his grasp of the steps which the Conservatives would have to take if they were to stand any chance of withstanding the hostile coverage which Labour were likely to generate. With three months to go to the start of the campaign he admitted it was still requiring an all-out effort to convince political correspondents that the Conservatives should not be written off but were instead fighting to win and had not given up the ghost. 'We are beginning to engage the media and get them to ask questions about Labour's policies but it's not easy to persuade journalists to take us seriously.' In two speeches the previous year he had outlined what he thought would be the news media's own responsibilities when reporting the 1997 general election. Without saying so in as many words, Mawhinney effectively identified the strengths of Labour's media strategy and put his finger on the Conservatives' weaknesses.

In what was by far the more thoughtful of the two speeches he told the Manchester Business School in February 1996 that he thought journalists were failing to serve the public interest when they allowed the news agenda to be dominated by reports about splits and leaks. He said that despite all the steps which the Conservatives had taken since 1979 to open up decision-making to public scrutiny and establish open government, reporters always considered that a leaked document was more interesting than one which had been published. Similarly, stories about splits between ministers, whether real or imagined, regularly took precedence over policy announcements. Mawhinney acknowledged that this trend had been fuelled by an 'explosion' in the amount of political broadcasting. He calculated that during the four terms of Conservative government since 1979 there had been a fivefold increase in the number of political programmes transmitted on Sundays. Therefore Sunday, which within living memory had not been a day for politics, had arguably become the 'busiest and most important day of the political week'. Ministers were regularly being asked to comment on soundbites taken out of context from interviews given earlier by their colleagues. 'This selective use of quotation can then be manipulated to create a wholly artificial and meaningless, but damaging, split.' Mawhinney renewed his appeal for a sense of perspective when he addressed the Westminster Media Forum the following November. No election campaign was likely to be free of outbursts of dissent by the 'odd backbencher or two' in each of the major parties, but journalists should not forget that the divisions and choices about which the public needed to be informed were between the parties and not within them. Mawhinney made no attempt to criticise his opponents, but he had pinpointed the two areas where Labour had built up particular expertise. In the months leading up to the election, shadow ministers had done all they could to feed the media's voracious appetite for leaked documents, and it was their researchers and advisers who helped scour interview transcripts for gaffes and inconsistencies which could then be exploited by Labour's spin doctors.

Mawhinney's brusque manner, and his urge to protest about news stories which he thought were biased or unfair, presented a perpetual problem for the party's senior press officer, Sheila Gunn, who was responsible for liaison with lobby journalists. She told me she was always trying to restrain him from making complaints. 'He'd keep saying this or that interviewer is too hard on ministers and shouldn't be allowed to get away with it. I'd tell him that if he kept complaining it would only be counterproductive.' Ms Gunn said her boss, Charles Lewington, kept getting the same routine from the chairman and from John Major. 'The Prime

Minister is always complaining about journalists like Simon Walters of the *Express on Sunday* and keeps telling Charles not to give them any more help. Charles keeps muttering about operating a blacklist, but I tell them it won't work and that we've got to go on talking to reporters.'

Mawhinney was especially angered by press reports in the autumn of 1996 which suggested that Cabinet ministers were protesting at 'heavy-handed' tactics in the way he was said to have upbraided them for being 'off message' and for failing to put across the government's line. After the *Daily Telegraph* had suggested that five ministers had made complaints to the Chief Whip, Alastair Goodlad, the paper's chief political correspondent, Robert Shrimsley, assessed Mawhinney's record. He paid tribute to the chairman's success in creating what party insiders had acknowledged was a 'modern, lean, mean fighting machine' out of a near-bankrupt Central Office. 'Hurricane Brian swept through Tory HQ. Old-fashioned staff soon found life deeply uncomfortable. In little time he had crafted Central Office to his own technocratic image.' Shrimsley said it was Mawhinney's misfortune that his shortcomings were often seen in public. While his manner of tackling his opponents was effective, the public did not warm to his somewhat brutal manner. Peter Oborne, writing in the *Express on Sunday*, reached the same conclusion. Dr Mawhinney had turned Central Office into a Rolls-Royce machine through a series of astute appointments, but he remained a 'dour Ulsterman who does not think fast on his feet'.

My own assessment of Mawhinney's manner when being interviewed was that his lacklustre delivery derived in part from an inner sense of caution and a fear that he could all too easily put the boot in and live to regret it. My suspicions were confirmed after the launch, early in January 1997, of the Liberal Democrats' pre-election pledges to spend more on education and health. Paddy Ashdown said he intended to avoid the presidential style of campaigning which Blair and Major were adopting. 'No doubt if we are attacked, we will respond. No doubt we will be pungent in our response, but you will not see a campaign from the Liberal Democrats that is based exclusively on negative or personal attacks.' At the start of his news conference Ashdown posed with two of his fellow MPs, Simon Hughes and Don Foster. All three were wearing ties of varying shades of yellow which they adjusted in unison for the benefit of the television crews and photographers. Ashdown's nonchalant performance had clearly irritated Mawhinney, as I discovered when we walked together across College Green. We were discussing the way the three MPs had preened themselves for the benefit of the cameras when the party chairman turned to me and said he just could not stand Ashdown. Some Conservative MPs had already taken to describing the Liberal Democrat leader as 'Pious Paddy' and it was obviously a sentiment Mawhinney shared. 'I do find him very annoying and I've been wondering how best to attack him. He is very saintly. Do you think I'd be able to get away with calling him the Reverend Ashdown?' I told Mawhinney that was pretty punchy and would certainly make a newsy soundbite, but he obviously had second thoughts because I waited in vain to hear him deliver it.

Mawhinney's willingness to endorse negative campaigning was signalled in the clearest possible terms in August 1996 when he gave the go-ahead for a controversial advertisement which featured a photograph of Tony Blair with demon-like eyes. It appeared in only three Sunday newspapers and, despite being lambasted by Labour, immediately acquired a cult status, spawning countless lookalikes and being lampooned mercilessly by cartoonists. The advertisement was a spin-off from an equally eye-catching image which had been unveiled the previous month to promote the Conservatives' 'New Labour, New Danger' campaign. Posters and advertisements showed a pair of vivid red curtains with two red, bloodshot eyes staring out. The curtains were said to represent the front behind which New Labour was hiding, and the pair of eyes were the ones which would peer into the everyday lives of ordinary citizens. Within a few weeks of these flaming red posters appearing all over the country, the shadow transport minister, Clare Short, inadvertently gave substance to the Conservatives' lurid imagery. For some months she had been highly critical of Labour's leading spin doctors, Peter Mandelson and Alastair Campbell, because of the way she believed they were briefing journalists against her. In one highly publicised instance, Blair's office informed reporters that colleagues were 'questioning her competence and profes-sionalism' after she suggested on GMTV's *Sunday Programme* that under a fair tax system people like her 'would pay a bit more tax'. Ms Short told me she considered the character assassination being authorised in Blair's name was tantamount to political thuggery. She expanded on her criticism in an interview for the *New Statesman*, in which she said she sometimes called Blair's advisers the people who lived in the dark. 'Everything they do is in hiding . . . Everything we do is in the light. They live in the dark.' Ms Short's graphic description was pounced on by Mawhinney who asked if it could be incorporated immediately into the 'New Labour, New Danger' campaign.

Charles Hendry told me that Central Office was determined to respond that weekend, although the *New Statesman* had only been published on Thursday, and the task of devising an instant advertisement for the Sunday newspapers was given to the Conservatives' three long-standing media advisers, Maurice Saatchi, who led M&C Saatchi, the Conservatives' advertising agency, Peter Gummer, chairman of Shandwick International, and Sir Tim Bell, chairman of Lowe Bell Communications. The advertisement which Saatchi presented to Dr Mawhinney for his approval showed a photograph of Blair with a big grin on his face and red, demon-like eyes. Beneath it was the slogan 'New Labour, New Danger' together with a reference to Ms Short having said that 'dark forces behind Tony Blair manipulate policy in a sinister way'. Charles Lewington told me subsequently that he was with Mawhinney when Saatchi made his presentation. 'He warned us that the advertise-ment was bound to provoke a storm of criticism. Actually Maurice was really much more nervous about putting the demon eyes on Blair than either of us were. We both agreed to it straight away. It was a tremendous image but we knew what the implications would be.' The advertisement made front-page news that weekend and the *Mail on Sunday*, which was one of the three newspapers to carry it, said Brian Mawhinney had sanctioned publication without reference to either John Major or Michael Heseltine, who were both on holiday.

Maurice Saatchi's fears were well founded: the advertisement produced widespread protests. Peter Mandelson said there appeared to be no limit to the depths to which the Conservatives would sink in personal-ising their negative attacks on New Labour. 'Tony Blair is a practising Christian and, by any standard, a man of decency and integrity. Whatever you think of his political views, to portray him as the devil is a crass, clumsy move.' Mandelson was supported by the Bishop of Oxford, the Right Reverend Richard Harries, who declared that the vilification of politicians was a puerile exercise, and that 'when that vilifying draws on satanic imagery it is not only silly but potentially dangerous'. He appealed to political parties to resist the temptation to go in for 'personal abuse and dirty tricks'. But the advertisement was defended by the Secretary of State for Defence, Michael Portillo, who said the Conservatives had to expose the dangers of New Labour. 'We have applied the symbol of the red eyes, which stand for danger, to Tony Blair in order to make the point that behind the smiles and the soundbites there are policies which are deeply dangerous to our country.'

The controversy was given fresh life ten days later when the Prime Minister included Maurice Saatchi and Peter Gummer in a list of fourteen new life peers. Labour's environment spokesman, Frank Dobson, said that by making the two awards Major had given his personal seal of approval to the 'most negative election campaign ever' and plunged the peerage system to new depths. 'No coronets and ermine will cover up Maurice Saatchi and Peter Gummer's role in dragging British politics lower than the gutter. When they're deciding which title to take one of them will be the Lord of the Lies.' Labour considered their protests had been vindicated when the Advertising Standards Authority gave its verdict on complaints that the campaign had breached the advertising industry's code of practice. It ruled that the advertisement had depicted Blair as 'sinister and dishonest' and should not be repeated. Matti Alderson, director general of the ASA, said that both M&C Saatchi and Central Office should have known better because they must have realised that it was an offensive portrayal of a politician. But *Campaign*, the weekly magazine for the advertising industry, named it as the most powerful advertisement of the year. Stefano Hatfield, *Campaign*'s editor, said the demon eyes image made Blair's character a legitimate subject of debate in the election. 'In classic style it picks up on a nagging doubt about whether Blair is sincere.' Brian Mawhinney considered the 'impartial and authoritative' vote of confidence which they had been given by *Campaign* showed that the Conservatives were not just the best messengers but also had the best message. 'The real dangers lurking behind the facade presented by Blair were brilliantly communicated to a massive audience.'

Buoyed up by the notoriety of their demon eyes image, the Conservatives began 1997 with a new advertising campaign, devised by Maurice Saatchi. It illustrated yet another stark image of the supposed dangers of New Labour. Posters and advertisements showed a young couple, their faces haggard with distress. A red tear ran down the woman's cheek. The slogan said: 'New Labour, New Failure'. Lewington hoped the red tear advertisements would prove as effective as the demon eyes campaign, but he feared that without Labour's help they might not prove as controversial. 'Labour do look as if they are learning their lesson and so far they've not drawn attention to the red tear campaign. They realised that their attacks on the demon eyes gave that image enormous credibility. Our advertisements now get front-page treatment in the national press. Maurice Saatchi always says that it's not the advertisement itself which creates news but all the protests about it which generate interest and notoriety. Don't forget that in the 1979 general election, it wasn't Margaret Thatcher but Denis Healey, by kicking up such a fuss, who made the Saatchis so famous for their "Labour Isn't Working" poster.' Charles Hendry said the reason why Mandelson kept on complaining about the 'New Labour, New Danger' posters and advertisements was because the reaction they were getting from Labour's focus groups showed that they were working. 'Mandelson has been a tremendous asset to the Conservative Party. He's given our campaign much more mileage than we could ever have hoped for.' Hendry insisted that Major was 'entirely happy' with the strategy and had backed the demon eyes advertisement.

Lewington had explained to me that the great strength of the 'New Labour, New Danger' slogan was that it provided a structured theme which could be adapted endlessly to highlight different dangers; but his confident predictions about the appeal and durability of their message proved ill-judged. The campaign foundered on a series of posters which showed a colour photograph of a lion with a large, superimposed blood-red tear running from its eye. Underneath the picture was the slogan: 'New Labour, Euro Danger'. After running for four weeks the posters were withdrawn in March 1997 amid a flurry of newspaper reports revealing unease in the party's high command at the failure of the advertisements to bring about any improvement in the Conservatives' opinion poll ratings. Advertising industry researchers were quoted as saying that the lion with the red tear was the least popular of the 'New Labour, New Danger' series because it associated the Conservatives with negative feelings, like failure and sadness. The poster was described as being beyond contempt by Ken Dampier, of Dampier Communications, who told the *Independent* it was one of the worst campaigns he had seen after twenty-five years in the business. 'The idea that because there's a change of political party in power that in some way will leave the British lion shedding tears is pathetic.' Conservative MPs queued up to say their constituents could not understand what the poster was trying to get across, and *The Times* reported that it was disliked even by the Prime Minister. According to Robert Shrimsley, the *Daily Telegraph*'s chief political correspondent, John Major had complained about Central Office's failure to try out their advertisements before they were launched, and Norman Blackwell, head of the No. 10 policy unit, had urged Brian Mawhinney to 'get a grip' on the campaign and stop handing over so much power to Lord Saatchi. Shrimsley said the reason why the advertisements were not tested in advance was that M&C Saatchi feared that details would leak out to the news media. When he was asked on *Breakfast with Frost* why the 'New Labour, Euro Danger' campaign had been terminated, Mawhinney insisted that it had succeeded in getting across the message that if Labour were elected they would destroy jobs. He denied that the posters were taken down because they had been a flop: 'I couldn't run everything in perpetuity.'

Later that week Mawhinney unveiled the Conservatives' next poster, which featured a photograph of Tony Blair and the accompanying message: 'Tony & Bill. £30 billion spending promises. Who pays?' M&C Saatchi's latest creation was to prove equally unpopular with Tory MPs, who claimed that most people could not fathom out what it meant. Michael Fabricant, the Conservative MP for Mid Staffordshire, was so dissatisfied with the campaign that he contacted Lord Saatchi direct. 'I do think the theme "New Labour, New Danger" worked well to begin with. It did prepare the public for the launch of a new product, but I told Maurice Saatchi there was no point carrying on with thematic advertisements because what we wanted was a more detailed campaign, which did more to explain the dangers of New Labour, but he said he hadn't been given any such instructions and he was still doing thematic posters.'

Despite Peter Mandelson's public protestations, Labour were developing a negative pitch in their own posters. One presentation put forward for Tony Blair's approval portrayed the Prime Minister looking like the Mr Men cartoon characters. According to an exclusive report in the *Express on Sunday* by its political editor, Simon Walters, artwork prepared by Labour's advertising agency, BMP, depicted John Major as 'Mr Weak, Mr Spineless, Mr Dither and Mr Panic'. Walters claimed that both Mandelson and Campbell were in favour of using the posters but that Blair had ordered the campaign to be scrapped because he did not approve of personal attacks and feared it might backfire. It transpired later that Labour would have been unable to run the campaign because BMP failed to persuade the trustees of the late Roger Hargreaves, who invented the character, to release the copyright. Campbell told me that Blair would, in any case, have refused to give his permission. 'Tony didn't like negative advertising of that kind which didn't have a purpose.' Nevertheless, the weekend after newspaper reports of the 'Mr Men' rebuff, Labour's deputy leader, John Prescott, unveiled a poster which did represent a highly personalised attack on the Prime Minister. Two profile photographs of Major's face were joined together at the back of the head so that he looked both ways. To the left of his face the poster said: '1992: "Tax cuts year on year"' and to the right it had the words '22 tax rises since 1992' and 'Enough is enough'. A picture of the poster was used to illustrate a signed column by Blair in that Sunday's edition of the *People*, and the *Independent*'s media page said the switch by Labour to negative campaigning showed that the critical focus of Labour's advertising had been tightened. 'Honest John is being portrayed as a two-faced liar.'

Major was said to have regarded the advertisement as being particularly offensive. His annoyance was reflected on *Breakfast with Frost* in an interview with Michael Dobbs, author of the political thriller *House of Cards* and a former deputy chairman of the Tory party. He said Labour had gone ahead and published the poster without seeking Major's permission – contrary to established practice in the advertising industry, according to which the subject of an *ad hominem* advertisement is consulted before the image is passed for publication – which was exactly what Mandelson had accused the Conservatives of doing with their Blair poster. Danny Finkelstein told me that he thought Labour would find that the poster was a mistake. 'I could have understood it if Labour had gone for Major for being weak, but he doesn't come across as two-faced and he's certainly not duplicitous. Don't forget he went out on his soap box in the 1992 election. If Labour had used the Tory party torch facing both ways that might have been different.'

Arguments over the opposing poster campaigns were about to dwindle to a sideshow. Mid-March marked the moment when the Prime Minister would have to begin the countdown towards holding the general election on his preferred date of 1 May. After so many false starts, the pace was at last quickening. Major's speech in Bath to the annual conference of the Conservative Central Council was intended to pave the way for the official announcement. Political journalists knew for certain that their long wait was almost over when Jonathan Haslam's guidance shifted, almost imperceptibly to an outside observer, towards the confirmation they were looking for. His statement to the lobby was short and to the point: 'I am not going to rule out an election statement.' Haslam's briefing coincided with the regular Thursday morning Cabinet meeting and, as ministers departed for Bath, the Prime Minister and his advisers began work on a speech which Major hoped would prove a rallying cry to his dispirited party.

Any hopes the Prime Minister might have had that Conservative MPs would set aside their factional differences and at least give him a clear run at Bath were dashed next day when the pro-European MP Edwina Currie fired off yet another broadside on *The World at One*. She said that if the Conservatives lost the general election, a leadership contest should be held cleanly and quickly. 'If we are going to have a leadership contest, please don't make us wait, John.' When Brian Mawhinney addressed the conference at the opening session, his faced looked as black as thunder and he spoke with deadly precision. 'To every Conservative, one message: if you don't have something to say that will help us win, don't say anything at all.' He held his pose for some moments, grim-faced, hoping no doubt that the gravity of his warning would sink in. Mrs Currie, however, far from feeling restrained, became more strident. On *Channel Four News* she renewed her appeal to the Prime Minister to go quietly if the Conservatives were beaten. 'Please don't make us wait, John; please, John, don't make us hang around.' Michael Heseltine did his best to minimise the damage, insisting that Mrs Currie's remarks were 'not of any interest'. Mawhinney, still grim-faced, told the *Nine o'Clock News* he realised the challenge they faced. 'The Conservative party is running behind in the polls. We are not coasting to victory. We are going to have to work ferociously hard to change public opinion.'

In his own Bath speech the next day, 15 March, Major put himself firmly in the centre ground of British politics. 'For those for whom life is a struggle, for those who don't have the best education or a decent home or job, many of them look to us, many of them are Conservatives. I know them, I came from them, I care for them, and I long to see them too have some of the finer things of life.' He warned of the danger which a change of government could pose to the economic management of the country. 'I say to "time for a change" merchants, find me a better country in the world in which to live than here in Britain today.'

The weekend papers offered Major no encouragement. An NOP opinion survey for the *Sunday Times* suggested Labour had a twenty-five-point lead which, it said, bolstered the conviction that Blair was unstoppable and Major doomed. In his weekly column, Richard Harris commiserated with the Prime Minister as he prepared to make his announcement next day. There were few more lonely and fateful decisions than the timing of a general election, Harris said, and he had come to the conclusion that the Conservatives might have fared better if they had gone to the country the previous October: the longer the 'dreary and interminable' wait for polling day had gone on, the more it had favoured Labour, just as the Conservatives under Margaret Thatcher had benefited from Jim Callaghan's decision to soldier on through the first few months of 1979. 'I can't help feeling that John Major has made a grim situation desperate, that he, like Callaghan, has turned what might have been a close race into what begins to look, increasingly, like a sea change.' But however gloomy the predictions, Major put on the bravest possible face for Monday's hectic comings and goings in Downing Street. After a final Cabinet meeting, Major set off for Buckingham Palace. On returning from his audience with the Queen, Major faced the cameras in Downing Street to announce the dissolution of Parliament. It was a fluent, positive performance. He said that in the previous eighteen years there had been a dramatic change in the lifestyle of the British people, 'a revolution in choice, in opportunity and in living standards.' Major said he guessed that most people had waited 'a long time for this general election'; but although elections were a tough and gruelling business they were also 'a lot of fun' and he was looking forward to campaigning in every part of the country. Major was as good as his word and campaigned that afternoon in Luton. Out came the famous soap box, as it did in the 1992 general election, and again Major was heckled – this time mainly by supporters of the Referendum Party rather than the activists of the Socialist Workers' Party who had harried him with their banners five years previously. Major hoped it would be a lucky omen. 'The last time I came to Luton we had a reception just like this. Three weeks later we won both the Luton seats and the general election.'

Many of the next morning's newspapers had special election supplements. There was much comment about the length of the campaign and the fact that voters would have to wait six and a half weeks until polling day. According to the *Express*, a forty-four-day campaign was the longest since 1918; the nearest parallel was in 1945 when forty-one days elapsed between Winston Churchill calling the election and Clement Attlee winning it. George Jones, the *Daily Telegraph*'s political editor, found another wartime parallel. A Gallup opinion survey showed that Labour had extended their lead to an unprecedented twenty-eight points, putting the Conservatives further behind in terms of public support than any governing party at the start of an election campaign since opinion polling began before the Second World War. But for politicians and journalists alike, it was the *Sun* which was required reading that morning: blazoned across the front page, in three-inch-high capital letters, were the words: 'The Sun Backs Blair'. That one front page symbolised the start of what would become a far-reaching shift in the loyalties of the popular press.

Blair and his press secretary, Alastair Campbell, had gone to immense lengths to woo the tabloid papers; their efforts, in his three years as party leader, to win over the papers owned by News International had taken the Labour leader all the way to Queensland to address 200 of the most influential editors and managers in Rupert Murdoch's worldwide media empire. The *Sun*'s denigration of Neil Kinnock in the 1992 campaign still evoked bitter memories in the Labour Party, and its post-election headline, proclaiming that 'It Was The Sun Wot Won It' for the Conservatives, was still a chilling reminder of the influence which newspapers could exercise. In a two-page leading article, the *Sun* explained why it was ready to put its trust in Blair: 'The Labour party say they have changed. They say they are fit to govern. So today the *Sun* says: Let's give them the chance to prove it.' John Major was a decent man, who did his best, but he was a follower and not a leader. 'We must face facts. The clapped-out Tories don't deserve to win . . . The country is sick and tired of them.' The *Sun*'s declaration that Blair was the 'breath of fresh air this great country needs' itself made front-page news in several newspapers. However, Campbell was decidedly restrained in the press gallery that afternoon when I asked him for his reaction. 'I always thought the *Sun* would come out for us but I am surprised they did it right at the start of the campaign.'

Under the banner headline 'Knocked off his soapbox', the *Daily Mail* said the decision of Murdoch's biggest-selling newspaper to back Blair was a first-round body blow to Major. It would take a monumental or unforeseen blunder for Blair to lose the election. 'Bereft of both public support and a parliamentary majority, John Major, like Mr Micawber, has waited for something to turn up for the beleaguered Tories. But nothing did . . . ' By opting for the longest peacetime campaign of the century, Major had allowed himself yet more time for 'something to turn up'. Michael Heseltine was one of the exponents of playing it long. He told the *Independent* that he stood by the prediction he gave during the Wirral South by-election that the Conservatives would win by a majority 'nudging upwards' to sixty seats. He was convinced that New Labour were all 'transatlantic packaging'. 'Our task is to strip off the packaging and reveal the product. We've got six weeks to do that . . . and once you do strip off the packaging, Labour become defensive and edgy; scared.'

5

Holding the Line

Labour began the six-and-a-half-week offensive leading up to polling day in an unparalleled position. Never had any British political party been so far ahead in the opinion polls at the start of a campaign: victory in the general election, it seemed, was theirs for the taking. The chance to fight the Conservatives from a position of such overwhelming strength was a unique opportunity for Labour. The superiority of their organisation in the many marginal constituencies which would decide the outcome of the election had been established beyond question. The Conservatives were no longer the formidable fighting force which they undoubtedly were in the Thatcher years. They had also had to cede to Labour their former pre-eminence in influencing and often shaping the news agenda of the day. John Major's minority government was on the brink of defeat not just as a result of its own mismanagement, or the way it had been hounded by opposition parties across the floor of the House of Commons, but also because it had been harried mercilessly through the news media. In the long pre-election build-up Labour had shown great expertise in the art of orchestrating unfavourable publicity for their opponents. Many of the disasters which had befallen the Prime Minister were largely of his own making, but Labour had done their damnedest to make sure that the unpopularity of his hapless ministers and the follies of his administration were paraded night after night on the country's television screens, and written about day after day in the newspapers.

As campaign manager Peter Mandelson surveyed the prospects from his party's newly established media centre in Millbank Tower, he faced what for a Labour communications chief was, by any standards, an exceptional election encounter. The task before him was not to fight back as the underdog but to manage political success and preserve Tony Blair's reputation as a decisive party leader. After all the dire trials and tribulations of previous elections, Labour were now in command, enjoying the most favourable media climate which the party had experienced for a generation. The challenge was twofold: Mandelson had to make sure that news reports which were damaging to Labour were obliterated as quickly as possible, while at the same time sparing no effort to thwart the Conservatives' increasingly desperate attempts to swing the news agenda in Major's favour. As the campaign unfolded, those who worked for the news media would have to come to terms with what could sometimes be an unpleasant side to New Labour, a ruthless efficiency which took no account of journalistic niceties or hurt feelings.

John Major's pivotal role in his party's campaign was cruelly exposed as the weeks went by. Without his presence the Conservatives' whole election strategy would have collapsed because, in effect, what they were putting before the country was a Prime Minister who was seeking to get re-elected on his own personal manifesto. His government could not point to a harmonious Cabinet, let alone a united party. By contrast, the momentum which had built up behind Blair was so powerful that there seemed to be almost nothing which could stop New Labour from taking office. But so great was the fear that the Conservatives' powers of recovery might not have been entirely exhausted that Labour could take no chances. They had to be prepared to fight Major every inch of the way. Nonetheless, no campaign team could have imagined that their opponents would prove quite so suicidal, and that Conservative ministers and MPs would end up tripping over one another in the rush to humiliate themselves and their party. By the mid-point of the campaign the news coverage seemed have to fallen neatly into two distinct categories. On the one hand there were positive reports about the plans and intentions of a Blair government; on the other, a sequence of daily episodes in the Conservatives' long-running horror story. Labour succeeded in having their cake and eating it: they had the freedom, for much of the time, to display their political wares with virtual impunity, while also being able to take every opportunity to twist the knife in their opponents.

Of the many tactical errors which flowed from Major's decision to go for a protracted campaign, by far the most enfeebling for his party was his failure to achieve a clean break to the parliamentary session. That had certainly been the Prime Minister's intention. In his Monday morning statement in Downing Street in which he announced the dissolution of parliament on 8 April and an election on 1 May, Major had said proroga-tion would take place that Friday. As this would leave only a week in which to complete the government's parliamentary business before MPs said their farewells and departed from Westminster, the next morning's newspapers predicted a last-minute scramble by ministers to salvage as much as possible of their outstanding legislation. Tucked away on an inside page of that Tuesday's edition of the *Financial Times* was a report by its political correspondent, James Blitz, which heralded a ruinous start to the Conservatives' campaign. Blitz said Major's decision to prorogue Parliament that Friday had scuppered the chances of the House of Commons Standards and Privileges Committee completing its investigation into the financial affairs of Neil Hamilton, the Tory MP at the centre of the cash-for-questions affair. According to Blitz, the Commissioner for Parliamentary Standards, Sir Gordon Downey, had expected to complete his report by the end of that week but, as no select committee could sit after that Friday's prorogation, Sir Gordon's findings could not be presented, considered or published until after the general election had taken place and the new House of Commons had assembled on 7 May. Sir Gordon was said to have been surprised by the timing of prorogation because he had anticipated the House sitting until after Easter, thus giving the select committee a full week in which to consider his report.

The political significance of Blitz's account of the fate of the Downey inquiry was noticed by Roger Lowry, an aide to the Liberal Democrats' chief whip, Archie Kirkwood, who suggested that Major should be challenged about it that afternoon during Prime Minister's questions. As luck would have it the Liberal Democrat MP Simon Hughes had the first question on the order paper, and straight away he tackled Major about why MPs were being sent away in such a hurry that Friday. Hughes was speaking so slowly and deliberately, and being heckled so loudly, that the Speaker, Betty Boothroyd, was forced to intervene. Amid much laughter, she gave him some advice: 'Come on, Mr Hughes: Spit it out . . . Produce your voice, Mr Hughes.' At last he managed to make his point, claiming that the cash-for-questions report would be 'hidden until after the general election'. Such had been the commotion in the chamber that Major was able to take advantage of it: one of the reasons for making his announcement on the Monday and arranging for Parliament to be prorogued on the Friday, he said, was to give Hughes time to finish his question. As to the substantive part of the question, he said he had 'no knowledge' as to when Sir Gordon's report would be presented to the select committee.

Hughes' question was just the reminder which political correspondents had needed. Half an hour later, at the afternoon lobby briefing, the Prime Minister's press secretary Jonathan Haslam was pressed further about the status of Sir Gordon's report in view of the imminent prorogation. Haslam said it was the responsibility of Sir Gordon, and not the government, to decide when to publish his report. 'The select committee acts independently . . . I have no idea about their plans for publication.' Haslam was then asked about an undertaking which Major had given on *Breakfast with Frost* the previous October, when he had said that the cash-for-questions inquiry would be completed well before the election. 'That was a long time ago,' said Haslam. 'Clearly it has taken Sir Gordon longer than anticipated. There has been new evidence coming forward which none of us knew about.'

Labour were quick to realise the significance of Major's answer, and within an hour their campaign spokesman, Brian Wilson, was touring the studios at Millbank, offering to be interviewed about what he described as the government's calculated attempt to suppress publication of the Downey report until after the election. I asked him if he knew exactly what Major had promised the previous October. He said he was not aware of the precise words, but he could find out within an instant by ringing Labour's media centre on his mobile phone and by asking the rebuttal unit to search for the transcript via the Excalibur computer system. Five minutes later Wilson was reading me the full quote from the screen on his pager. He showed me what was clearly the crucial part of Major's answer: 'It is very much my wish, my hope and my expectation that this will be cleared up well this side of a general election.' As we stood there on the steps to the Millbank studios and looked at the words on his pager, I could sense that Wilson was absorbing the full import of Major's reply and that he realised the relevance for the election of the Prime Minister's failure to honour his own undertaking. Labour lost no time in supplying newsrooms with a full transcript of the interview, which served to underline how, in answer after answer, Major had gone out of his way to express his determination to see Sir Gordon's investigation completed as expeditiously as possible. 'I have said to Gordon Downey get on with it, settle it as quickly as you can, go back to the committee as quickly as you can, and I say now publicly to the committee, "I want you to publish that report when you've done it." What I do not want is this kicked into the long grass for ever.' These were no throw-away lines but a heartfelt and deliberate statement. Major's rather dismissive answer to Simon Hughes at question time that afternoon certainly did not do justice to the gravity with which he had approached the problem six months earlier. Within twenty-four hours of calling the election, the Prime Minister had left himself exposed to accusations about two issues which would dog his campaign: parliamentary sleaze and whether he could be trusted by the British people.

Major was open to the twin charges that by allowing the cash-for-questions affair to go unresolved he had broken his word, and that by proroguing Parliament so quickly he was attempting to cover up Sir Gordon's findings until after the election. Late that afternoon there seemed to be no appreciation on the part of the Prime Minister's advisers, either in Downing Street or in Conservative Central Office, of the dangers he faced. There was certainly no evidence of any contingency planning or clear strategy as to how to answer journalists' questions should the fate of the Downey report be seized on by the news media during the election campaign. Charles Lewington told me that the Downey report was not an issue which concerned him. 'The more Sir Gordon looked into things, the more evidence he found and the longer it took. But this is entirely a matter for the select committee.' Events were to move swiftly that evening as Labour and the Liberal Democrats sought to put the government on the spot. John Prescott and Paddy Ashdown both issued copies of letters they had written to the Prime Minister appealing to him to arrange for the Downey report to be completed and, if necessary, published the week after prorogation.

So anxious were Labour to get the issue of parliamentary sleaze back on to the news agenda that they were willing to jeopardise another of their spoiling operations, this one aimed at undermining the publication next day of the latest unemployment count. The total was due to show a further significant fall and was bound to be hailed by ministers as another sign of economic success. Labour's thinking appeared to be that if the validity of the jobless figures could be questioned in advance of their official publication, this would lessen the impact of the favourable publicity which the government was hoping for. A leaked set of the statistics had been obtained by the *Mirror*, whose political editor, Kevin Maguire, was anxious to get their story trailed on the *Nine o'Clock News* that evening. This was the third time in a matter of months that the *Mirror* had secured a leak of government figures. On earlier occasions, however, they had not always been totally accurate, so the newsroom decided to wait for the official news release next day. At a lobby briefing the previous month, Jonathan Haslam had rebuked the BBC for broadcasting the *Mirror*'s incorrect figures and said it was time BBC journalists stopped 'slavishly' following what the tabloids claimed were leaks. This time, when the *Nine o'Clock News* failed to run the story, there was a complaint from Charlie Whelan, press officer to the shadow Chancellor Gordon Brown, who protested – not for the first time – about the BBC's news judgement. 'Those leaked figures shouldn't have gone to the *Nine o'Clock News* but to *News at Ten*. They'd have broadcast them. The judgement of the *Nine o'Clock News* is terrible.' The leaked figures were spread across two pages in the *Mirror* next morning under the banner headline '68,200 new lies. *Mirror* exposes Tory dole fiddle'. Beneath it was a picture of Blair and the caption: 'He knows the *Mirror* reports the truth.' In the event the leak proved to be entirely accurate and when the figures were published later that morning they showed that the jobless count in February had fallen by 68,200. It was the twelfth consecutive monthly fall, bringing the seasonally adjusted number of people out of work and claiming benefit down to 1.7 million, the lowest level since 1990. In what was clearly a choreographed attempt during news conferences and interviews to talk up the significance of the lowest unemployment figure since he became Prime Minister, Major said he hoped the country was not going to throw away the government's achievements. 'Today's news is proof that Britain is booming . . . People's hard work has created a turbo-economy, which is making life better right across the country.'

However, Major's failure to clear the decks at Westminster had dashed any hope of the Conservatives achieving favourable publicity from the first high spot of his campaign. The focus of attention at the House of Commons remained firmly on the efforts of Labour and the Liberal Democrats to ensure speedy publication of the Downey report.

Concerted moves were made by opposition MPs to force the government's hand. After the Speaker ruled that it was 'constitutionally not possible' for the Standards and Privileges Committee to continue its work after prorogation of the House on Friday, Tony Blair and the entire shadow Cabinet took the unusual step of signing an early day motion calling for prorogation to be postponed. Although they had been caught off guard to begin with, the Conservatives tried desperately to limit the damage. Michael Heseltine told *Channel Four News* that the government had done everything in its power to provide Sir Gordon with the resources he needed but ministers had no control over the length of time it would take the Parliamentary Commissioner to complete his report, nor over the duration of the select committee's consideration of it. The Deputy Prime Minister accused the Labour leader of a hypocritical attempt to divert attention from the third largest fall in the monthly unemployment figures since records began. 'What is appalling, and a leap into gutter politics, is that Labour are so appalled at this manifestation of Tory success that they have contrived this totally artificial row about sleaze to get the headlines to appear to be sympathetic to them and push unemployment falls down the agenda.' Brian Mawhinney could scarcely conceal his anger at the way their plans to promote the drop in unemployment had been so comprehensively overshadowed. 'Tony Blair and Gordon Brown look for a smear, look for a diversion to stop the people of Britain focusing on the good news. You are now seeing the first example of the Labour Party playing dirty tricks.' But at the very moment the Conservatives were trying to hit back at Labour, the select committee was planning yet another surprise: it emerged later that evening that an interim report would be released the next day announcing the Commissioner's findings in relation to some of the MPs whose conduct had been investigated.

The report was published at noon that Thursday, the last full day of the session. Sir Gordon said he was satisfied there had been 'no contravention of the rules' by fifteen of the MPs whose conduct he had investigated. They included one Liberal Democrat and three Labour MPs. However, his conclusions with regard to the allegations which were outstanding against ten other MPs, including the former minister Neil Hamilton, would have to await his final report. In exonerating some of those MPs who had received payments to their campaign funds from the lobbyist Ian Greer, Sir Gordon said he recognised that if the cases were 'simple and clear-cut' it would seem unnecessary for the MPs concerned to enter the election campaign with these allegations outstanding against them. Inevitably, the Commissioner's failure to clear the other ten MPs seemed destined to provoke a storm of parliamentary protests that afternoon. There could hardly have been a worse curtain-raiser for Major's final appearance at the despatch box for his last round of Prime Minister's questions. Blair, his transcript of Major's *Breakfast with Frost* interview at the ready, declared it was 'absolutely outrageous' for Major to continue to stonewall and refuse to postpone prorogation until the final dissolution of Parliament on 8 April. But the Prime Minister, against a barrage of Labour interruptions and shouts of 'hear, hear' from Conservative MPs, refused to change the date of prorogation. He said it was 'improbable in the extreme' that the task of considering Sir Gordon's report, and the thousands of pages of evidence which went with it, could be done 'fairly and properly' in just a few days. Blair stood his ground, saying that justice demanded that the report be published. 'Has not this parliament ended as it began, with the government breaking their word? If the Prime Minister fails to have this report published, when everyone knows that he could, it will leave a stain on the character of his government that will be erased only by a new government with a fresh mandate.' Major had to shout back his reply to make it audible over the uproar: 'The stain, if stain there will be, is upon a Labour front bench that has smeared and smeared and smeared again.'

'Game, set and match!' shouted David Shaw, the Conservative MP for Dover, who immediately rallied to Major's support. By the standards of House of Commons theatre, it had been an electrifying performance; but the Prime Minister had made yet another damaging error in thinking he could fight an election with the unanswered questions from Sir Gordon's investigation hanging over the heads of several prominent Conservative candidates. Next morning's *Guardian* printed what it claimed were transcripts of the evidence which had been given in secret to the Commissioner by Neil Hamilton and another Conservative MP, Tim Smith, who had resigned from his post as a junior Northern Ireland minister in 1994 when it was first revealed that he had accepted cash payments from Mohamed Al Fayed, the owner of Harrods. In a front-page leading article, the *Guardian* said it was publishing the transcripts of their 'secret confessions' because it believed elections should be 'fought in the light, not in the dark'. Failure to publish all of Sir Gordon's findings amounted to concealment from Parliament and the public of the 'secret and squalid' motives which led MPs to table their questions. 'John Major, honest John, as he used to be advertised . . . has sneeringly resisted every attempt to rewrite these arrangements . . . The Prime Minister and Parliament itself have singularly failed to protect the essential rights of the voter. It is because we believe that this balance needs to be redressed that we today publish the essence of Sir Gordon Downey's investigation.' Alan Rusbridger, the *Guardian*'s editor, gave a series of radio and television interviews defending the paper's publication of the transcripts. 'We wanted to give an indication of the confessions which the MPs have made in private. One of the nauseating aspects of this whole thing is that MPs have been confessing dishonesty in private and then going on television in public saying, "I am innocent, please vote for me."'

Sir Gordon deplored the *Guardian*'s conduct: 'The selective leaking of evidence is against the interests of natural justice . . . a gross breach of the trust placed in those to whom the documents were sent, in confidence.' Major had rarely looked so annoyed when out campaigning. On being challenged by reporters he gave a terse answer: 'The story in the *Guardian* is total and complete junk.' Major had himself been implicated in the *Guardian*'s disclosures concerning Tim Smith, as it was alleged that after Smith told the Cabinet Secretary, Sir Robin Butler, that he had taken money from Al Fayed, the Prime Minister allowed him to remain a Northern Ireland minister for ten days before he resigned. Major took the unusual step of asking his press secretary, Jonathan Haslam, to go to the House of Commons that Friday afternoon to give political journalists his account of what had happened. Extracts from the Prime Minister's diaries indicated that he did not have prior knowledge of what Smith had told Sir Robin. Haslam's unexpected visit to the press gallery was a sign of the concern which the *Guardian*'s allegations had aroused in Downing Street. At his final lobby briefing of the session the previous afternoon Haslam had told journalists that, because of prorogation, the government's information service would be adopting a 'lower-key mode', and unless a matter of national importance arose he did not expect to meet the lobby again until the day after the general election.

The two MPs at the centre of the controversy both mounted a robust defence of themselves and succeeded that evening in retaining local support. Tim Smith said that he had written to the Speaker to protest at the *Guardian*'s conduct, which he considered amounted to a 'contempt of Parliament and an abuse of the rights of justice'. He won unanimous support at the annual meeting of his constituency association in Beaconsfield in what he said afterwards was a 'spontaneous motion of confidence'. Neil Hamilton emerged from the annual meeting of Tatton Conservatives to say he felt very upbeat and that he had been 'quite humbled' by the degree of support he had been given.

As the two MPs had secured the backing of their constituencies, ministers were left with no option but to fall in behind and offer public support, although it made for some bruising encounters. Michael Portillo, the Secretary of State for Defence, accused the *Channel Four News* presenter Jon Snow of playing 'Labour's game' by persisting in his questions about the advisability of Hamilton and Smith being allowed to stand as Conservative candidates. Snow refused to be deflected and Portillo looked uncomfortable as he kept repeating that his party had to allow natural justice to take its course. 'Yes, they are fit and proper to be candidates. The principle by which we run this country is that people are innocent until proved guilty.' Diana Madill, who presented *Breakfast with Frost* in Sir David's absence, had a similarly tense confrontation with Michael Heseltine after she challenged him about reports that the Prime Minister was privately urging the MPs who had not been cleared by Sir Gordon to stand down as candidates. Heseltine rounded on her, saying it was a lie and that he personally would be quite prepared to go out campaigning with Hamilton and Smith. 'I would be happy for them to come to my constituency and for me to go to their constituencies. We have a system in this country that you are innocent until proved guilty . . . We only had this extraordinary story about the recall of Parliament because Labour are trying to hide the unemployment figures with gutter levels of opportunist campaigning. Out in The Bull and Bush people realise this country is booming.' Some Conservative MPs were confidently predicting that Labour would find it difficult to sustain their allegations about parliamentary corruption once the campaign got under way. David Tredinnick told me he thought the Tories would benefit eventually from having got the sleaze issue out into the open so early in the election. 'In the end the way it has happened might actually help us. I think we will get a clear run from now on for the rest of the campaign.' Tredinnick's rosy assessment was not shared by party strategists at Central Office, who were keen to find issues which would put Labour on the defensive.

One announcement which had been rather overlooked during the furore over the Downey report was Major's decision to open negotiations with BBC and ITV over the possibility of a televised debate between the party leaders. Michael Dobbs, the former Conservative deputy chairman who had been chief of staff to Norman Tebbit during the 1987 general election, had been asked to head up the Conservatives' team of negotiators. There had been speculation for some weeks that the Prime Minister had been warming to the idea, and senior broadcasters and producers had spent a considerable amount of time discussing a range of formats for the programme. When he announced the date of the election Major told journalists that he thought a televised discussion with Blair would 'enhance the democratic process' provided it was 'a responsible, long and detailed debate'. However, it was not until his last meeting with backbench Conservative MPs, two days before prorogation, that the Prime Minister finally announced that he had given the go-ahead to the negotiations. Charles Lewington said there was much banging of desks in the 1922 Committee meeting when Major declared that he was 'relishing the chance to take part in a debate and pin Blair down on the detail of Labour's policies'. Once Lewington was asked to give his assessment of the rival bids it was clear Major had taken a close interest in the way the proceedings were likely to be conducted.

The BBC was proposing a ninety-minute programme, of which an hour would be allowed for debate between Major and Blair under questioning from David Dimbleby. There would be a separate stand-alone interview with Paddy Ashdown and closing statements from all three. Lewington said Major's reservation about the BBC's proposal was that the two half-hour question-and-answer sessions would be strictly controlled by stop-watch. A total of six topics would be covered, each being allocated nine minutes, and Major and Blair would each be allowed to give three two-minute responses on each subject. 'Major thinks the BBC's format is far too rigid and very similar to the way American television does presidential debates. He believes the BBC's programme would give Blair too many opportunities to trot out his soundbites.' Lewington said ITV's ninety-minute programme would begin with short opening statements from all three party leaders and a question to each of them from Jonathan Dimbleby. After a commercial break there would be the first of two half-hour debates. Major would begin and Blair respond. After a separate stand-alone interview with Ashdown, and another commercial break, the second debate between Major and Blair would follow, with additional questions from Sue Lawley and Michael Brunson. Both the BBC and ITV programmes would have audiences, though they would not participate, and the Prime Minister had welcomed that.

Lewington said Major was looking forward to the possibility of a serious debate but believed that Blair was now getting 'cold feet' about the whole idea. Journalists had been hearing for some days that Major's advisers in Downing Street and Central Office were urging him to take part. Most of his Cabinet colleagues were in favour of a debate; they believed that as he was up to speed on so many issues, because of the detailed preparation he did for Prime Minister's questions, he would demonstrate a much wider grasp of national affairs than Blair. Hugh Colver, a former Tory communications director, told Radio 5 Live that, having been rather cool about the idea to begin with, Major had realised he had 'nothing to lose' by taking part.

Although the Conservatives seemed fully conscious of the opportunity which a televised debate would provide Major to demonstrate the breadth of his experience, the party's spokesmen could not resist the opportunity to score points against Blair whenever they were asked how the negotiations with the BBC and ITV were progressing. Brian Mawhinney claimed that once Michael Dobbs began discussions with the broadcasters, it soon became clear that Labour were running scared and did not like the idea that Major would be able to pin down Blair. Michael Heseltine derided Blair's chances if either the BBC or ITV came up with what he described as a proper debate. 'Blair will try to choose ten- to fifteen-word soundbites which he'll use to give viewers the impression he knows what he is talking about. We want him to debate the facts, which is why John Major would walk all over him.' Heseltine claimed Labour were trying to wreck the chances of a debate by insisting on the audience taking part and asking questions. 'What Labour want to do is send in people to cheer for Blair and to boo Major . . . Blair is conducting the most professional, phoney campaign this country has ever seen.' Peter Mandelson took the provocation in his stride and told Sky television that the Conservatives should stop getting so agitated. 'Major should relax and stop trying to impose conditions. He should allow the public to be invited into the debate and let them put their questions to the politicians.' Lord Irvine of Lairg, the shadow Lord Chancellor and a long-standing friend and adviser of Tony Blair, was conducting the negotiations for Labour, and Mandelson said Lord Irvine's task was to 'clear away the obstacles' to the debate which Major was seeking to impose. 'We want the debate to happen in a way which suits the audience. It is very important that we don't have just one person putting the questions. Let the debate take place in a way which is interesting to the viewer and with a formula acceptable to the public.'

While Labour gave every indication in public of seeking to expedite the negotiations, Alastair Campbell revealed no great enthusiasm for the idea when tackled by journalists. He told me he was concerned that all the fuss over the arrangements for a televised debate might become more important than the politics. 'We don't care a stuff if Major does or does not want a debate. It would be OK by us. What we don't welcome is the idea of a television debate becoming a dominant issue in the campaign with all the bother over who should be the interviewer. All we need is Tony Blair and John Major in a room, and no fuss. You guys are obsessed about this and it's all that media people talk about, yet television debates always end in a draw.' Campbell rounded off what I took to be a pretty clear steer that he thought a debate was unlikely by insisting that the argument about the role to be played by Paddy Ashdown was a problem for the broadcasters, and not for the Labour Party. Once Lewington had revealed the details of the programme formats being proposed by the BBC and ITV, the Liberal Democrats' campaign manager, Lord Holme, protested at the way they were being treated. 'The idea that only the two great men, Major and Blair, are allowed to have a debate, and then the interviewer goes across to Ashdown who's stuck in a room on his own, is quite unacceptable.'

Charles Kennedy said the Liberal Democrats had already taken legal advice because the broadcasters knew their programmes would have to be balanced politically. He was sure they would be supported in court action by Alex Salmond, leader of the Scottish National Party, and Dafydd Wigley, the Plaid Cymru leader, unless the BBC and the ITV had second thoughts. 'The broadcasters will find themselves in a legal minefield if they try to impose a two-party debate on the whole of the UK and don't give a voice to the other parties.'

Having lost out in publicity terms over the improvement in the unemployment statistics, the Conservatives were determined to start the second week of their campaign on a high and take full advantage of the latest trade figures, which showed a £3 billion fall in the balance of payments deficit. Michael Heseltine and Kenneth Clarke were heralded by a musical fanfare as they walked on to the platform for the morning news conference at Central Office. They spoke against a backdrop of two flashing signs. The top one, on a blue background, said: 'Britain Is Booming'. Beneath it was a red sign bearing the words: 'Don't Let Labour Blow It'. Clarke told the assembled reporters that Britain had enjoyed the longest and strongest recovery of any major European country. If that success could be repeated over the next five years, then by the year 2002 British living standards would have improved 100 per cent in twenty-five years. John Major, out campaigning in the West Country, said the trade figures showed that all the economic indicators were set 'extremely fair' and he was confident their message would not be buried as it had been the previous week by stories about sleaze. 'You can't drown out the fact that this country is performing more successfully than anywhere else in Europe.' Major had also leapt enthusiastically on a report in that morning's *Daily Telegraph* which quoted from a leaked copy of Labour's business manifesto and said that Blair had acceded to one of the key demands being made by the trade unions. Robert Shrimsley, the paper's chief political correspondent, said the document showed that Blair had rejected intense lobbying by the Confederation of British Industry and had agreed that firms would be 'forced by law to recognise and negotiate with unions where they are supported by a majority of the workforce'. Shrimsley's front-page splash was backed up by a leading article written by the *Daily Telegraph*'s political columnist, Boris Johnson, who was standing as a Conservative candidate in Clwyd South, and who described Labour's pledge to the unions as being 'pregnant with potential trouble'. Major said the news would be a nasty blow to many businessmen, as it tipped the balance back in favour of the unions, who were Labour's paymasters.

Labour tried to play down the issue, as the party had made no secret of its pledge to grant union recognition where this was agreed to by 'a majority of the relevant workforce in a ballot'. Margaret Beckett, the shadow trade and industry secretary, said Labour's approach was perfectly fair and she was not aware of its having been opposed by the CBI. But the story caught the imagination of the *Daily Mail*, which published next morning what it called a union hit list of the sixty-three companies which would 'immediately be dragooned' into granting recognition. Among the business leaders quoted, saying she feared she would face 'harassment' from the unions, was Kay Coleman, the Oldham textile firm chief executive whose membership of the Conservative Party had been publicised earlier in the year after a search had been conducted on the Excalibur computer system at Labour's media centre. When I was interviewed that morning on *Today*, John Humphrys asked me why the Conservatives were seeking to make so much of the story. I explained that one reason why they were trying to play up fears about the unions was that they hoped it might elicit favourable treatment in newspapers whose proprietors had been critical of John Major but might now give a boost to the Tories if they thought there was any danger of the print unions getting special privileges under a Labour government. Humphrys made a comment about this sounding like 'going back to the bad old days'. Labour were furious that the union story had even been mentioned on the programme. On arriving at Labour's news conference I saw that Alastair Campbell, head down, was making a beeline in my direction. He wasted no time in getting to the point: 'Your two-way on *Today* was outrageous.' He then gave me an earful about my brother George Jones, the *Daily Telegraph*'s political editor. 'Your brother's paper is just a dreadful Tory rag. You should tell him to resign.' Campbell's tirade was, perhaps, only to have been expected: the Conservatives could hardly contain their excitement that morning at having succeeded at last in getting journalists to look at the small print of one of Labour's election pledges.

At most morning news conferences in Conservative Central Office, Brian Mawhinney looked as if he was smiling through gritted teeth when welcoming journalists, but on this day for once he had seemed genuinely pleased to see the assembled company and promptly announced that because of a 'devastating revelation' about Labour's link with the unions, the planned launch of a new Conservative policy statement on school testing had been postponed. The flashing signs at the back of the platform had been updated: 'Britain Is Booming. Don't Let The Unions Blow It.' Michael Heseltine said that for the Conservatives it was the most important day so far in the campaign. 'Union power has now become one of the central issues . . . If Labour and the unions win, Britain loses . . . Companies would become battlegrounds in which different unions, with separate agendas, fight out historic rivalries and enmities, each seeking to secure their own toehold on power. It would be yesterday's demarcation disputes run riot over today's industrial peace.' The first journalist to ask Heseltine a question was the *Guardian*'s political editor, Michael White, who said he was glad to see the *Daily Mail* and the Tory party 'back in tandem'. But he thought stories about union-bashing did not ring true to anyone under forty. Heseltine was ready with an instant put-down: 'Sadly, Michael, neither you nor I are under forty. You understand this issue, so does the *Guardian*.'

Labour's discomfort at being forced to spell out exactly what their pledge entailed was all too clear as their news conference progressed. Gordon Brown was asked if recognition ballots could be held within units of a firm or whether they would be restricted to a company's entire workforce. He surprised journalists by announcing that Labour would be adopting the procedure practised in the United States where a third party, perhaps a judge, sorted out recognition disputes and gave a ruling as to what constituted 50 per cent of the workforce. 'This system has been operating in the United States for sixty years and is backed by Republicans and Democrats. At the time, even President Reagan said he supported it.' The idea that Labour intended to follow American practice was new to me, and once the news conference had finished I joined other reporters who were asking Labour's chief spokesperson, David Hill, for more details about Brown's announcement. 'Yes, we are still thinking about the details,' said Hill. 'Obviously this sort of development adds spice to the story. Our clarification will come out in the coming weeks.' I was amazed that Hill had been so frank: the last thing I had expected was for Labour to start making up policy on the hoof in the middle of an election campaign, especially over an issue as potentially troublesome as union recognition.

An hour after I had left Labour's media centre, Hill rang the BBC with further clarification. He told me Brown had not made a new announce-ment as the intention all along had been to refer demarcation disputes to the existing Central Arbitration Committee, which would be given an expanded role. Half an hour later, in an interview for *The World at One*,

Robin Cook confirmed that Labour would be asking the CAC to undertake this task. When I went back to Hill to ask why he had not explained this earlier, he acknowledged his omission. 'The Central Arbitration Committee was an organisation about which I knew very little until an hour ago.' In view of the metamorphosis their policy had undergone, Labour's education and employment spokesman, David Blunkett, could hardly complain about some forceful questioning next morning on *Today*. He said the Conservatives' refusal to accept what Labour were proposing meant they were to the right of Ronald Reagan. But Ian Lang, the Secretary of State for Trade and Industry, kept up the attack at their morning news conference, claiming that at last Labour's cover had been blown.

Danny Finkelstein, the Conservatives' head of research, said that once he heard Gordon Brown making up Labour policy as he went along, 'a little light went on in my head'. 'When Labour's spokesmen pick up a policy which they haven't rebutted countless times before, they just don't know the detail. Our best tactic would be to look for other policies which they haven't had to rebut because they could be just as weak on them as well. When you're in an election it's always difficult to turn propaganda into news, but if you're on the ball you can do it and we've certainly done that with Labour and the unions.' Brown's press officer, Charlie Whelan, was irritated by the way the Conservatives had managed to keep the story going for so long and he was highly critical of my reporting. I pointed out that if Brown chose to make unexpected policy announcements he could hardly complain. Whelan finally accepted my point that journalists had been surprised to hear that Labour intended to follow American practice on union recognition and he agreed that if Brown had said all along that this was simply a matter for the CAC, there would probably not have been much of a story. 'The reason Gordon went hard on the American angle was because that was the line he was told to take. There's always a meeting before the news conference and that's where we are given the line.' In his assessment of Labour's difficulties, the *Sunday Times*' political editor, Andrew Grice, said the party had been pushed into a 'damage limitation exercise' for the first time in the campaign. He said Brown had been blamed for 'appearing to make policy on the hoof' although his allies had said he was 'reading from a brief prepared by David Blunkett's employ- ment team'.

There was certainly no equivocation about the line Labour were taking when Tony Blair sought to put an end to further speculation on the third day of the controversy. He told that morning's news conference that workers would have a choice as to whether they wanted to be in a union. British practice would be in line with that in the United States, where a majority could vote for union recognition. No one had suggested President Reagan was a 'pinko' for having backed the right to choice. But Blair reiterated his blunt warning to the unions: there would be no return to the 1980s, to secondary action, flying pickets and strikes without ballots. 'Even after every change that we are proposing as a Labour Party in government, Britain would remain with a more restrictive trade union legislation framework than any country in the western world, including the United States of America.'

Blair's stark warning could hardly have been more timely, because that afternoon Lady Thatcher made her first foray into the election campaign. In a dramatic gesture for the benefit of photographers and television crews, the former Prime Minister held up her hands in mock surrender outside her party's headquarters to emphasise her conviction that a new Labour government would give way to the unions. 'It wasn't the Labour Party who fought the bully boys in the miners' strike or down at Wapping. It was the Conservative Party. We got trade union law right and Britain is booming . . . The trade unions have demanded new legislation, and Blair's response? Surrender. We never surrendered.' Her forceful intervention made compulsive viewing in television news bulletins and Michael White described it in the *Guardian* next day as vintage Thatcher, 'reminiscent of Gloria Swanson's final descent down the staircase in the last reel of *Sunset Boulevard*'.

Another of the Conservatives' doughty media performers, the Home Secretary, Michael Howard, had also tried to seize the initiative that day after two small bombs, planted by the IRA, exploded at a signal box in Wilmslow, near Manchester, on the main railway line to the north-west. He issued an immediate statement saying that the 'disgraceful bombing' which had taken place was a reminder both of the threat which the country faced and of the fact that voters could not trust Tony Blair and Labour to be 'tough on terrorism'. Howard's statement, which pointed out that Blair had never once voted for the renewal of the Prevention of Terrorism Act, prompted a sharp protest because Labour said it breached an understanding agreed with the government the week before that the political parties would not seek to exploit public reaction to terrorist incidents during the election campaign. Blair said Howard's attempt to make political capital out of the Wilmslow bombs was reprehensible and his desperation to score points had exceeded his judgement. But the Home Secretary was unrepentant and, in a display of fast political footwork, he tried to shift the blame for the breakdown in the bipartisan approach to terrorist incidents on to Labour's deputy leader, John Prescott. While being interviewed that afternoon in Luton, Prescott had said the Northern Ireland peace process broke down when Major decided he had to 'make all sorts of deals in order to stay in power'.

The dispute provoked a pointed exchange of letters between the Labour leader and the Prime Minister. Blair told Major that he detested terrorism and that the Home Secretary's press release, seeking to make political capital out of the Wilmslow bomb outrage, was an 'extraordinary act of attempted opportunism' in view of the cooperation Labour were giving the government to prevent terrorists getting the oxygen of publicity. Major defended Howard, saying his remarks accurately recorded the long-standing differences between the Conservatives and Labour over the Prevention of Terrorism Act. Howard had condemned the bombing but he 'did not visit the scene of the outrage and did not encourage publicity for it otherwise'. Major said he had not discarded the five years he had spent seeking peace in Northern Ireland in order to make political deals to stay in power; Prescott's assertion was untrue, and beggared belief coming from someone who aspired to be a minister. Howard, who had briefed political journalists himself during the day in order to put his side of the story, remained equally robust in maintaining his criticism of Blair's voting record on terrorism. The Home Secretary considered he had succeeded in damaging Labour, and, when interviewed for the *Nine o'Clock News*, offered no apology, refusing to withdraw his charge that Blair could not be trusted to be tough on terrorism. 'That is the truth. I've said it before and I shall say it again.' Howard appeared to have savoured the opportunity to provoke Blair, and the calculated way in which he exploited the bomb explosions confirmed the suspicion of political correspondents that he would like to have been allocated a more prominent role in the Conservatives' campaign.

Howard's attempt to embarrass Blair was short-lived, as was Lady Thatcher's rallying cry against Labour's approach to the unions: the Conservatives' mounting confidence that they had finally succeeded in turning the news agenda away from parliamentary corruption was about to be shattered. Late that afternoon the former Northern Ireland office minister, Tim Smith, announced that he would bow to mounting unease within his constituency and stand down as the Conservatives' candidate in

Beaconsfield. In the five days since he had been given the support of the annual party meeting, local confidence in his ability to fight the election had ebbed away. Smith's position had, slowly but surely, become untenable. He had admitted accepting from Mohamed Al Fayed around £18,000 in cash, packed into envelopes, without declaring the payments; and then, in the aftermath of the *Guardian*'s disclosures about his evidence to Sir Gordon Downey, he had acknowledged publicly that his behaviour fell below the standards people were entitled to expect. He made a short but dignified statement: 'I now believe that it is in the best interests of this association if I withdraw my candidature from the general election. I regret that the action of the *Guardian* newspaper, in support of the Labour Party, has made my course of action inevitable with its complete disregard for parliamentary privilege and natural justice . . . I would like to see the re-election of the Conservative government led by John Major.' Brian Mawhinney, although looking somewhat chastened that evening on *Newsnight* at the latest turn of events, was clearly relieved that Smith had stepped aside. 'Many will feel he made an honourable judgement . . . If you are asking was he being levered out, that was not the case . . . If his association had been happy to continue with him, he would have been a candidate of good standing, but, out of respect for the Prime Minister and not wishing to be a distraction, he has made his decision. I respect and admire that.'

Smith's rapid departure inevitably focused the media spotlight ever more sharply on Neil Hamilton's position as the Conservative candidate in Tatton, but, despite persistent questioning by Jeremy Paxman, Mawhinney insisted that natural justice had to run its course in the case of the former trade minister and that the Conservative Party would go on running their affairs on a devolved basis. 'We don't sit in Central Office and force candidates on associations . . . There is a huge difference between the positions of Tim Smith and Neil Hamilton out of their own mouths. Hamilton vehemently denies he was taking money, and people are innocent until and unless proved guilty.'

While Mawhinney was being interviewed, newsrooms had been alerted to an even more sensational development. The next morning's edition of the *Sun* contained what it said was a seven-page world exclusive alleging that the Conservative MP for Beckenham, Piers Merchant, had been having an affair with Anna Cox, a seventeen-year-old 'blonde Soho nightclub hostess'. Merchant was photographed in the *Sun* with Cox, who had been helping him canvass in his constituency. The MP denied there had been an affair: 'That may well be me kissing her in the pictures but I see nothing wrong in that. I am sure my wife will not be the slightest bit concerned.' To illustrate what was described as the Merchants' 'show of togetherness', later editions of the paper carried a photograph of the MP kissing his wife Helen on the doorstep of their home after he had been shown the *Sun*'s disclosures. Merchant's determination to resist pressure on him to stand down, and his readiness to fight back against the *Sun*, caused consternation within the Conservative Party hierarchy; but, as with Smith and Hamilton, there was no sign of any contingency planning or a clear line of command in orchestrating responses to the demands of the news media.

Michael Heseltine began what became a weekend of high drama by indicating in the clearest possible terms that he considered Merchant should do the honourable thing and stand down as candidate for Beckenham. Interviewed on *Today*, the Deputy Prime Minister left listeners in no doubt about his own feelings: 'It is an embarrassment, a diversion from the real issues of the general election. We are bound to feel let down, but these judgements are left to local people and I have not the slightest doubt that his family and his association will want to consider very carefully the consequences of this for the party at large.' Heseltine feared that a pattern might be emerging in the behaviour of those newspapers which backed Labour. 'First we had the *Guardian* story about sleaze to cover up the unemployment figures, and now the *Sun* has this story when we are exposing Labour on the unions. It is amazing how these two newspapers have come to Labour's rescue.'

The Conservatives' news conference was a subdued affair. John Gummer, the Secretary of State for the Environment, tried valiantly to generate interest in his party's glossily printed green manifesto, but it was the *Sun*'s revelations which were required reading that morning. Kenneth Clarke, who was sharing the platform, said he agreed with Heseltine's assessment. 'Of course public life demands the highest possible standards and I think those standards still apply across public life. It would be a disaster if these sorts of things dominated our headlines for the next few days and decide the government for the next five years.' Afterwards Danny Finkelstein seemed resigned to the fact the Conservatives' policies on the environment would probably sink without trace. As journalists crowded round to discuss Merchant's likely fate, the general conclusion was that Heseltine had left the MP without visible support and that the party leadership's dearest wish was that he would fall on his sword. Finkelstein did not seek to disabuse us. 'What Heseltine said speaks for us all . . . it's now up to the local association.' Later that morning John Major took the same tough line: 'I think Piers Merchant will want to explain the stories in the press to his constituency association . . . But we will need to find out what has happened, that will have to come first.' Michael Portillo was the only minister who cautioned against what he considered was the rush to make a judgement. 'We are a fair country and we allow people to put their case . . . What I think would be really damaging would be trial by media, the lynching mob, decisions and judgements made on incomplete evidence, people condemned who have not had a chance to speak up in their defence.'

Portillo's defiant note reflected the determination of a growing number of Tory MPs to stand firm if they felt they had been set up by a tabloid newspaper or were being hounded unfairly by people who were seeking to gain financially from their disclosures. Jerry Hayes, the Conservative MP for Harlow, was one of the few backbenchers who had withstood allegations about his private life and succeeded in resisting pressure for his resignation. He had vehemently denied allegations published in the *News of the World* in January 1997 that he had 'cheated on his wife with an under-age gay lover'. Hayes said that his relationship with Paul Stone, a Conservative Party activist and formerly his unpaid researcher at the House of Commons, was 'purely platonic', and subsequently won a unanimous vote of confidence from his constituency party. Stone was paid for his disclosures by the *News of the World*; moreover, he was a client of the public relations consultant and publicist, Max Clifford, who claimed at the time that he was working on another three stories which he hoped to get published before the general election and which would 'expose the sleaze and hypocrisy' of Conservative MPs.

Hayes had always been popular with journalists and had rarely if ever shied away from publicity, so he was able to put his experience and knowledge of the news media to good use in fighting to clear his name. He told me that the first thing he did on being interviewed by the *News of the World* about Stone's allegations was to take his wife and young family away from the constituency as he was determined to protect them from media intrusion. That weekend nineteen cars containing reporters, photographers and television crews were parked outside his home. 'I knew that the first thing I had to do was avoid being interviewed on the doorstep. However clever you might think you are at avoiding journalists' questions, you are never in control in such situations and you must avoid doorstep interviews.' Hayes said his next step was to write to the *News of the World* to say he felt no personal animosity against the paper's journalists or the deputy editor, Rebekah Wade, whose by-line had appeared on the story. He hoped that his letter might lessen the chances of the *News of the World* taking a vindictive stand if it followed up the story in subsequent editions. 'Obviously if a paper like the *News of the World* is offered a sensational story about an MP they're going to take it, so there is no point in taking it out on the journalists.' Hayes said he wanted to put his side of the story, as did his wife Alison, but he was anxious they should do it in a controlled way. He therefore arranged interviews with two journalists who he hoped would be sympathetic, Lynda Lee-Potter of the *Daily Mail* and Nigel Nelson, the political editor of the *People*. 'I wanted the interviews and any photographs to be done on my terms.'

As perhaps was only to be expected, once the *Sun* had published its disclosures, Piers Merchant's home was similarly besieged by the news media, but he appeared to have adopted the first of the Hayes guidelines for survival because neither he nor his family was prepared to be interviewed or photographed. Nevertheless, Merchant's resolute stand would test almost to destruction the patience of Tory party strategists, while exposing yet again the impossible task which John Major faced in seeking to fight an election on behalf of a party whose constituency associations had complete autonomy.

Labour's spin doctors could hardly contain their delight at the way the story about trade union recognition, which had dogged them all week, had suddenly disappeared without trace. As journalists arrived for the morning news conference, Peter Mandelson, who according to his habit had positioned himself strategically at the entrance, told me he thought Michael Heseltine was really getting desperate if he imagined he could blame Labour for what had happened to Piers Merchant. Mandelson said he was on record in a speech he had given the previous week as having made it quite clear that he hoped the 'Max Clifford factor' would not play a part in the election campaign. David Hill had less compunction about admitting that Labour would continue to draw attention to the conduct of Conservative MPs. 'Of course sleaze will be topping off our news conference.' Labour's issue of the day was the government's record on VAT, but Gordon Brown declared that weak leadership was at the heart of the election and Major had failed to act against MPs who were unfit to be candidates. 'Where there are known and admitted facts, it is time the Conservatives showed leadership and put their house in order.'

In what looked like a calculated attempt to divert attention from their embarrassment over Piers Merchant, the Conservatives held an unexpected news conference to protest at what they said was Labour's decision to impose a deadline of midnight on the negotiations for a possible televised debate between the party leaders. Michael Dobbs, Major's chief negotiator with the broadcasters, claimed Labour had been deploying wrecking tactics for some days in the detailed discussions which had been taking place with the BBC and ITV. He understood Labour were 'planning to pull the plug' on further talks. Dobbs insisted that he had been negotiating in good faith: the Conservatives were the only party which had accepted the principles laid down for the debate. 'We think the broadcasters' proposals are responsible and we are happy to keep discussing them.'

Mandelson's riposte was to accuse Dobbs of playing games and using the prospect of a televised confrontation between Major and Blair as a stunt to provoke Labour. 'Every time we thought we were close to a deal, the Conservatives decided instead to play politics.' Alastair Campbell was in no doubt that the Conservatives had breached the confidentiality of the negotiations simply to distract journalists from their discomfort over Piers Merchant. 'It's just a diversionary tactic to get you lot on to something else and away from sleaze. They've been negotiating in bad faith all along. They don't really want Major to meet Blair on television. What they do want to get up and running is a story about a possible debate and it's the only story they've got to sell. The idea we don't want Blair to be cross-questioned is balls. What we didn't want was a format like Prime Minister's questions. We wanted the audience to ask the questions.' Campbell said Labour were not going to waste any more time on the negotiations. 'If all the Conservatives can dream up is a story about a row over a television debate they're obviously in need of a campaign strategy. What the BBC should be doing is asking their campaign team what they've done with their brains.' Campbell suggested I start off in the House of Lords by asking former Tory chairmen like Lords Tebbit and Parkinson if they had any idea why Mawhinney and his colleagues had lost the plot.

I did not get the chance to carry out Campbell's instructions as I was on early duty next morning at Broadcasting House, monitoring the latest developments over Piers Merchant. As it was Good Friday the Conservatives were hoping it might be possible to keep a low profile and avoid having to answer awkward questions about the likelihood of a meeting over the Easter weekend between Merchant and officers of Beckenham Conservatives. Roderick Reid, deputy chairman of the Beckenham party, told *Today* that he had left ten messages on the MP's answerphone but had not heard from him for twenty-four hours. Anthony Gordon Lennox, the party's broadcasting officer, had been against fielding a spokesman, but it was eventually agreed that Mawhinney would do a pre-recorded interview for *Today*.

In the studio at Millbank, Mawhinney sounded rather disconsolate as John Humphrys cheerily ran through the subjects to be discussed: 'Sleaze first, then substantive matters.' After a short pause and a sigh, the party chairman responded: 'The shorter the former, the larger the latter, the better.' Mawhinney revealed that the executive of the local party were intending to meet Merchant 'fairly soon' that weekend and they would be examining the *Sun*'s allegations. 'This is a matter for Piers Merchant's association, for himself and his family. I have no doubt they are all giving this serious consideration.' When pressed about his inability as party chairman to influence the outcome of the association's decision, he said the constitution of the Conservative Party had stood them in pretty good stead for a long time. 'The relationship between the voluntary party and the parliamentary party has been a lot better than in Labour and I don't think we shall be rushing to change it on the basis of one or two stories about MPs.'

Mawhinney brightened up considerably when asked about the prospects for resurrecting the negotiations for a television debate. He insisted the Conservatives could do business on the basis of the proposals put forward by the broadcasters. 'BBC says it can happen. ITV says it can happen. I say it can happen. Blair is terrified, he's chicken.' Accusing Blair of chickening out was hardly likely to aid the resumption of talks, but it was the first time the Conservatives had pointed an accusing finger so firmly at Blair himself and, in the absence of developments in Beckenham, it gave a hard edge to my report that lunchtime. In view of Labour's statement that they remained committed to the idea of a debate, *The World at One* tried without success to persuade Mandelson to set out the conditions on which Blair would agree to take part. After refusing point blank to grant an interview, Mandelson ended up having a heated ten-minute conversation with the programme's presenter, Nick Clarke.

Obviously Labour's campaign manager had no intention of responding to Brian Mawhinney's attack on Blair, being only too well aware that if he were to do so in person it would fuel the story and might provide the Conservatives with further useful ammunition with which to attack the Labour leader. It seemed to me that Michael Dobbs had made a tactical error in thinking that Labour could somehow be bounced back into the negotiations if it could be shown they were responsible for the impasse. Even so, I formed the clear impression that Labour were only too happy to use Dobbs' miscalculation as a way of accomplishing a speedy exit from what the leadership had clearly concluded was an unnecessary and unprofitable diversion. John Underwood, a former Labour communications director, told *Today* that it was obvious the campaign team had reached the conclusion that Blair had nothing to gain by taking part. The Conservatives saw a confrontation on television as the 'last throw of the dice' for the Prime Minister; as Major looked all set to lose the election unless he could 'pluck a miracle out of the air', Underwood considered Labour had every reason to want to deny him that chance.

I thought that one way to explore the reasons for the breakdown in the talks, and to test the sincerity of Labour's public statements in support of a televised confrontation between the party leaders, would be to seek an interview with Lord Irvine of Lairg, who had been conducting negotiations on Blair's behalf. Dobbs had made himself available, but David Hill was emphatic: Labour were not going to put up Lord Irvine to answer my questions. Lord Irvine did, however, give his side of the story in an article in the *Independent* on Easter Monday. He said the two conditions which he had wanted to see fulfilled were the involvement of a studio audience and a face-to-face encounter involving Major, Blair and Ashdown. 'The Tories did not want a studio audience at all. Their aim was an elitist format, with questions coming from the chairman and a professional panel of interviewers.' Lord Irvine said the negotiations had seemed to be making real progress. He had understood that Dobbs had yielded and agreed to both a studio audience and a three-way leaders' debate. 'But all that changed . . . The Tories' negotiating position was put into reverse. They were trying to revert to their original proposals. I am sure that Dobbs was being instructed from on high that he had conceded too much and had to be tougher. I therefore imposed a deadline for an agreement to be reached on Thursday, before the Easter break began . . . If Dobbs had been in sole charge, the deadline would have concentrated minds wonderfully and there would have been an agreement before Easter.' Lord Irvine said nobody should be taken in by the 'Tory misinformation machine'.

For me, the most revealing point in this article was Lord Irvine's acknowledgement that the question of whether the 'debate would or would not take place was itself becoming a distracting issue'. He seemed to have confirmed what I thought, that Labour had nothing to gain by continuing the negotiations. The imposition of a deadline horrified the Labour MP and broadcaster Austin Mitchell, who, writing in the *Sunday Times*, said that he considered Mandelson's 'weasel words of withdrawal' were a sad blow to democracy. 'I feel ashamed that my party has been negotiating in bad faith and imposed impossible deadlines . . . The broadcasters have finally overcome their mutual antipathy, developed simple proposals on how to stage debates and are prepared to share the project . . . The voters' appetite and expectations have been roused. To throw all that away would be as shaming for Labour as it is insulting to democracy.'

Most political columnists agreed with Mitchell's verdict that Labour had made a calculated decision to withdraw from the negotiations. Chris Buckland, writing in the *Express*, thought Labour knew it would be 'crackers' to give Major the chance to score a 'knock-out blow' in a television debate. Bruce Anderson, in his column in the *Observer*, said he believed that an unconvincing performance by Blair on *Newsnight* when interviewed by Jeremy Paxman at the start of the campaign had led Mandelson to the conclusion that Blair was 'not to be trusted at more than soundbite length'. The *Daily Mail's* leader writer, rather than carping at Mandelson's behaviour, was effusive in praising Labour's immaculate timing in 'cheekily accusing the Tories of bad faith' when Blair could 'run for cover in the happy knowledge that few hard questions would be asked' because political correspondents were preoccupied with the Piers Merchant affair. 'With a spot of spin-doctoring, even the most ignominious retreat can be made to look like a kind of victory . . . Labour has once again demonstrated the art of effective political campaigning. If only the Tories could begin to match that ruthless efficiency.'

Little did I know, when I heard Mandelson refusing to be interviewed by *The World at One* that Good Friday lunchtime, that within a matter of hours Labour would be demonstrating yet again the ruthlessness of their political campaigning and, in the process, making doubly sure that the argument about the breakdown in the negotiations over the television debate became a non-story. A news flash from the Press Association news agency, timed at 4.29 p.m., was the first instalment of what, at least for many journalists, would turn out to be the most engaging story of the 1997 campaign. To begin with there was just one sentence to go on: 'Labour's candidate in Neil Hamilton's Tatton constituency, Jon Kelly, is to stand down tomorrow in a bid to force the Tory to resign.' David Hill gave me instant confirmation of the story. Labour were calling on the Liberal Democrats' candidate in Tatton to stand down as well and they hoped a non-political candidate would come forward to fight the election on an anti-sleaze ticket.

My first broadcast was half an hour later on *PM* and my immediate reaction was to say that I thought the highly publicised withdrawal of Labour's candidate in Hamilton's constituency would keep sleaze right at the top of the news agenda and that the search for a Mr Clean or a Mrs Clean to fight the seat would make a tremendous news story. On walking out of the studio to return to the reporters' room, my bleeper went off. There was a message on my pager to ring Alastair Campbell urgently. He told me my interview on *PM* had been a disgrace. 'Our candidate is standing down not to make sleaze news but to bury sleaze. This is a genuine attempt to force Hamilton out so that the general election can be fought around other issues, without sleaze getting in the way.' I made sure that my next report for Radio 4, for the *Six o'Clock News*, used Campbell's words, saying that Labour regarded this as a genuine attempt to try to stop sleaze dominating the campaign. But I also included my original line that the effect of it would be to keep sleaze high on the agenda and that Labour were looking for a 'Mr Clean or a Mrs Clean' to stand as an anti-sleaze candidate. I considered my original assessment was both fair and accurate and that Campbell was being rather disingenuous in complaining yet again. My suspicions were confirmed on Easter Sunday when Campbell's assistant, Tim Allan, asked me rather sheepishly if I had 'enjoyed Labour's spin-doctoring' about their candidate in Tatton. 'It was the smart thing to do on Good Friday, wasn't it? Journalists wanted a new story so we obliged. It was quite good spin-doctoring, wasn't it?' I smiled as Allan asked his rhetorical questions, sensing that he had probably been amused by the dressing-down I had been given by Campbell. Charlie Whelan was even more revealing than usual when giving me his version of what happened. He said it was Gordon Brown's idea to put up an anti-sleaze candidate against Hamilton. 'We decided to go for it a couple of weeks ago, even before Jon Kelly knew anything about it, and we started looking for an anti-sleaze candidate. Timing it for Good Friday was perfect for Labour because it kept sleaze in the news.'

Far from the Easter weekend providing a break for the politicians, it was dominated by further feverish activity. News bulletins on Saturday morning were dominated by the preparations being made later that day for the withdrawal of Jon Kelly in Tatton. The Press Association quoted Blair's office as saying that the plan to try to shame Hamilton into stepping down rather than face an anti-corruption candidate was the 'brainchild' of Kelly himself. Charles Lewington, who was being bombarded for news of Piers Merchant's fate in Beckenham, described Kelly's withdrawal as a pathetic stunt by Labour's spin doctors which did not alarm the Conservatives. 'Labour know there's no chance of anyone else winning that seat; it's one of the safest in the country. It's typical of the Labour antics we've come to expect.'

Journalists had been led to believe that the Beckenham meeting would not take place until the following Tuesday, but late on Easter Saturday news came through that the association had met that evening and had endorsed Merchant as their candidate by forty-three votes to three. Roderick Reid, the deputy chairman of the local party, told journalists that the MP denied the allegations which had been made by Anna Cox and that the resulting vote of confidence in him was overwhelming. In an exclusive interview in next morning's *Sunday Times*, Merchant said he was definitely the victim of a 'very carefully orchestrated set-up' by the *Sun*. However, like Jerry Hayes, he had taken immediate action to avoid further unwelcome publicity, taking his family away from their constituency home and refusing to be photographed or give radio and television interviews. According to the *Sunday Times*, the MP had three points of advice for his fellow politicians: 'One: be permanently on your guard. Two: expect hidden photographers everywhere. Three: never kiss anybody, especially not before or during an election.'

Merchant's swift endorsement might have been greeted with some relief by the Conservatives had it not already been overtaken by yet another body blow to their campaign: the resignation of the Scottish Conservative chairman, Sir Michael Hirst. In a letter to the Prime Minister, Sir Michael said that as a result of a 'past indiscretion' in his private life he felt his chairmanship of the Scottish party 'could become untenable' and he did not want to jeopardise the work which had been done in preparation for the election. 'I will not allow a personal deficiency on my part to put all this at risk. Only by taking immediate action to resign can I hope to minimise the damage to my family and to the party.' Major's reply spoke volumes for the Conservatives' beleaguered position. He said that he was very sorry on personal and political grounds to be losing Sir Michael but he fully understood his position and supported the decision he had made 'so speedily and in such a courageous and honourable manner'.

Over the subsequent two days Tory spin doctors made great play of the decisive way in which Sir Michael had responded to the difficult position he had found himself in; but party strategists committed yet another tactical error in thinking that the dignified departure of their Scottish chairman might have some influence on Neil Hamilton. Eventually, as the Prime Minister tried to clear the decks ready for the launch of the Conservatives' manifesto, he had no alternative but to run up the white flag of surrender and allow Hamilton to go forward to his final showdown. For Charles Lewington it must have been the nadir of a nightmare weekend as the media strategy the party had been pursuing was turned on its head.

Beckenham Conservatives began the rout. By snubbing so publicly Michael Heseltine and the other senior figures who had called for Piers Merchant to fall on his sword, they had demonstrated the supreme power of a local association, and the signal they sent to Hamilton was that defiance paid off. In their desperation to persuade Hamilton to reconsider his position and follow the examples of Sir Michael Hirst and Tim Smith, Lewington and his colleagues at Central Office had encouraged senior Conservatives to call publicly for the MP to stand down. After the comprehensive rebuff they had suffered in Beckenham, Lewington said the Merchant case would not be reopened and they realised there was no point in trying to lean on members of the Tatton constituency association. Major could not go through the embarrassment of being turned over by another local party, so the only option left was to highlight the 'courageous and honourable' action of Sir Michael and hope that peer-group pressure could be used to make Hamilton understand the damage the sleaze issue was inflicting on the party. Lewington was keen for as many Tory MPs as possible to add their weight. Easter Sunday's edition of *The World this Weekend* was chosen as the platform from which to make this ill-fated appeal. James Cox, the presenter, had asked to interview Michael Heseltine or Brian Mawhinney but neither was prepared to take the risk of being humiliated. Sir James Spicer told the programme that he thought all the candidates who had been caught up in the cash-for-questions affair should put the party's interests first. Reluctant though he was to say it, he considered natural justice might have to be cast aside. Sir Teddy Taylor added his support, saying that if the MPs concerned stood down they could always seek re-election to Parliament at a later date if they were found to have been innocent. By far the most influential of the three grandees wheeled out that lunchtime was John Townend, an executive member of the 1922 Committee. He had declined all morning to give an interview, but shortly before the programme went on the air Lewington rang through to say he would be appearing. Townend urged all Conservative candidates to examine their consciences and put the future of the party before their personal interests. 'We have to consider natural justice, but sometimes we have got to sacrifice our own position for the greater good . . . We have got to lance the boil.'

Hamilton was unmoved by these fresh entreaties, as should have been evident all along from an interview which he had given to that weekend's edition of the *Sunday Telegraph*. In an attempt to prove his innocence, he had released confidential minutes of his evidence to Sir Gordon Downey. 'It's all-out war now. I am obliged to retaliate against the deluge of lies by revealing the truth.' That evening Lewington sounded pretty despondent as it became obvious that Hamilton was digging in. He said John Townend had been 'pretty forceful' in building up peer pressure but the message Central Office was getting back from Tatton was that support for Hamilton remained solid. 'If Hamilton doesn't go, we'll have to respect that decision. We can't turn this into Armageddon.'

Lewington could hardly have been franker about the failure of his efforts that weekend to encourage Hamilton to respect opinion within the party. He seemed, understandably, keen to look ahead to the launch that Wednesday of the Conservatives' manifesto. The priority for Central Office was to try to ensure a clear start to the week ahead and the last thing Lewington wanted was any further confrontation over sleaze or unwelcome publicity. Easter Sunday was a lovely sunny day and the Prime Minister had been spending the weekend at Chequers. There had been talk of a photo-call at the nearby Bernard Arms but Lewington said that Major and the family had decided instead to take it easy in the swimming pool. Kenneth Clarke had also been out enjoying himself. Producers on *Today*, who had been trying without success to contact the Chancellor, were told he had gone to the pub and had not taken his bleeper with him. My report for the morning bulletins on Easter Monday reflected the rather low-key pace of the Conservatives' campaign and what I thought was Lewington's attempt to prepare the ground for their retreat in Tatton.

Major waited until late Sunday afternoon before finally calling a halt to the disastrous attempt to lean on Hamilton. In a letter to constituency association chairmen, he said that he abhorred lapses of behaviour in public life but the accuracy of the allegations against some MPs was being contested vigorously. Although he could not publish Sir Gordon

Downey's report as it was not his to release, the House of Commons had draconian powers which he would not hesitate to use if Conservative MPs were criticised. He acknowledged that there had been pressure for some constituency associations to be disbanded, so that new parliamentary candidates could be imposed, but under the party's constitution 'the selection of a candidate is the responsibility of the association and the decision to contest the seat is for the candidate'. With this statement, he intended to draw a line under the Hamilton affair in the hope that the launch that week of the party manifestos would wipe sleaze off the news agenda.

Labour insisted they were just as anxious as the Conservatives for the election to move away from allegations about financial impropriety at Westminster. Alastair Campbell said Tony Blair felt a burning need to lift the election campaign. 'We think there has been too much in the news about sleaze and it could turn people off voting, which might in the end benefit the Tories.' To demonstrate their change of approach, Labour intended to unveil a new poster campaign on Easter Monday morning: it would be a blaze of colour and, like all their advertising up to polling day, would carry a positive message. Campbell said Blair had ordered the removal of the poster showing a two-headed Major facing both ways. 'It's been hugely effective and we know Major hates it, but Tony is determined to reject the conventional wisdom that only negative advertising works.' Blair and John Prescott duly joined an army of children dressed in red sweatshirts to unveil the brightly coloured posters which all carried the slogan 'Britain Deserves Better'.

Fresh from the poster launch, Campbell proceeded to brief reporters on the campaign tours which the Labour leader would be making. Usually they would be travelling in a convoy of three coaches, with enough room for support staff, journalists, broadcasters and photographers. 'Between them Tony Blair and John Prescott will visit every one of the ninety key seats at least once, and Tony aims to hit sixty towns and cities between now and polling day. Tony is the most potent force in British politics; John is our Mr Motivator and Tony is our great persuader.' Campbell said Blair would not be giving endless doorstep interviews. 'He is not a rent-a-quote and there is a limit to the things which he can do in a given day.' Campbell was convinced Labour's strategy for the first two weeks of the campaign had been vindicated. 'Major's ratings on trust, truthfulness and leadership have fallen and Blair's have risen, and Blair has broken through as the one positive thing in the campaign so far, which is why we are trying to get above sleaze.' Campbell's breezy talk about rising above sleaze did not, however, hold Peter Mandelson back from doing a BBC interview in which he made sure Labour took full advantage of the letter to Conservative associations which explained why further attempts to pressurise Hamilton had been abandoned. Mandelson said Major was incapable of sorting out his own party. Sleaze would 'dog the Conservatives until polling day'. And Campbell himself, despite having lectured journalists that morning on Labour's determination to campaign on issues other than parliamentary corruption, was quick off the mark in alerting me to an interview for the *Mirror* next morning in which Blair had made it clear he would have sacked Hamilton on the spot.

On occasions like this the impudence of Blair's press secretary left me speechless, although one could not but admire his sheer gall. While haranguing journalists who failed to portray the Labour leader in a positive manner, Campbell was simultaneously doing all he could to push Major ever deeper into the mire. Piers Morgan, the *Mirror*'s editor, had conducted the interview and he reported that sleaze held no problem for the next Prime Minister: 'He makes it clear he would sack any Labour MP caught with his nose in the trough. Without exception, without dithering and without delay.' Major had no alternative but to face the issue head-on at his first formal news conference after the Easter holiday and answer questions about the repercussions of the weekend's events. The morning newspapers made grim reading: 'Major lets sleaze MPs off the hook' was the headline in the *Express* over a report by the deputy political editor, Jon Craig, on the 'premier's dramatic U-turn'. In the event the news conference went far better than party officials expected. Major calmly took every question which was thrown at him and explained in a patient but deliberate way why he would not over-rule constituencies or their candidates. 'Everyone who retains the support of their constituency party and who protests their innocence has a right to stand and fight the election upon the policies and the philosophy that they support. That applies explicitly to Neil Hamilton . . . I am not going to bow to the witch-hunt mentality of saying that anybody who faces unsubstantiated charges must leave public life. I don't think asking people who may be wholly innocent to stand aside is leadership. It may be partisan political vindictiveness and self-interest but I don't regard it as leadership.'

One quip by Major which lightened the proceedings, and made a change from his otherwise dogged delivery, was a sharp jab at Labour over their retreat from a televised debate. He taunted Blair for refusing to take part in a head-to-head confrontation: 'Turkeys may not vote for Christmas, but chickens apparently run away from broadcasts. I have accepted the proposals; it is up to the Labour Party to see whether they will.' In recycling Brian Mawhinney's jibe of Easter Saturday that Blair had chickened out, Major signalled the start of the funniest sideshow of the campaign. Charles Lewington was already making arrangements to hire the musician and actor Noel Flanagan, who was to be dressed in a bright yellow chicken suit and given instructions to try to get himself photographed next to Blair. A menagerie of weirdly dressed animal characters spent the campaign pursuing the party leaders across the country, providing an endless supply of amusing pictures and plenty of witty captions but throwing precious little light on the reasons why the negotiations had failed. Michael Dobbs was confident their chicken stunt would remind voters that it was Blair who had pulled out. 'If I was Peter Mandelson I'd probably have advised Blair to do the same thing but I wouldn't have got so close to the election and still allowed Blair to go on saying he wanted a head-to-head debate. If Blair and Mandelson had backed off six months ago they would have got off scot free.' Hiring the chicken to harass Blair was, in a way, sweet revenge. Some prominent Conservatives, including Brian Mawhinney, had moved to safer constituencies for the election because boundary changes had turned their previously safe seats into marginals. Labour had taken delight in publicising those Tory MPs who had availed themselves of what was dubbed the 'chicken run', and a party activist dressed as a chicken had even been sent to chase after the Tory MP Nick Hawkins, who had departed from Blackpool South to the less risky terrain of Surrey Heath.

Paddy Ashdown, sensing that the Liberal Democrats might get sidelined as the Major v. Blair contest went the distance, laid on a timely reminder at his first morning news conference of his resolve to remain above the relentless sparring of the two main parties. Political correspondents were entertained to a Punch and Judy show, set inside a cardboard Palace of Westminster, which Ashdown hoped would demonstrate the futility of knockabout politics. Major as the battered wife, dressed in Tory blue, and Blair as her husband in Labour red, beat each other about in true seafront style. To reinforce their message, the Punch and Judy theme was incorporated into the Liberal Democrats' one and only poster which Ashdown unveiled across the Thames at Vauxhall Cross. Lacking the hundreds of thousands of pounds which the Conservatives and Labour were to spend on poster advertising, the party had to concentrate its

meagre resources on this one fixed hoarding, which cost £15,000 to rent
for the four weeks up to polling day.

The fun and games of the morning were just an interlude before the
serious politics of the day. In this week, which brought the publication in
sequence of the manifestos of all three main parties, the spin doctors at last
had some new policies to promote. Word spread quickly round the press
gallery that ahead of the Conservatives' launch next day, exclusive
briefings had been given to the political correspondents of four newspapers: *The Times*, *Daily Telegraph*, *Daily Mail* and *Express*. Of the four
stories being trailed in advance, by far the most significant was that in the
Daily Mail, which had been given details of the government's plans for a
radical reform of the personal tax system. In a bid to bolster traditional
family values, the manifesto promised that if the Conservatives were re-
elected they would allow married men or women who gave up work to care
for children or sick or elderly relatives to transfer their personal tax
allowance to their spouses.

When Labour's press officers heard what was afoot they immediately
set about the task of costing the various pledges. David Hill rang me late
that evening to say that on their calculations the Conservatives' promises
would cost a total of £13 billion, which included £3 billion for the changes
to married couples' allowances and £5 billion for another manifesto
pledge, revealed by *The Times* and the *Express*, to cut the basic rate of
income tax to 20p in the pound. Labour's spin on the figures sounded a
little far-fetched, given that the *Daily Mail* was suggesting the entire
package would cost only £1 billion, but Hill would not hear of this. 'The
Conservatives' proposals are entering the realms of fantasy. Where is the
money going to come from? This must be the most costly and irresponsible manifesto ever published.'

As the *Daily Mail* correctly predicted, the new tax relief for married
couples was the centrepiece of the programme announced by John Major,
who described it at the launch as the 'boldest and most far-reaching'
manifesto published by any party since 1979. He estimated that allowing
married partners to transfer their personal tax allowances would help
almost two million families and add up to £17.50 to their weekly income.
When challenged about Labour's claim that the government had broken
ninety-two of the promises made in the 1992 manifesto, he retorted that
no one ever asked him about those things which had turned out better
than he ever thought they would. 'I didn't promise that we would have
growth outstripping the rest of Europe, but we have. I didn't promise we'd

have interest rates at a lower level than we've known for generations, but we have. I didn't promise we'd have inflation at record low levels for the last three or four years, but we have.'

Major's stirring performance, and the absence of any questions about sleaze, encouraged the two principal authors of the manifesto, David Willetts and Danny Finkelstein, who briefed journalists afterwards on the various proposals. Willetts said they had tried to write something which was shorter than usual and did not get bogged down in political history or trivial pledges like safeguarding hedgerows. Finkelstein was mightily relieved that the document was out at last. 'I do hate knowing the contents of the manifesto and not being able to tell my contacts.' He insisted that the cost of helping married couples would be only £1.2 billion. 'We purposely played down our pledges on inheritance tax and capital gains so that we could concentrate on the married couples' allowances.' A more detailed briefing was given later by the Chancellor, Kenneth Clarke, and the Chief Secretary to the Treasury, William Waldegrave. Political correspondents were ushered into a small side room where Clarke was puffing away on a cigar. As Waldegrave, who was sitting beside him, kept waving the smoke away from his nose and eyes, Clarke asked Charles Lewington if there was any reason why his off-the-record briefing was having to be held in a 'smoke-filled room'. Clarke denied that the tax breaks for married couples amounted to social engineering. 'I don't think getting £17.50 a week is going to make anybody rush out to hear the sound of wedding bells.'

After the Conservatives' upbeat launch, it was Alastair Campbell's turn that afternoon to try his hand at spinning a line about the policy proposals to be announced next morning at the unveiling of Labour's manifesto. He said that as it was Blair's objective to meet head-on the fact that people were extremely cynical of politicians, Labour would not be following Major's example of 'spraying around promises in a desperate bid for support'. Labour had no significant new policy proposals to announce because their programme had been worked out over the previous three years and the manifesto would set out the ten-point contract which Blair was offering to the British people. The basic pledges, like smaller class sizes, taking 250,000 young people off benefit and the promise not to put up income tax, had all been approved by the membership. 'We don't have to repeat the panic attack which has seized Major and copy the Conservatives' cobble together.' When I pointed out that the commitment not to increase income tax had only been announced in

January, and therefore had not been included in the pre-election manifesto approved by the party in the autumn of 1996, Campbell said it was 'obvious to anyone who knew anything' about the Labour Party that that was the way they were going to go on tax.

His rather laidback canter through Labour's proposals left me wondering what stroke Campbell had up his sleeve, as I was sure he would have thought of some way of giving the manifesto a newsy send-off. Campbell's many years in tabloid journalism had taught him a trick or two in reheating old stories. I was not to be disappointed. He had mentioned early on in the briefing that Blair had written out the ten-point contract while sitting in the garden the previous weekend; right at the end of his remarks, without prior warning, he told us he had some photocopies of it for distribution. I caught just the flicker of a smile on Campbell's face as the assembled journalists rushed forward to grab copies for themselves. He knew there was every chance that the two-page document in Blair's handwriting, complete with corrections, would appear in most newspapers next morning and would very likely be printed alongside stories about the Conservatives' manifesto. Campbell's intuition was spot-on. Most of the nationals used it as an illustration and some reproduced the entire ten pledges, helpfully pointing out Blair's problem in spelling the word 'developing'. (Blair's first try, which was crossed out, had two 'p's in it by mistake.) Campbell's orchestration of the coverage had looked effortless, but few former journalists could match his flair for promoting political news in a way that excited the popular press.

I took my copy of Blair's pledges back to the BBC's studios, so that I could use it as an illustration in my report for *Breakfast News*, and found to my surprise that the production team was hard at work trying to obtain copies of handwritten documents from Major and Ashdown. A handwriting expert had already been booked for interview next morning, providing another useful spin-off from Campbell's attempts to publicise Blair's ten commitments. The Liberal Democrats were having the greatest problem because Ashdown wrote everything directly on to his word processor, but eventually the head of press and research, Nick South, tracked down a copy of a handwritten parliamentary question.

Although Campbell's advance billing for the unveiling of the manifesto had been lighter in tone than the Conservatives' determined efforts to hype their launch, the occasion itself achieved far greater impact. Labour had spent years perfecting the running of news conferences and, as they had demonstrated in both the 1987 and 1992 elections, they could turn the presentation of a political speech or policy launch into an event which would be remembered. Publication of the Conservatives' manifesto had been effective and workmanlike, and their newly opened press conference room at party headquarters provided an authoritative backdrop for John Major; but the launch lacked flair and did not seem to have done much to inspire political journalists. The setting for Tony Blair was a far larger and loftier room at the Institution of Civil Engineers and there was space for four or five times as many people as had been crowded together in the cramped accommodation at Central Office. In addition to the reporters, broadcasters and technicians there were party workers and other guests. As everyone settled down, to the accompaniment of the music from Labour's campaign song, 'Things Can Only Get Better', there was a far greater sense of anticipation. In front of the audience was the New Labour set, incorporating the Union flag, and alongside large drapes bearing the slogan from the latest poster, 'Britain Deserves Better'. The whole atmosphere seemed more uplifting, and I was told by a BBC cameraman, Giles Wooltorton, that this was partly because of the way the room had been lit. He said the Conservatives tended to use theatre lighting, which made the colours on their set appear much brighter, but it did give their news conference room a closed-in effect, whereas Labour had tried to suggest a feeling of openness.

As there was so much more space, there were ample seats at the front for the shadow Cabinet, who filed in first. When Blair mounted the platform, he knew the routine: he stood facing the photographers and television crews, accepting their instructions to turn in sequence so that each of them got a clear shot as he held the manifesto up to his face. He did not smile, indeed his face was deadpan; no political sketch writer would be able to say he was grinning or looked smarmy. Sitting beside him on the platform were John Prescott, Gordon Brown, Margaret Beckett and Robin Cook; this line-up, in comparison to Major's solitary presentation, highlighted the unity and team spirit which Labour believed they could offer. Blair said the manifesto did not promise the earth, but the ten commitments they were making were a programme for national renewal and they affected what moved and concerned people in the country: schools, hospitals, crime, jobs and industry. 'We want to be held to them. They are our bond of trust, most of all my bond of trust with the people of Britain.' His answer to one of the questions underlined the sense of occasion which the event seemed to be generating. Blair had already succeeded in conveying the feeling that the country was on the brink of a momentous event but, after being challenged to justify his assertion that he would be 'implacably tough' in the face of industrial unrest, he somehow found the words to encapsulate that sentiment. He would not turn the clock back: 'This is the historic opportunity for the Labour Party, this election, to become a modern party of progress and justice . . . This is our historic opportunity. If we blow this opportunity, we blow our place in history. It's as simple as that and we have got no intention of doing that.'

Blair was well practised in one essential technique for party leaders at election news conferences: the choice of questioners. Once questions are called for, a strict pecking order has to be followed because the first half-dozen answers are as important as the opening statement and the opportunities which they provide must not be wasted through inept selection. Party leaders are required to know and remember the first names of the leading broadcasters because television and radio rule the roost, for several interlocking reasons. Sky TV and Radio 5 Live, as well as other channels, may well be taking a feed of the news conference, so the possibility of live transmissions must not be overlooked. Also, the answers given to the radio and television journalists are the ones most likely to be selected for use in news bulletins and programmes and, as a way of lending added authority to their reporting, shots of leading broadcasters asking pertinent questions are frequently included in the television broadcasts. Therefore no political leader, knowing that an answer to a question from the BBC or ITN is likely to be seen by millions of viewers, is going to ignore the presence of their correspondents. This close – some would say cosy – arrangement helps the politicians because they think they come across as being human and approachable if they are seen to be on good terms with the friendly faces and voices who are so well known to viewers and listeners. And, perhaps most importantly of all, the spin doctors like it too, because they know that by and large the broadcasters have to ask simple and straightforward questions and do not usually have the time to get bogged down in the nit-picking queries about policy detail which so delight political correspondents on newspapers. Blunt, controversial questions are rarely a problem because they can be answered in short, pithy soundbites; in any case, to prepare for just such an eventuality, the party leader will invariably have gone through difficult areas beforehand and rehearsed what to say.

Blair's handling of questions at his manifesto launch began in textbook fashion: the first went to Robin Oakley, political editor of the BBC, and the second to Michael Brunson, ITN's political editor. For the third question he called out the name 'Adam', but then found that for a moment, dazzled by the television lights, he was thrown by the mass of faces in front of him and could not pick out the location of Sky TV's political editor Adam Boulton. The newspaper correspondents who were sitting beside me cackled at Blair's embarrassment. They have been grumbling for years about the preference given to broadcasters, and believe that the political parties are now so carefully stage-managing their news conferences, and deliberately taking up time with the softer questions of television and radio, that the news media as a whole have suffered and are losing out on the chance to expose politicians to a thorough grilling on the detail of their policies.

Foreign journalists and broadcasters, who had been refused access to the Conservatives' manifesto launch because of lack of space, were welcomed with open arms by Labour and the consequent doubling in the size of the media contingent helped to give the impression that this was not just an important national occasion but a world event. By any yardstick this was a supremely well-organised launch, and after its conclusion Peter Mandelson, not unnaturally, stood in the foyer as journalists departed, brushing away their plaudits with a modest wave of the hand. A group of American journalists were particularly persistent in their questions to him, which were directed mainly at aspects of political presentation. One correspondent, who had muttered something to the effect that New Labour was just a public relations firm which would be out of office in two years, demanded to know what was going to be done about Blair's 'big old grin'. Mandelson paused for a moment before replying: 'That big old grin you refer to is just another product of the Tory lie machine.' Another American reporter wanted to know if New Labour were playing it too safe. Mandelson dodged the question but said it was difficult to know whether anyone was really listening out there in the country at large. 'There will be febrile activity by the political parties for the next three weeks and then the public will wake up in the final week to see whether anything has changed and if they were wrong in their original judgement.'

As Blair was about to leave there was a sudden flurry of activity. Word had reached Mandelson that the Conservatives' chicken was prowling outside, armed with a placard which said 'Chicken Blair Won't Debate'. Labour's campaign manager, never one to be upstaged by his opponents' photo-opportunities, immediately set to work shooing party workers outside with strict instructions to block the chicken's progress and ensure Blair an untrammelled exit. Help was at hand, because the *Mirror* had hired a headless chicken to chase after Major, and soon scuffles were breaking out all over Westminster as party officials fought off the attention of what appeared to be the bedraggled inhabitants of a deranged zoo. A rhinocerous and two mangy-looking foxes joined in the fun, as did two bears who laid out a political picnic in Whitehall complete with a placard which asked: 'Is Tony Bear in it for the honey?' A grim-faced Alex Aiken, the Conservatives' chief press officer, made the mistake of trying to evict the headless chicken from the forecourt of Central Office, but after being given the runaround he ended up providing the *Mirror* with plenty of free publicity as his picture was splashed across next morning's newspapers.

Try as they might, there was no way the Liberal Democrats could recapture the heady atmosphere of Labour's launch when they published their manifesto the following day. Journalists were given a preview by the party's campaign manager, Richard Holme – which was just as well, because the room at Church House used for the launch itself proved to be far too small and quite a few correspondents failed to get in. Lord Holme said there would be no surprises or gimmicks because their policy proposals had been agreed for over a year. 'What we intend to put forward is a manifesto containing practical, commonsense policies which can really make a difference after eighteen years of Conservative government. Our manifesto is the only one which comes from a consistent and coherent set of principles. The centrepiece will be making Britain the world's No. 1 learning society in the next century.'

Paddy Ashdown defended his party's plan to increase the basic rate of income tax from 23p to 24p in the pound in order to raise £2 billion a year to invest in education. 'Only the Liberal Democrats will actually make a difference in schools where teachers are now being sacked and classes are rising to forty or above, because only the Liberal Democrats have the clear commitment to do something about it now, not to wait until resources allow, but now, today, as soon as we are elected.' In addition to an extra 1p on the basic rate, the Liberal Democrats also proposed a new top rate of 50p in the pound on earnings of over £100,000 a year and said this would finance an increase in personal allowances. As a result half a million people would be taken out of tax altogether. However, under their proposals for opportunities at work, the manifesto quoted a different figure and stated that their policies would have the effect of 'cutting the benefits bill and reducing tax for 99.5 per cent of all income tax payers'. Anthony Bevins, the *Independent*'s political editor, challenged Ashdown on the figures. There was a short and pointed exchange between them which was quite unlike the almost reverential tones which had been adopted when Blair was questioned at the Labour news conference. Bevins ended up telling the Liberal Democrat leader to reprint his manifesto. 'You will need to look at it, because it's rubbish. It's not true that you are reducing income tax for 99.5 per cent of all income tax payers.'

Blair, who flew to Glasgow that morning for the launch of Labour's Scottish manifesto, was also experiencing some turbulence in his campaign. Previous visits to Scotland by the Labour leader had provoked some dissent, but his suggestion in an interview for *The Scotsman* that the tax-raising power of a Scottish parliament would be comparable to that of an English parish council produced consternation among supporters of Scottish devolution and gave his opponents a field day. The front page of the *Evening Standard*, which bore the headline 'Blair's First Clanger', was held aloft by Brian Mawhinney as he warmed up the audience for the Prime Minister at the Conservatives' first set-piece election rally in the Royal Albert Hall. Major changed his speech at the last moment to attack what he described as the 'total and utter chaos' in Labour's plans. 'For years Labour have been telling Scotland they would give them a tax-raising parliament. Now Blair implies that a Scottish parliament would be no more than a parish council . . . With his words Blair both insults Scotland and breaks the promise he's given them for a long time. This is the man who only yesterday asked Britain to trust him.' At the Conservatives' news conference next morning, Michael Heseltine widened their attack on Blair's trustworthiness. On the screen behind the Deputy Prime Minister there was a moving display of a yellow, squawking chicken and the slogan 'You Can't Trust Blair'. Heseltine was in his element: 'Yes, Mr Blair, it's a question of trust. Why should anyone believe a word you say when you change your mind on all the major issues of our time?'

Regular appearances by the Conservatives' chicken had not alarmed Peter Mandelson. He thought that by turning the dispute over the television debate into a comedy turn, the Tories had lost the argument and that his tactic of seeking to distance Labour from the row had been vindicated. 'Now that the Conservatives have descended to chickens and insults we know we have seen them off.' But the twists and turns over the proposed powers for a Scottish parliament, a developing debate about Labour's plans for privatisation and questions about the impact future sell-offs would have on Gordon Brown's budgetary plans had all conspired to put Labour firmly on the defensive. When I questioned Mandelson at the manifesto launch about the approach he had adopted the previous week during the apparent confusion over their policy shift on union recognition, he said his advice was that the party had to be 'steady, steady and very, very firm'. As Labour were again discovering to their cost that the Conservatives could make breaches in their defences, I wondered what tactics Mandelson might be recommending and whether the spin doctors might have come up with yet another diversionary tactic.

6

Under Siege

In deciding to abandon all further attempts to influence the selection of the Conservative candidate in the Tatton constituency, the Tory leadership had been forced to acknowledge that they were up against a redoubtable husband and wife team. Neil and Christine Hamilton were battle-hardened, having withstood month after month of media vilification during the seemingly endless parliamentary inquiries into the hotly disputed allegations of the cash-for-questions affair. Whenever I had seen them walking together along the corridors of the Palace of Westminster they appeared invincible. Christine Hamilton, who worked full-time as her husband's secretary, had a forbidding manner and would look journalists straight in the eye, as if throwing up a defensive ring around the MP. I knew that if I was going to attempt to penetrate that protective shield, and try to speak to him, I had better have a good reason; otherwise she would see me off within an instant.

The tragedy for the Conservative Party was that this formidable political partnership had finished up trying to defend – in the opinion of most parliamentarians – the indefensible. Newspaper stories alleging that Conservative ministers and MPs were guilty of parliamentary corruption had started to undermine John Major's authority soon after he won the 1992 election and, by the end of the parliament, the issue of 'sleaze' had come to haunt the Prime Minister. The row over his failure to ensure that the Select Committee on Standards and Privileges was allocated sufficient time both to complete its proceedings and to arrange for the publication of Sir Gordon Downey's findings on the cash-for-questions allegations before Parliament was prorogued for the general election had effectively wiped out the first two weeks of the Conservatives' campaign. Further opprobrium had been heaped on Major's head following the unsuccessful attempts of the Tory leadership to persuade Hamilton to follow the example of the Beaconsfield MP, Tim Smith, and step down as candidate in Tatton. However, the launch of the party manifestos succeeded in steering the election back towards policy issues and, by the end of the third week, Tory party strategists at last had a spring in their step.

For once, that weekend's Sunday newspapers looked encouraging for the Conservatives. Much of the coverage was directed towards investigating and assessing three issues: the repercussions of Tony Blair's apparent comparison of a Scottish parliament to an English parish council, and the implications of Labour's perceived policy shifts over trade union recognition and the privatisation of state-owned assets and services. In a pre-arranged interview that Sunday morning on *Breakfast with Frost* John Major sounded positively enthusiastic, confident that the start of the fourth week of the campaign heralded a change in Tory fortunes. He went straight on to the attack, accusing Blair of 'slithering and sliding around' after having used the word 'trust' twenty times when launching Labour's manifesto. 'Labour had three years to prepare their manifesto but in three days it has begun to fall apart, on the Scottish parliament, on trade unions and on privatisation . . . If Blair says trust is important why weren't these changes included in Labour's manifesto when it was launched just days ago? . . . Their manifesto is falling apart before our eyes. Three days, a big change every day.'

Major's onslaught led the political coverage in the lunchtime and early evenings news bulletins; but another Press Association newsflash was about to shatter what until then had looked like being a relatively quiet Sunday evening. It was timed at 7.01 p.m. and stated that the BBC war correspondent, Martin Bell, intended to put himself forward as an anti-corruption candidate to stand against Neil Hamilton in Tatton. Phil Murphy, the PA's political editor, did not say in his release where the information had come from, but there was no doubting its authenticity. He told me subsequently that he had no intention of revealing where his tip-off originated: 'I jealously guard my sources.' Nevertheless, as events unfolded, and Bell crossed the line from journalism to politics, the tell-tale footprints of Labour's spin doctors were all over the story.

Only the week before, after the withdrawal of Jon Kelly, Labour's candidate in Tatton, and the furore over the Conservatives' failed attempt to lean on Hamilton, Alastair Campbell had told me that he was confident Labour would eventually find someone of sufficient standing to become an anti-sleaze candidate. He said it needed a public figure of the stature of Frances Lawrence, widow of the murdered London headmaster, Philip Lawrence, to win the support of the local Labour and Liberal Democrat party members. Terry Waite, the former Beirut hostage, and the former

Chief Inspector of Prisons, Judge Stephen Tumim, were two other names which had been bandied about in the newspapers as possible candidates. As Campbell put it, 'If someone does come forward who is really respected then Tory MPs will say to Hamilton "it's shoot yourself time", and he'll have to resign.'

Martin Bell was approached in the first instance by Tom Stoddart, the Labour Party's official photographer, after he had opened an exhibition of Stoddart's war photographs at the Royal Festival Hall. As Bell was to recount on numerous subsequent occasions, it was at a dinner after the opening that Stoddart took him by surprise and said: 'You're what we're looking for in Tatton.' Bell said his initial silence when the idea was put to him must have been taken as acquiescence because he received a succession of telephone calls next day, the first of them from Alastair Campbell, who had been alerted by Stoddart to Bell's interest in becoming the candidate. Once his 'political innocence' had been verified – a process which included a call from Paddy Ashdown, whom he had known from time spent together in Bosnia – Bell found himself being whisked off that Sunday morning and driven to Tatton by the Liberal Democrats' vice-chairman, Tim Clement-Jones. After meeting the local executives of the two parties, and once it was reaffirmed that Kelly and his Liberal Democrat counterpart, Roger Barlow, would stand down, an announcement was issued. Labour made immediate arrangements for Bell to hold a news conference in London the following day.

Instead of waiting for the news conference, my instructions were to get to Tatton as quickly as possible to obtain Hamilton's response and report local reaction. As I drove north on the M1 that Monday morning I felt a slight pang at the thought of missing the daily round of news conferences at Westminster, but I realised Bell's intervention meant that the Hamilton saga had taken off yet again and that this time there was no way of predicting how it might end up. If Bell did go the distance and fight the seat, I knew there was every likelihood the contest would become as highly publicised as recent by-elections, and the news media would descend on the constituency in force. The sleaze issue had already wrecked the start of the Conservatives' campaign, and now it was poised to return to the headlines with a vengeance. Voters in the constituency would get the chance to set aside their traditional allegiances and support a non-political candidate. The true extent of the danger this posed to the Conservatives had not yet dawned on the party leadership. They had no way of knowing that Tatton would be held up as an example to voters in the rest of the country of how it was possible to target an otherwise impregnable Conservative MP and, I would suggest, help to encourage the notion that tactical voting might achieve the same result in other constituencies where there were substantial Tory majorities. I certainly had no inkling as I headed out of London that I would end up reporting a story worthy of a political melodrama, including an MP who could be cast as the villain, his scheming wife, and a hero in an off-white suit with a beautiful daughter who would dazzle and beguile a bunch of hard-bitten, cynical journalists. As Bell's audacity slowly sank in at Conservative Central Office the reaction hardened. Michael Trend, the deputy chairman, derided his candidacy as a cheap stunt by Labour's spin doctors aimed at diverting attention from a 'wobbly week when their policies have been unravelling by the hour'. Charles Moore, the *Daily Telegraph*'s editor, told *Today* it was 'absolute madness' for Bell to think he could become a white knight and a moral guardian of standards in public life. 'It's ludicrous for a BBC correspondent to become an anti-sleaze crusader. Journalists should not put themselves on pedestals.'

On arriving in the constituency, my first stop that Monday lunchtime was the village of Nether Alderley, near Knutsford, where I joined a large contingent of reporters, television crews and photographers who were already staking out the Hamiltons' home, a large converted rectory looking out across the Cheshire countryside. Bell was due to hold his news conference in London early that afternoon, but Christine Hamilton was doing her best to prevent her husband being completely upstaged. Their lunch guest was the local television celebrity Bill Roache, who as Ken Barlow had become the longest-serving cast member of *Coronation Street*. While careful to acknowledge that Bell was a 'very honourable journalist', Roache said that the BBC correspondent had nothing to do with the constituency and was allowing himself to be used as 'a bit of a tacky device' by Labour and the Liberal Democrats. Neil Hamilton looked on approvingly, but once we sought his reaction to the likely impact of Bell's emergence as an anti-sleaze candidate, his wife said he could not answer reporters' questions as that was forbidden by the Representation of the People Act.

Under the RPA 'personal electioneering' on television and radio is considered unlawful if practised by a candidate in the pending period before an election, and Mrs Hamilton regularly quoted the provisions of the Act if she caught journalists in the constituency trying to cross-question her husband about his personal position. Herself free from any such restraint, she said that in her view Bell had a 'flaming cheek' and his arrival in Tatton would only stiffen the couple's own resolve and that of the local Conservatives, who together had stood 'shoulder to shoulder' for over two and a half years, fighting Mohamed Al Fayed, the *Guardian* and most of the rest of the British press. 'It's just complete nonsense for Bell to flip in here with a few hours' notice and say, "Hamilton should go. I'm going to stand" . . . If you think we're going to chicken out, you're all mad.'

Bell told his news conference in London that his decision to offer himself as an anti-sleaze candidate was rapidly turning into a more daunting experience than war reporting in Bosnia. He kept insisting that he hoped Hamilton would agree to stand aside, so that he could become the shortest-lived political candidate with the shortest-lived political career. 'I would much rather run the trenchlines of Dobrinja or tackle snipers' alley in my armoured vehicle, Miss Piggy, than be going through this. I really would. This is one of the scariest things that has ever happened to me and I wouldn't be doing this unless I really believed that people wanted me to do it.' However, on the drive north late that afternoon, Bell kept hearing on his car radio Mrs Hamilton's strictures about his 'flaming cheek' in standing against her husband. When he arrived at his hotel he told me that her criticism had really fired him up. I quickly formed the impression that Bell had gone through something of a conversion on the road to Knutsford and had rather taken to politics. 'Yes,' he said, 'it really is going to be a David and Goliath situation.' On seeing me smirk, Bell paused and smiled himself. 'Yes, I know, you're going to say I'm already talking in soundbites.'

My first job early next morning was to get film of him eating his breakfast. The hotel manager walked with me through to the dining room and, as we approached his table, I moved forward and said: 'Please, Mr Bell, may we get some pictures of you having breakfast?' He looked startled. 'Why are you calling me Mr Bell? What's the point of that?' I said that was how I usually addressed politicians and explained that it was unwise to use first names when filming because there was always the danger that, as a broadcaster, one might use them on air; such familiarity angered some listeners and viewers and could be interpreted by others as indicating a degree of collusion. Whenever I spoke to a politician I liked to indicate to him or her that there was, at least as far as I was concerned, an imaginary barrier between us, and I reminded Bell that he had, after all, crossed the line from journalism to politics. Bell's pained expression made me realise that I had obviously touched a sensitive spot. Bridling somewhat, he demanded to know, first, what instructions I had been given by the BBC as to how to report the story of his becoming a candidate, and secondly, what my advice would be on the question of whether or not he should resign immediately from the BBC. On the second point I said that in my opinion he should leave the Corporation, because he had clearly taken a calculated decision in accepting the chance to become the anti-sleaze candidate, and from what I could see he was already relishing that challenge. Bell, who had been immediately suspended on unpaid leave when he took up the candidacy, said that was his thinking too. He admitted to having a 'crisis of conscience' as to what to do but felt that if he did resign it would indicate to local Labour and Liberal Democrat party members that he was serious about standing and that for him there was no going back. So I was hardly surprised when, two hours later, we heard that Bell had resigned from the BBC. Bell's daughter Melissa was also at the breakfast table, taking notes, and as they discussed their tasks that morning, he said he must get his suit off to the cleaners as soon as possible.

Melissa, who was twenty-four and a marketing executive with Reuters news agency in Brussels, had taken leave immediately in order to become her father's campaign manager. She was tall, of striking appearance, and had a habit of elegantly flicking her blonde hair behind her ear. I could see the television crew were taking the trouble to film her from several different angles. Although I was not sure whether the pictures would be needed, it was obviously sensible to take full advantage of the opportunity to film father and daughter together. With my producer Julian Joyce we began compiling a report for the *One o'Clock News* – but no sooner had we finished editing than we heard that Neil and Christine Hamilton were on their way to Knutsford for a face-to-face meeting with the war correspondent who had invaded their constituency. They had obviously decided beforehand to stage a high-profile confrontation and when we reached Knutsford Heath, Bell and the Hamiltons were surrounded by reporters, television crews and photographers. Their altercation had clearly reached a critical point and although, for once, Mrs Hamilton had decided that her husband was not going to be silenced by the RPA, she was still doing much of the talking:

Christine Hamilton: Do you accept that a man is innocent unless proved guilty?
Martin Bell: Of course I do.
Christine Hamilton: Do you accept that my husband is innocent?

Martin Bell: Let's just see what comes out. I don't know. I'm standing
    here . . .
Christine Hamilton: Why aren't you prepared to wait for . . .
Martin Bell: Look, this is an ambush. A lot of local people have asked me to
    stand here. The impetus comes from local people. Let them just
    choose between us.
Neil Hamilton: I would just like to say then that you are prepared to give
    me the benefit of the doubt on the allegations that have been made
    against me?
Martin Bell: Absolutely, absolutely.
Neil Hamilton: Good.

The moment Bell gave his verbal assurance that he accepted that
Hamilton was innocent until proved guilty, the couple's demeanour
changed. Armed with this concession they began backing away, evidently
surprised that their ambush had been so successful. Hamilton said he had
no wish to hijack the whole of the news conference which Bell had been on
the point of giving to waiting reporters. Having realised by now that he
was the one who had given ground, Bell told the Hamiltons they had not
done badly: 'I'm supposed to be the guy who manipulates the media.' Mrs
Hamilton, taking full advantage of her moment of glory, gracefully walked
away with her husband, and for the benefit of the cameras, pointedly
clasped his hand, providing a perfect end shot for the television coverage.

    As for the journalists and broadcasters, we could not believe our good
fortune. The battle royal we had just witnessed on Knutsford Heath was
undoubtedly going to be one of the high spots of the entire election
campaign, and we knew it would provide a dramatic trailer to the meeting
that evening of Tatton Conservatives who were having to decide whether
to keep Hamilton as their candidate. Bell looked somewhat put out when
asked why he had given way. 'I was ambushed by the Hamiltons and I have
to say it was the scariest ambush I've ever been in. I thought I should treat
it like a Serbian road block, that I should placate and conciliate, but it was a
political mistake.' Paul Eastham, the *Daily Mail*'s political correspondent, thought Bell's tactical error, in the first place, was to have walked
across to the Heath when the Hamiltons arrived. 'The tanks were already
on the lawn. He should have known better.' Michael Brunson, ITN's
political editor, agreed. 'Bell should have stayed in his hotel once the
Hamiltons turned up, and if he'd been watching me on the 12.30 ITN
news and heard what I was saying, then he'd have known not to go there.'

To help Bell regain the initiative, Alastair Campbell faxed through the draft of a letter to be sent to Hamilton setting out what Bell considered were the MP's admitted wrongdoings. The letter also outlined how Bell intended to fight the election, standing as an independent candidate, campaigning on an anti-corruption platform. Bell said: 'The Labour people from whom this idea came wanted me to go on to the attack in a confrontational way so I let them help me draft the letter, but I think I was ill advised and after that I never talked to Alastair Campbell again during the campaign.'

When we came to edit our report of the Knutsford Heath confrontation for the evening news bulletins there was so much material we were spoilt for choice. As Bell was still not officially a candidate, and as Labour and the Liberal Democrats had yet to hold meetings formally endorsing the withdrawal of their candidates in his favour, both the BBC and ITN considered coverage of Bell's spat with the Hamiltons should not be restricted by the provisions of the RPA, and the story led the news. Inevitably, among the many images of the day to be included in my report were the pictures of Melissa. Even without my drawing it to the video tape editor's attention, he instinctively selected the shot of Bell's daughter flicking back her blonde hair.

Hamilton secured a resounding vote of confidence at the meeting of Tatton Conservatives. An unsuccessful attempt was made to force a secret ballot, but on a show of hands there was a two-to-one majority in favour of his re-adoption. Next morning we had to start filming in preparation for the meeting that evening of the constituency Labour Party, which had to approve a resolution to support Bell. Our first stop was Nether Alderley to get some fresh, daytime pictures of the Hamiltons. As usual the pack were waiting at the end of the drive, discussing tactics. Mrs Hamilton would not let photographers or journalists encroach on her property unless invited in for an interview or photo-call, and even then, once the business was completed she would frog-march us down the drive, repeatedly saying 'shoo, shoo' as though we were a gaggle of troublesome geese. Today, after their success the previous evening, she was only too happy to be filmed with her husband and we talked about the best location. 'Oh, by the way, is this top bright enough for television? Actually, I'd better go inside and tart myself up, I mean tart up my lipstick.' I marvelled at her attention to detail and her ability, despite all the setbacks they had suffered, to exploit any opportunity to counter the adverse publicity which her husband had received. Almost without my asking she had realised the significance of Labour's meeting that evening and the opportunity it gave her to portray Bell as a Labour Party stooge.

The danger of Labour's becoming too closely associated with Bell's campaign was clearly exercising the deputy leader, John Prescott, whose job it was to reassure local party members that their candidate, Jon Kelly, had made the right decision in offering to step down. Prescott hurried into the meeting, not saying a word. Bell and Melissa followed a little later. Waiting journalists were told by Labour's regional press officer, Martin Liptrot, that there would no media access to the meeting, and Prescott's refusal to be interviewed was an indication of the seriousness with which Labour were taking the Hamiltons' tactic of undermining Bell's credibility as an independent candidate. There were some harsh words at the meeting about the unprecedented decision to deny local people the chance to vote Labour, but a secret ballot showed that support for the anti-sleaze candidate was overwhelming and Prescott and Bell, who made sure they left separately and were not filmed together, both said they were delighted by the result.

Bell's long experience behind the camera was of enormous benefit to him in the campaign: for example, he made sure, when on walkabouts in the constituency, that he allowed time for the television crews to get well in front of him, so that they had ample time to focus and get clear shots of his approach. Usually walking a few paces behind him was an off-duty BBC cameraman, Nigel Bateson, who had taken an unscheduled holiday to act as driver and minder. 'Martin's watched my back enough times. I thought I might as well watch his for a change.' Bell's fame as a war correspondent acted like a magnet for other celebrities. Colonel Bob Stewart of the Cheshire Regiment, a friend from his days in Bosnia, and the former deputy chief constable of Greater Manchester, John Stalker, were among the first to visit the constituency and give their endorsement.

Within a matter of days Bell had shown that he could add the words 'political operator' to his curriculum vitae. However, he was taking his initiation rather too fast for our comfort, because within a matter of forty-eight hours he had developed one of the more irritating traits of the modern politician: a propensity to make complaints to the BBC. The report which attracted his ire was by my colleague Paul Newman and was transmitted on the *One o'Clock News*. It included what broadcasters describe as a 'vox pops', a short sequence of comments from the public, which had been recorded that morning when Bell did a walkabout and talked to passers-by. Bell's objection was that only one clip from the vox pops was used in Newman's report and it was one that was critical of him. He considered that unbalanced and unfair as he had spoken to a total of twenty-five people, of whom only three had reservations about his decision to challenge Hamilton. Newman's difficulty that lunchtime was that all the other interviewees in his report were praising Bell and, as there was no balancing material in support of Hamilton, he had been anxious to reflect the fact that there were at least some critical voices in the constituency, so had used a clip from the vox pops expressing some reservations. In fact, the remarks to which Bell took exception were hardly condemnatory, taking the form of questions from a middle-aged man. 'What do you know about education?', he asked; 'What experience have you had?' Bell replied himself with a question: 'What about having two children?', to which the man responded: 'But in terms of being a politician? Surely electors want a professional politician representing their interests?' At a news conference that afternoon, Bell gleefully regaled the story of his first official complaint to the BBC as a parliamentary candidate. 'It's unbelievable . . . The only person they used in the report was one who opposed me . . . I left the BBC and standards decline so fast.' Newman was as baffled as I was at all the fuss, not least when we discovered that Bell had rung through with his complaint direct to the editor in the news studio gallery while the *One o'Clock News* was still on the air.

In the course of his news conference, when explaining why he had decided to leave the BBC, Bell said he realised that he had 'crossed the line' from journalism into politics. Afterwards I complimented him on using the phrase I had mentioned at breakfast on his first morning in Knutsford, but I could see that he thought I was trying to cause mischief and that I needed reminding of his new status as a parliamentary candidate. 'Yes, it was great making a complaint to the BBC. I knew exactly which number to ring and precisely whom to talk to. I think the BBC is bending over so far to be balanced in reporting this story that you are going to end up being unfair to me. And, if you do that again, don't expect the first interview on election night; you can forget it.' I was rather taken aback to hear a distinguished former war correspondent start issuing threats against journalists whom I considered had given him fair and generous coverage. My immediate thought was that in the induction procedures which he had been through in the course of being approved as a candidate by Labour and the Liberal Democrats, he had paid too much attention to the advice he had been given by Alastair Campbell.

As I drove back to London it suddenly dawned on me why our trip to the Tatton constituency had been so enjoyable. For once in the campaign we had not been bothered or badgered by Labour's spin doctors, and for three whole days we had reported a story without finding that our news judgement was being constantly monitored and challenged by the political parties. However, this could not last, and in the event Bell's complaint was a timely reminder of what lay in store for me. Our last day in Tatton was described by the newspapers as Labour's 'Wobbly Wednesday' and, as I was to discover to my cost, the air would soon be blue with abuse: Labour's media monitors were on the warpath. The cause of their anger was that the Conservatives had not only identified weak points in Labour's policies but had also succeeded in generating some highly damaging publicity.

As soon as it was first mooted that Bell might become the anti-sleaze candidate in Tatton, the Conservative leadership realised that if Hamilton was re-adopted later that week they would have no option but to disengage as quickly as possible and leave him to his own devices. John Major had tried in his *Breakfast with Frost* interview the previous Sunday to make a virtue of the fact that Conservative constituency associations had complete freedom over the choice of candidates. He gave an undertaking that he would not challenge the selection process: 'I have not interfered in the selection of any candidate at any stage. It's not part of our constitution to do so and I will not do so.' Now, after all the favourable comment which Bell had received, strategists at Central Office believed their policy of disengagement was the right tactic. Danny Finkelstein told me that if they could continue to play down the significance of Bell's challenge in Tatton, and treat the contest as of no more importance than a by-election, they would be free to concentrate their attack on Labour. His judgement proved correct, and once Labour stumbled during a tortuous argument over plans for the privatisation of the air traffic control system, sleaze fell rapidly down the news agenda.

A report in the *Sunday Telegraph*, which predicted that in a speech to a City audience Tony Blair would promise to 'privatise everything', heralded the start of Labour's troubled week. In what was described as the final break with their former commitment to nationalisation, the paper said that Blair was ready to 'sell off billions of pounds'-worth of state assets'. In an interview for *The World this Weekend*, the shadow Chancellor, Gordon Brown, confirmed that a Labour government would establish a national register of assets held by government departments and then decide whether or not to keep them in the public sector. 'In the iron grip we will have on public spending and public resources, if there is no other clear use, we will get rid of assets which are of no further use to us.' Next morning on *Today*, the shadow Chancellor was asked whether the National Air Traffic Services would be among the assets to be sold off, because when the government had announced the previous year that air traffic control would be privatised, Labour had opposed it. Brown said Labour's concern all along had been about the 'safety implications of the sale', but that the privatisation of NATS would be looked at, on its merits, once they had compiled the national register of public assets.

At the root of Labour's difficulties was that at the start of the year, when the government was so constantly on the defensive, some of the party's policy shifts had received scant attention when they were first announced. At the time Labour were only too pleased to find that controversial decisions were arousing little interest in the news media or dissent within the party. On 23 February the shadow trade and industry secretary, Margaret Beckett, told *On the Record* that Labour was 'not ruling out' the sale of NATS because the likely proceeds of £500 million had been included in the Treasury's estimates and Labour would have no alternative but to accept the broad framework of the government's public expenditure proposals; but this U-turn was barely publicised. However, because this change in policy had not been highlighted at the time, even within the party itself, Michael Heseltine was now able to exploit what the *Daily Mail* claimed in a front-page headline was 'Labour's Broken Promise'. In an interview for *Panorama*, Tony Blair repeated the line taken by Brown and Beckett, that Labour would certainly look at the sale of air traffic control and did not rule it out. But the *Daily Mail* then claimed Blair had broken a promise given in a letter dated 5 February from the party's shadow minister for transport, Keith Bradley, stating that Labour were 'completely opposed to the privatisation' of NATS which would 'remain in the public service'. As the row took off a second letter was revealed, this time from the air traffic controllers' union, the Institution of Professionals, Managers and Specialists. Dated 21 March, it stated that the shadow transport team had confirmed that the position remained unchanged and that Labour would not privatise NATS.

The original pledge to keep air traffic control in the public sector had been set out in the strongest possible terms at Labour's annual conference the previous October, when Andrew Smith, the shadow transport secretary, condemned what he said was the government's 'crazy new scheme to privatise the air'. Labour would do everything they could to block the sale, and, he declared, 'Our air is not for sale.' As Smith had been so categoric, he was now tracked down by *The World at One* and interviewed at length about the apparent confusion. He sounded uncomfortable and appeared to be stonewalling for much of the time, but he stuck rigidly to the agreed line that once in government Labour would consider the future of air traffic control, although 'public safety must be paramount'. The interview with Smith was quite a coup, because a pager message had been sent to all shadow ministers in a desperate effort to coordinate Labour's response. According to the *Mail on Sunday*, the message was explicit: 'Urgent: do not comment on ATC'. A subsequent message said: 'Urgent: say we have never ruled out the privatisation of ATC'. The messages were described by the *Mail on Sunday* as an 'emergency plea' from Labour's 'panic-stricken' headquarters as 'Wobbly Wednesday' turned into the 'blackest day of a nightmare seven days racked by in-fighting'.

The World at One's editorial team had not been alone in believing that Labour had some explaining to do: the *Independent*'s editor, Andrew Marr, had also concluded that Wednesday morning that some of the party's policies seemed to be unravelling. His newspaper's front-page headline could hardly have been blunter: 'Tories smell blood as New Labour wobbles'. In a signed article, Marr said that for the first time since the campaign began the Conservatives were 'suddenly realising they are not dead yet'. He argued that general elections were political accelerators, speeding up argument and analysis. If Gordon Brown had not adopted Kenneth Clarke's borrowing and spending totals, Labour would not have been so vulnerable to the charge that there was a £1.5 billion tax hole in their spending plans; they would not have had to emphasise their readiness to embark on a new privatisation programme; and party spokesmen would not have contradicted themselves over selling off air traffic control. 'This,' he said, 'is how policies unravel.' Labour's habit of making policy changes by 'bounce and briefing' was regarded by Peter Riddell, political columnist for *The Times*, as the principal reason for the wobbles in their campaign. The slip-ups over privatisation and air traffic control were the result of the 'very centralised' way in which the leadership took decisions; a Labour government would find that initiatives could not be launched by 'nudge and wink'.

The warning by political commentators that Labour were dangerously exposed on some issues was reinforced when 900 firefighters in Essex decided to stage two days of strike action during the final week of the election campaign. Essex County Council said the strikers could face suspension or dismissal; the Fire Brigades Union countered by suggesting that disciplinary measures could provoke a national dispute. A fleet of Green Goddess fire engines was already on standby at the army garrison in Colchester, together with 300 men from the Airmobile Brigade. The timing of the union's decision could hardly have been more advantageous for the Conservatives. Their manifesto contained a commitment to tackle strikes in the essential services and a statement that, in order to prevent 'massive costs and inconvenience' to the public, they would legislate to 'remove legal immunity from industrial action which has disproportionate or excessive effect'. If the Fire Brigades Union was prepared to catapult its dispute to the front of the election campaign, Michael Heseltine was only too ready to respond, and he condemned the Essex strikes out of hand. 'We are not prepared to allow the British public to be put to the dramatic and dangerous inconvenience of strikes of this sort.' When John Prescott was interviewed the next morning on *Today*, he accused the Conservatives of trying to exploit the Essex dispute for political purposes, but he also defended the right of firefighters to go on strike. His sympathies were with a householder who might need help, but workers had a right to withdraw their labour. 'That right is something that has to be recognised but dealt with so that justice can be found between the different parties. Now that's about arbitration, it's about mediation, it's about getting good agreements.'

In view of the likelihood of industrial action, I asked Heseltine at the Conservatives' news conference later that morning if he would comment on what Labour's deputy leader had said. I thought my question to the Deputy Prime Minister was pertinent and clear: 'Doesn't Mr Prescott have a point that the right to strike should be recognised if accompanied by mediation and arbitration?' But instead of answering the question, Heseltine launched a ferocious broadside against Prescott, claiming that his support for the right to withdraw labour revealed 'the true instincts of the Labour Party and of the nature of the deal' that Blair had done with the trade unions. 'The essence of the deal is that they would be given recognition rights throughout the extent of British trade and commerce, with devastating consequences as every union fights to get a toe-hold on the production process.'

As I left Central Office to walk to Labour's news conference, I knew they would be anxious to play down the threat of strike action. I had heard the previous day that Peter Mandelson and Alastair Campbell had both been complaining about the way BBC programmes were 'nitpicking' on policy issues and that BBC journalists, in their determination to show their impartiality, were said to be exploiting every slip which Labour made as a way of suggesting that the party was split or divided. Nevertheless, nothing had prepared me for the torrent of abuse which greeted me on checking in at the Millbank Tower media centre. Campbell was incandescent, verging on the incoherent, as he went on and on about my report for the 9 a.m. Radio 4 news on Prescott's remarks about the Essex dispute: 'So that's the story, then, a trade union dispute . . . That was a nice easy question you asked Heseltine, wasn't it? It was just a free hit . . . I just love the way you guys in the BBC decide what the issue is . . . John Major only has to fart to get on the news. If Blair does something positive you don't report it . . .' By now David Hill and Charlie Whelan had joined in, jabbing their fingers, denouncing me as a prat and a wanker, as Campbell continued his tirade: 'What right has the BBC to set the agenda? The *Today* programme is just a radio version of the *Daily Mail*. You think it's the BBC's job to even things up for the Tories in the hope it'll make a difference.' Peter Mandelson, who on this occasion had remained aloof from the fray, gave me a supercilious look as he walked by, and, with a majestic sweep of his hand, tried to be as dismissive as he could about my reporting. 'So you've done it again, have you? You and the unions. The third world war would break out and you'd ask a question about the unions.'

My response on such occasions was always to try to get down on paper, as quickly as I could, the fullest possible account of the spin doctors' comments and complaints, but the sight of me writing furiously in my notebook only infuriated them even more. They knew I was preparing a book on the general election campaign and my habit of squirrelling away their observations for future use had long been a source of contention. Nonetheless, I knew I served a useful purpose, rather like a lightning conductor, because they had to find some way to vent their fury about the BBC and I think they hoped their practice of putting me firmly in my place would serve as a reminder to other BBC journalists of the dangers in stepping out of line. Occasionally, other political correspondents would look on in amazement at the public vilification of a fellow journalist. On this occasion Stephen Castle, political editor of the *Independent on Sunday*, had stood open-mouthed as Campbell berated me, interjecting rather hesitantly at one point to suggest that Blair's press secretary was engaging in 'rather crude browbeating of the BBC'. I understood the reasons for Campbell's anger and the sense of frustration he must have felt when stories got out of his control and were developed and analysed by various BBC news bulletins and programmes. Even so, I did think he demeaned himself by being unnecessarily abusive and I was often tempted to say he should have thought back to the days when he was the *Daily Mirror*'s political editor and then a columnist on *Today*. Although he was always proud to parade himself as a political propagandist, and did in my opinion write some pretty outrageous stories, he was at the time, as far as I could see, always treated courteously by Conservative MPs and press officers, who respected the freedom of journalists to adopt a partisan position if that was what their paper wanted. The BBC, which he was now so ready to lambast, had also played a part in Campbell's rise to prominence as a political commentator, because he had been provided with numerous broadcasting assignments, which had ranged over the years from presenting *The Week in Westminster* to giving the morning newspaper review on *Breakfast News*.

After the intemperate dressing-down he had given me that morning, Campbell must have realised he had made something of a fool of himself because he rang me that afternoon for a point-by-point discussion about his dissatisfaction with my reporting of the Essex firefighters' dispute. Campbell was so single-minded that nothing deflected him from the task in hand, which on this occasion, as he saw it, was to persuade the BBC to drop all mention of the firefighters' strike action. I explained that as Prescott had outlined Labour's approach to the dispute on *Today*, I considered that on grounds of news judgement it was right and proper to ask Heseltine for his reaction. Campbell would have none of it: 'Will you accept that the only reason Labour and the unions are a story is because you raised the question at the Conservatives' news conference? You knew your question was a free hit for Heseltine . . . Your job is to cover the general election, not to set the BBC's agenda . . . Labour's positive stories are not getting covered on the BBC, but according to the BBC our policy on air traffic control is a story, because that is damaging to Labour, just as the BBC thought Scottish devolution was damaging to Labour the week before.' As there seemed no way of curtailing the conversation, I realised that my only option was to turn the tables and put the frighteners on Campbell himself for a change. I asked if he could perhaps explain why, when Prescott had been interviewed on *Today* that morning, he had not mentioned the policy which the shadow employment minister, Stephen Byers, had enunciated at the TUC conference the previous September, that a future Labour government could not rule out the possibility of legislation to impose compulsory arbitration and the withdrawal of the right to strike in essential services. As the deputy leader had not referred to this, and as this was relevant to the Essex dispute, I asked if this in any way indicated yet another policy shift by Labour. Campbell paused for a moment and, having realised I had a point, terminated the conversation. However, he rang back triumphantly later that afternoon with a sarcastic apology about Tony Blair's failure to meet firefighters who were involved in the dispute when he visited Ilford, on the London–Essex border. Blair went there to unveil a memorial to a police constable who was shot and killed on duty when answering an emergency call. According to Campbell, the BBC correspondent, Jeremy Vine, had enquired if Blair was by any chance meeting firefighters that day as well as police officers. 'Sadly, we were unable to line up any firemen to meet Tony today, so I'm afraid the BBC has failed. Sorry, there won't be any shots of Blair with firemen for tonight's news.'

Labour's paranoia about stories linking the party to union disputes, and John Prescott's annoyance at the way the BBC had reported his support for the right of the fire crews to take strike action, were graphically illustrated when film of an interview he had given in Manchester was fed into the BBC's studios at Millbank. I had realised that something was afoot after receiving a call from Prescott's press officer, Jeff Postlewaite. He was on a train, returning to London with Prescott, and demanded a full explanation of the 'outrageous story' which I had done for Radio 4 that morning. I told him that in my report for the 9 a.m. news bulletin I had used the answer which Prescott gave in his *Today* interview, when he had said that the right of the firefighters to withdraw their labour had to be recognised but that he hoped the dispute could go to arbitration. Postlewaite listened in silence and made no further comment. Half an hour later we received the feed of an interview which Prescott had given to a BBC television reporter before leaving Manchester, and on watching it I could see instantly why Postlewaite was so agitated. Either Prescott had realised himself that he must avoid repeating his defence of the firefighters' right to strike, or perhaps that was what he had been advised to do after his remarks on *Today*, because when asked about the dispute he fluffed his answer.

The interview had been filmed close to where work was under way to repair the damage caused by the IRA bomb explosion in Manchester's shopping centre in June 1996. Prescott had been shown the reconstruction that morning and he had tried to link this in with his answer, but came unstuck: 'Of course we don't want to see a strike. A lot of talk is going on and firemen don't want the strike. There was a terrible tragedy here twelve months ago and the people who went in to rescue the people were the fire services, the ambulance crews, the emergency services and the police. We don't want party political bickering about trades unions but getting a settlement to those matters. That's already under way and I don't want to exploit these difficulties . . . ' At this point Prescott lost his thread completely and said: 'Oh shit.' He sighed and was obviously so distraught at making a mess of his answer that he threw his head down in despair, moving so violently that he completely disappeared out of shot. The reporter could be heard off camera asking if he was all right and reassuring him that the answer could be recorded again. I knew from my own experience that Prescott was often unhappy with the first few takes of an answer during a pre-recorded interview and regularly asked if it could be filmed again. He was usually so good-humoured, and tended to be so apologetic about his syntax, that interviewers and television crews kept on filming until he was happy with his answer, and, as happened with the Manchester interview, I knew of no attempt ever being made to broadcast replies which Prescott was dissatisfied with or to supply them as out-takes to comedy programmes which poked fun at public figures. Not every politician was treated so kindly, and there have been countless examples over the years of gaffes or other answers which interviewees were unhappy about being transmitted. On this occasion I took a note of Prescott's stumble because I thought it indicated the extreme sensitivity of Labour's spin doctors at the merest hint of support for the firefighters' dispute.

Postlewaite was a doughty defender of Prescott's interests and was frequently on the phone seeking to promote the deputy leader's speeches or to cover his back if journalists picked up gossip about him slipping up in public. There was a fair amount of the latter to do, for Prescott himself was so mischievous that he often could not help ruffling feathers. For example, when walking out of the Millbank studios one afternoon three months before the election, he passed Kenneth Clarke on the stairs. Clarke's arrival was being filmed and as Prescott walked by he challenged the Chancellor over the unemployment figures; but Clarke kept going and told Prescott to drop him a note about it. Prescott then turned round and, raising his voice, shouted after Clarke: 'Fiddling the unemployment figures and not telling us the truth about it. You'll be before the truth commission next. Lying all the time, Ken.' Word of Prescott's contretemps with Clarke was soon circulating in the press gallery. Anthony Teesdale, Clarke's political adviser, thought Prescott had sworn at the Chancellor, but nothing to that effect could be heard on the tape. Postlewaite was so determined to make sure of his facts that he spoke personally both to the producer, Tim Jones, and to the cameraman, Dave Longstaff. Prescott's determination to speak his mind could make interviewing him a rather hazardous assignment, because arguments could develop over which was the most appropriate answer to use in news bulletins. I was asked to interview him to get Labour's reaction to the resignation of the Paymaster-General, David Willetts, who had been criticised by the Select Committee on Standards and Privileges over the truthfulness of his evidence in the cash-for-questions investigation. Prescott said he thought Willetts should think of resigning as an MP as well as a minister. As this reply went further than Labour's official position I asked the question again, but he gave me the same answer and it was used in the *Six o'Clock News*. After David Hill complained about a BBC headline based on Prescott's answer, claiming that it was inaccurate because the party was not calling for Willetts' resignation as an MP, Postlewaite implored the newsroom to use an earlier answer from the interview.

Prescott's long service as an official of the National Union of Seamen meant he was popular within the union movement, but he realised that as deputy leader of the party he had to approach labour issues with caution because of the importance which would be attached to his remarks. He regarded me with suspicion as he knew of my interest in union affairs and if he was in a remote studio, having to be interviewed down the line, and heard me asking the questions he would pass some comment to the effect that I was the 'voice of trouble'. I think my presence probably did not help his syntax because in one notable encounter, shortly after his clash with Kenneth Clarke, I had to ask him to respond to unexpected support for Labour's policy on a national minimum wage from the former Conservative Prime Minister, Sir Edward Heath. Prescott kept referring to him as 'Sir Heath' and it was not until after half a dozen attempts and an 'oh shit' that he finally mastered his soundbite. Nevertheless, the abounding enthusiasm of Labour's deputy leader, and his ability to reassure traditional Labour supporters about the strength of Tony Blair's commitments, proved invaluable to the party during the election campaign as he criss-crossed the country in a specially adapted coach dubbed the Prescott Express. In a way he probably found it a blessing in disguise to be spending so much time away from the Millbank Tower media centre, because union stories were a recurring source of annoyance among the spin doctors, as was only too evident with Labour's extended moan about the BBC's coverage becoming front-page news. As far as the BBC's political correspondents were concerned the fifth week of the campaign could not have got off to a worse start, with all three of the Radio 4 early news bulletins on Sunday provoking complaints.

The agenda for the annual conference of the Scottish TUC had been published that morning, and among the resolutions were demands for the renationalisation of the railways and for the preparation of a blacklist of companies which failed to honour the minimum wage. Although reference to the Scottish TUC formed only part of that morning's political report, Peter Mandelson rang to complain after the 7 a.m. bulletin, accusing the BBC of following a Tory news agenda in having referred to it; Alastair Campbell reiterated Labour's complaint after the 8 a.m. bulletin, arguing that the proceedings of the Scottish TUC did not represent political news; and Charlie Whelan followed up with a call after the 9 a.m. news, insisting that the BBC was reporting the wrong story. Campbell also made a point of making a separate call to the newsroom of BBC television, but was told there was no point in him making a complaint because there had been only a short news summary that morning and the affairs of the Scottish TUC had not even been mentioned.

That afternoon Labour's dissatisfaction with the BBC's coverage became public knowledge and it was clear that a concerted move was under way to force not only the BBC but other broadcasting organisations to be more positive in reporting Tony Blair's campaign. Blair used a speech at Milton Keynes, unveiling a series of new posters which featured Labour's five election pledges, to try to break free from what he said was media cynicism and the Conservatives' negative strategy. He was not surprised that the television news ratings had been on the slide since the start of the campaign. 'You watch the news every night and it is tit for tat. They knock us, we knock them. What this campaign should be about are the things that are really concerning people in this country, not just one set of politicians knocking another set of politicians . . . If we can break through this news blackout on vision and conviction in this election and get through to the British people what we can actually do for them, then we can given them a sense of hope for the future.'

In a briefing for journalists after this speech, Campbell insisted that Blair was not trying to make a gratuitous attack on the BBC and Labour acknowledged that the Representation of the People Act might be partly to blame for the way television coverage was producing voter apathy. But Campbell felt that as a result of the Corporation's determination to observe the Act, and give the parties equitably divided amounts of air time, the resulting output consisted mainly of Tory criticism of Labour and Labour's subsequent rebuttals. 'People want to hear about the issues and Tony feels very strongly that we have to start gripping this election by the scruff of the neck and shaking people out of media-inspired cynicism. We do that by Tony being positive, positive, positive, every time the Tories are negative, negative, negative.' Campbell's remarks were widely reported, as was his advice to Carole Walker, a BBC correspondent assigned to cover Blair's campaign tour, that the party would prefer it if the BBC broadcast separate news packages examining the rival policies of Labour and the Conservatives. 'We don't even mind if you give them more time than us; we are not stop-watch crazy.' Newspaper journalists came up with different interpretations of Labour's motives. Steve Boggan, writing in the *Independent*, said that Blair and Campbell considered the BBC was being 'too fair' in allowing politicians to make negative jibes at each other, but Philip Webster, political editor of *The Times*, said the 'dramatic shift' in Labour's approach had been signalled to counter damaging Conservative attacks on 'alleged Labour U-turns on privatisation, the unions and devolution'. Peter Mandelson gave Blair's argument a further push in a signed article in the *Guardian* in which he said 60 per cent of the public viewed the campaign negatively and were turning away from broadcasts which they saw as a 'daily dogfight between the parties'. He thought there were two elections going on: 'the media bore which few are taking notice of, and the real election with people making up their mind on their experiences and their impressions, especially of the two main party leaders . . . The broadcasters' simplistic tit-for-tat coverage is playing into Tory hands. John Major's maxim for this election is if you can't beat them, bring them down to your level.'

Having studied Mandelson's article, and having seen the wide coverage in the newspapers of Blair's observations on the BBC's coverage of the election, I naturally expected that Labour would have laid on a positive story for their news conference that morning. However, on arriving at the media centre I was handed a clutch of press releases all attacking the Conservatives. Education was the main theme of the day and the shadow education secretary, David Blunkett, outlined a four-point challenge to Major in which he attacked the Tories for their 'complete failure' to raise classroom standards. We were all supplied with a dossier listing the government's shortcomings, entitled 'You can't trust the Tories with our schools'. The two other news releases listed the Conservatives' failures to represent the fishing industry and 'Tory broken promises on defence'. When I asked David Hill what had happened to the positive campaigning which Blair had promised he said the BBC obviously had difficulty understanding the difference between a negative campaign and an attacking campaign. 'Obviously we are still going to attack the Conservatives on their record but we are not going to abuse individual Tories in an unpleasant way. What we want to expose is the inadequacy of Major's record.' Charlie Whelan could see I was still puzzled. He insisted there was a difference between attacking the Tories and campaigning against them in a negative way. 'All our focus groups are showing that people don't like the way the Tories are attacking Blair for being "phoney Tony". So we're not going in for tit for tat campaigning, abusing personalities, but of course we're still going to attack the Tories' record. We had a go at the BBC because you're following the tit for tat agenda and that's why the BBC's ratings have fallen but ITN's haven't.'

I had forced Hill and Whelan to try to explain the difference between a negative and an attacking campaign out of sheer devilment, knowing full well that their tactics were nothing like as sophisticated as they were trying to pretend. Their plan was to use the news conference in London, and their press releases, to get across their negative attack while ensuring that Blair could be shown in an entirely positive light later that morning when he appeared in Birmingham and delivered a speech setting out Labour's 'twenty-one steps to better education in the twenty-first century'. Mandelson must have realised I had my pencil and notebook at the ready when I stopped and asked him if he could brief me on the significance of Blair's speech. He put on a show of mock surprise: 'That is the first time in your life that you have ever asked me a positive question.' He then made a point of ostentatiously calling over, in my presence, one of Blair's press officers, Tim Allan, in order to give him fresh instructions on what to say to the newspapers about the television coverage: 'Tim, in your briefings yesterday, you should have been critical of ITN as well as the BBC. You know, you were at fault in your briefings. You shouldn't just have criticised the BBC.' In *The Times* next morning, Philip Webster was in no doubt that it was critical news coverage which had prompted Labour's attack on media cynicism. 'The truth was that the aim was to up the tempo as far as Blair was concerned. And the fact that Blair had a long-planned speech in Birmingham on education was the perfect springboard.'

The Conservatives tried to take advantage of the debate over negative campaigning to press home their charge that Labour were always accusing

Major of lying and that Blair had authorised the 'most negative campaigning' of all the parties. Central Office supplied journalists with a long list of occasions when Blair and his shadow ministers had accused Major and the 'Tory lie machine' of dishonesty, two-faced betrayals and lie after lie. But, as so often seemed to be the case during the campaign, the Conservatives' attempts at rebuttal had no real impact and sank without trace. In comparison with Labour, their efforts to monitor and challenge the broadcasters were still sporadic and ineffective. No sooner had they developed a line of attack, begun to coordinate their news coverage and started to see it through to a point where it was beginning to damage Labour, than they were blown off course by yet another diversion.

If problems over the trade unions had caused Blair the odd bit of bother, they were as nothing when set against the continuing convulsions which the Prime Minister was having to contend with over Tory divisions on Europe. Major began the fifth week of the campaign in Newlyn, meeting Cornish fishermen, a visit timed to coincide with a meeting in Luxembourg at which the British fisheries minister, Tony Baldry, opposed proposals for a 30 per cent reduction in European catches – and one which was eventually to trigger a decisive change of direction in the Conservatives' election strategy. After a tour of the fish market and a meeting with local trawler skippers, he told reporters that unless there was a deal to stop foreign-owned boats buying up British fish quotas, the government would block progress at the European Union intergovernmental summit to be held in Amsterdam six weeks after the election. No Conservative news conference was complete without questions on a federal Europe and monetary union, and the Prime Minister reiterated the Conservatives' pledge to hold a referendum if the Cabinet and Parliament decided that Britain should join a single European currency. Major's next assignment was an interview with Radio 5 Live, and here he said that he was confident the government's wait-and-see position on the single currency would be supported by every Conservative candidate, even if ultimately they ended up opposing monetary union. 'All our candidates agree that we must negotiate and decide and that we are not going down the route of a federal Europe, although some of them have reached conclusions as to what they think should happen at the end of all the discussions.'

'Negotiate and decide' was the formula which candidates were expected to embrace when writing their personal election manifestos; but Tory Euro-sceptics had made threatening noises long before the start of the campaign about their determination to express outright opposition to a single currency. Many of them felt they were under tremendous pressure to be more forthright, especially if they were standing in marginal constituencies, because of the threat they faced from the candidates of the Referendum Party and its far less well-endowed rival, the UK Independence Party. Both groups were highly critical of the Maastricht Treaty and each had attracted support from staunch opponents of monetary union. The Referendum Party was launched in the summer of 1995 by the billionaire financier Sir James Goldsmith and, with an almost limitless supply of funds from his personal fortune, undertook repeated advertising campaigns in support of its demand for a referendum on whether Britain should join a federal Europe or return to a common trading market within an association of sovereign nations. Complete withdrawal from the European Union was advocated by the UK Independence Party, which said its sole objective was to prevent Britain becoming a 'province of a bureaucratic European superstate'. The UKIP was founded in 1993 by Dr Alan Sked, a history lecturer at the London School of Economics. It fielded twenty-four candidates in the 1994 elections to the European Parliament, gaining an average share of the vote of 3.3 per cent. Between them, the two new parties looked like securing enough votes to threaten sitting Conservatives in constituencies which were held by majorities of a few thousand votes or less.

The first member of the government to breach the wait-and-see formula and express her opposition to monetary union was the junior agriculture minister, Angela Browning, who faced a Referendum Party candidate in her constituency of Tiverton and Honiton. The week before the Prime Minister's visit to Newlyn, she published an election newsletter setting out her concerns over a single currency. Her principal objection was that Britain would have to hand over its gold and foreign currency reserves to a central bank in Frankfurt; that would result in tax and interest rates being determined in Europe; and that would mean the 'end of sovereignty of the nation state', a move which she could not support. After reporters had spent much of the day chasing her round her constituency, Mrs Browning finally made a statement outside her party headquarters in Exeter. She insisted she was not out of step because she agreed Britain should keep its options open. 'I don't feel that what I have said has been at all incompatible with what the Conservative Party has said.' However, at the start of the campaign John Major had declared that it would be a 'complete fantasy' to suggest that any minister would contradict the statement made in the manifesto that it was in Britain's 'national interest to keep our options open to take a decision on a single currency when all the facts are before us'. He was utterly confident that in their individual election addresses ministers would 'precisely mirror' the national manifesto. Once news reports emerged that Mrs Browning had gone well beyond the neutral phraseology of 'negotiate and decide', Major did his best to smooth over any differences. 'She makes it clear that she wouldn't agree to a transfer of national sovereignty over tax and spend policies. Well, let me make it absolutely clear, neither would I, neither would the government.'

As journalists gathered round Central Office staff after the Conservatives' news conference, Danny Finkelstein tried to play down the significance of the leaflet. 'We knew this story about the election addresses was coming, but the way it's come out isn't too damaging. Labour would have liked it to emerge in a much more dangerous way, later in the campaign.' However, Mrs Browning's departure from the tight wording of the manifesto opened the floodgates to other dissenting voices and the Tory Euro-sceptics were soon having a field day. Sir Peter Tapsell, fighting Louth and Horncastle, promptly supported Mrs Browning's contention that if Britain joined a single currency it would cease to be an independent nation, and he could hardly have been any more explicit in his own election leaflet: 'I give you this pledge: I shall never vote to join a single European currency.' By the end of the day Lord Tebbit was predicting that 200 Conservative candidates would publish election addresses pledging they could not support a single currency.

Labour derided Major's failure to show leadership. Gordon Brown said Conservative candidates seemed to be saying what they liked. 'They are now a disorganised rabble, breaking apart with dozens of separate manifestos.' In order to keep the story in the news and cause Major maximum embarrassment, Labour's media centre immediately began collecting and scrutinising Tory election literature from constituencies all over the country. By that weekend Labour's press officers had compiled a list of fifty-five Conservative candidates whose election addresses showed they were opposed to a single currency. Nevertheless, by the time the Prime Minister met Cornish fishermen the following Monday, his advisers thought they had succeeded in containing the controversy because the leaflets appeared to be coming from well-known Euro-sceptics whose views were no surprise. Charles Lewington believed Major's tough words on fishing quotas would help unite the party, and was annoyed that they had not been given much more prominence on the *One o'Clock News*; he rang in to complain, saying he hoped later bulletins would reflect the 'brilliance' of the position Major had outlined.

The optimism of Tory strategists was short-lived. That afternoon a television crew from *Newsnight*, which had been filming in the Mitcham and Morden constituency of Dame Angela Rumbold, obtained a copy of her election address, in which she too declared her opposition to a single currency. Dame Angela, a party vice-chairman, who faced candidates from both the Referendum and UK Independence parties, was determined to speak her mind. 'I tell my electorate what I think about everything else, surely I should do that on Europe . . . I will be calling for a "no" vote. I will not vote for it.' At his news conference next morning, Major rallied to Dame Angela's defence, brushing aside questions from reporters who asked if she would be disciplined or removed from the vice-chairmanship of the party. 'She's a backbencher, she's not a member of the government. She is entitled to express her views . . . I expect ministers to support the Conservative manifesto and make it clear they support the manifesto.'

Major had effectively boxed himself in, because while he was defending the right of candidates to have their say, he was also making it abundantly clear that members of the government were bound by collective responsibility and would be sacked if they stepped out of line. Again Danny Finkelstein assured me Central Office was relaxed. 'We think we're handling this the right way. We're pretty confident no more ministers will break ranks.' Despite his calm words, however, I knew Finkelstein was trying to make the best of a bad job, because party officials had shown great anxiety that morning. Charles Lewington had complained about the way BBC news bulletins were leading on Dame Angela's defiance and the Home Secretary, Michael Howard, had suggested to *Today* that, rather than trying to manufacture a Tory split, the programme should be reporting the controversy over the way Britain had been forced to pay £250,000 to treat a Brazilian who was suffering from AIDS but who was too sick to be deported. But the Euro-sceptics had seized both the initiative and the news agenda. They had strong backing from the *Daily Mail*, which that morning began publishing a roll of honour of those Tory candidates who were prepared to 'stand up to be counted in the Battle for Britain' by declaring 'loud and clear' that they would not surrender the pound. 'The *Mail* salutes them . . . The conspiracy of silence on Europe is being well and truly shattered . . . They are ensuring that the most momentous challenge to this nation's independence since the end of the war will not go by default.' And Major faced further difficulties on Europe. The stand which Britain had taken the previous day in opposing a further cut in the fish catch had failed to win over other fisheries ministers, who ended their two-day meeting by imposing significant quota reductions. Tony Blair accused the Prime Minister of having talked tough, but getting nothing done. 'Mind you, Mickey Mouse would get a better deal than this lot.'

Continuing efforts were made during the day by Central Office to try to divert attention away from their problems on Europe, but the Tory party's high command was powerless to control events and, more alarmingly, appeared to lack any effective means of two-way communication with their own candidates, let alone ministers: hour by hour, the news organisations, aided and abetted by Labour's media centre, were discovering fresh examples of dissent in Conservative election literature. *Newsnight* notched up another coup that evening when it revealed that the junior health minister, John Horam, had published an election leaflet saying that he was 'opposed to the Euro replacing the pound sterling'; before the evening was out, he was followed by James Paice, an education and employment minister, who said a single currency would lead inexorably to political union, for which Britain was not ready. David Maclean, a Home Office minister, was named in the *Sun* next morning as the third member of the government to have challenged the wait-and-see policy.

Maclean denied he had breached government policy and he was supported in this by the party leadership. Central Office told journalists that Horam and Paice would not be sacked because they had subsequently indicated their full support for the government's policy. The two ministers acknowledged the lack of clarity in their election literature. Horam said he supported the government's position of negotiate and decide, otherwise he would not be in the government and 'could not expect to be in it, in the future'. Paice was equally apologetic, saying that upon reflection he should have made his support 'crystal clear'. *Newsnight* tried unsuccessfully to obtain Kenneth Clarke's reaction to the rash of ministerial dissent but the Chancellor, who was opening an office block in Nottingham, kept walking away when asked questions by the programme's political correspondent, Mark Mardell. Clarke appeared to enjoy the chase and showed by his power of repartee the ease with which he could extricate himself from a difficult doorstep encounter. 'This is quite the silliest attempt to hold an interview which even *Newsnight* have tried for some considerable time . . . I am opening an office block.' Next morning the Foreign Secretary, Malcolm Rifkind, did not escape quite so easily from a spat on *Today*. When John Humphrys said the government's explanation for allowing Horam and Paice to keep their jobs was like something out of 'Humpty Dumpty', Rifkind blamed journalists for misrepresenting the ministers' remarks and accused Humphrys of believing it was his job as a *Today* presenter to take remarks out of context. 'I think Humpty Dumpty would be proud of you, Mr Humphrys, you live in a fantasy land.'

As was only to be expected, with the story hotting up so quickly, there was a good turnout at the Conservatives' news conference that morning but journalists had no inkling of the surprise Major had in store for them. We had been expecting the Prime Minister to take full advantage of newly released figures for unemployment and the public sector borrowing requirement, which both showed further falls, but he passed over the statistics in a couple of sentences and then, with no warning and without notes, launched himself into a passionate justification of the way he was meeting the challenge posed by monetary union. In the time he had been in politics, he said, there had been no issue of such magnitude, nor one that had been so woefully misunderstood. If a single currency was successful and it did deliver a zone of low inflation across Europe, it could improve living standards immeasurably; nevertheless, after the way the European exchange rate mechanism fell apart and caused immense damage, he had to be cautious. 'But can anybody honestly put their hand on their heart and say they know for certain what the outcome would be if we were to decide now, precipitately without the details, that never in any circumstances were we going to decide to enter a European currency? . . . I'm often told it would be a great advantage if I would rule the whole thing out or rule the whole thing in; it would be splendidly decisive, they say. So splendidly decisive you would send a British Prime Minister naked into that conference chamber . . . I will negotiate in the interests of the United Kingdom as a whole, not in the convenient party political interests of the Conservative Party. If that's unhappy politically for some, then I regret that. I have to answer to my conscience and my nation and history for what I actually decide to do . . . And I'm going to keep to the position of negotiate and decide, in the interests of the British nation, because, rightly or wrongly, only in that fashion do I judge I can get the best deal for the British nation . . . But don't ask me to expose every aspect of my negotiating hand now, convenient though it may be for some . . . Whether you agree with me, disagree with me, like me or loathe me, don't bind my hands when I am negotiating on behalf of the British nation.'

Major seemed to be electrified by his own words, holding up his hands and gripping them together to emphasise his point about needing the freedom to negotiate. Few of his news conferences had been so powerful and, after so many setbacks in their campaign, party officials seemed genuinely impressed by his heartfelt defence of the wait-and-see strategy. Journalists crowded round the Tory spin doctors to hear their explanation of what had prompted the Prime Minister's eloquent defence of the government's negotiating position – and the crushing rebuke which he had delivered to the two ministers who had expressed their personal opinions. Major said Horam and Paice had been foolish and he intended to make it absolutely clear to members of the next government that they would be bound by collective responsibility. Danny Finkelstein thought Major was right to have retained the two ministers and then to have seized the opportunity to come out fighting, turning the election campaign on to what for the Prime Minister was strong territory. 'The Conservatives will be the net gainers from this because no one could see a brilliant performance like that from Major without realising he is the best man to negotiate for this country. Major has the power of being in a position to negotiate with our allies whereas Blair's only position is one of not wanting to fall out with the *Sun*.' Charles Lewington agreed that Major was right to confront a federal Europe and a single currency head-on. 'All Blair will do is trot out his soundbites and silence the rest of his party.' David Willetts believed that by setting out his stall as a negotiator the Prime Minister had shown he was closer to the instincts of middle England than Blair. From what I could gather there was no doubt Major believed that if he could demonstrate to the voters that the Conservatives were in a better position than Labour to protect Britain's interests in Europe, then there was still a chance they could win the election. At his meeting with fishermen in Cornwall he had been concerned to find out how few people were aware of the Conservatives' promise of a referendum on a single currency and he intended to do all he could to reinforce that pledge.

Immediately after the news conference Major recorded a five-minute party election broadcast. He was so fired up that he spoke off the cuff and did three takes, straight to camera. The election broadcast which had been due to be shown that evening was scrapped. Sheila Gunn, who served as Major's personal press officer during the campaign, said events moved quickly once he was told the previous evening that Horam and Paice had defied the government's line on negotiate and decide. 'What happened was that John Major thought about it long and hard overnight. Then he came into our morning pre-meeting at Central Office, which was an hour before the news conference, and said he wanted to go hard on the single currency. It was his decision. He thought the unemployment figures would be overshadowed anyway by the fuss over Horam and Paice and he felt that he had to tackle Europe straight away.' The language and delivery in the election broadcast were more conversational than at the news conference but he nevertheless tried to inject the same fervour in outlining his response to what he regarded as the defining issue on the doorstep. 'Everybody in this country who plays cards would never put their cards face up on the table and then expect to win the game . . . There has been no matter like this in peacetime, in the living political memory of anyone. This is of such importance that in those circumstances, there would be a referendum . . . open to every adult in the country . . . I will not take Britain into a single currency. Only the British nation can do that. Upon that, you may be certain.'

Next morning's newspapers were divided in their response. The *Daily Mail* considered the Prime Minister had bowed to overwhelming party pressure and made his 'most dramatic personal pledge yet in defence of the pound', but the *Sun* claimed Major's emergency appeal to voters had failed to stop three more ministers defying him. The verdict of the *Financial Times* was that it was a huge gamble to put Europe at the centre of the Conservatives' campaign and the *Guardian* took the view that Major's eleventh-hour bid to stamp his authority on his strife-torn party looked 'doomed to failure in the face of renewed Euro-sceptic defiance'. One of the three additional members of the government named by the *Sun* as having expressed opposition to a single currency was the education and employment minister Eric Forth, whose election leaflet indicated that he could not accept any further transfer of power from Britain to Europe. Central Office, anxious to minimise reports of continuing dissent, denied this constituted a breach of collective responsibility, although Forth said he stood by his constituency literature. 'I've not heard from the Prime Minister. He's far too busy to look at what we're all saying in our election material.'

Repeated attempts were made to talk up the virtue of allowing candidates the freedom to express their reservations about monetary union. The former transport minister, Steven Norris, who was not seeking re-election but was assisting the campaign team in London and the south-east, told me he believed a relaxed attitude would help the Conservatives. 'If our candidates are allowed to speak their mind on

Europe, and express their own views, it will strike a chord with voters because we can compare it with Labour's Stalinist and scripted approach.' After I explained in an interview on *Today* what Norris and the other Tory strategists were thinking, Peter Mandelson told me he thought my broadcast was a party political for the Conservatives. 'Of course the Tories are trying to strike a note with the public, but the clear view out there in the country is that while people think Major is a decent man, they don't admire him and he's being hacked to bits by his lunatic party. What the Conservatives are trying to do is lift themselves out of the mire in an attempt to outflank Labour. We anticipated this would happen, which is why we've been stressing a negative tone towards the single currency from the outset of our campaign and why Labour's commitment to a referendum is now being put up in headlights.' Alastair Campbell thought Major's tactic of not sacking the two ministers and making a personal appeal to the country had not been a total disaster. 'To be fair, he did make the best of a bad job.' Tony Blair told Labour's morning news conference that he could not believe the Conservatives were still falling apart over Europe less than two weeks from polling day. 'I do understand why the news media have an occasional outbreak of generosity towards the Tories, but if Labour was tearing itself to pieces like the Conservatives, my flesh would be hanging in strips off the walls.'

After hearing how Labour were reacting to the Prime Minister's unexpected move to put the single currency at the forefront of the Conservatives' campaign, journalists set off for Central Office, not knowing there was yet another surprise development in store. Major was again in do-it-yourself mode, working out his election strategy as he went along, but this time it would take a little longer for the implications of what he had said to be understood and accepted, even by his closest Cabinet colleagues. He opened the news conference by holding up a copy of the draft agenda for the European summit to be held in Amsterdam the month after the election. Among what he described as the federalist proposals which were to be discussed were further controls on employment, an extension of qualified majority voting and a common defence plan for Europe. 'Our European partners believe in this direction . . . Our view in many respects is the polar opposite.' What suddenly caught the attention of reporters was Major's acknowledgement, in response to a question, that there was nothing to stop MPs being given a free vote on any decision reached by the Cabinet about future British membership of a single currency. 'Of course, within the government, the government are bound by collective responsibility. But there are many precedents on great constitutional matters for there to be a free vote amongst backbenchers. That's a decision to be taken nearer the time, but certainly I wouldn't rule that out. It is a possibility as far as backbenchers are concerned.'

Journalists immediately began checking the words which Major had used, trying to work out whether this was a throwaway remark or part of a calculated attempt to follow through his strategy of attempting to convince voters that he was the best-equipped leader to negotiate for Britain on monetary union. There had been no inkling beforehand that he was ready to offer what we knew would be seen by Tory Euro-sceptics as a significant concession. The former rebel MPs, from whom the Conservative whip had been withdrawn because of their failure to support the government on crucial European issues, had always said that if the Prime Minister had allowed a free vote on the Maastricht treaty he would have avoided the splits which had so damaged his party. Major was about to set off for a campaign tour in the north-west, but before he left Central Office he made it clear to journalists that the offer he had made would become government policy. Since the British people would get a free vote on entry into a single currency through a referendum, he thought it would be illogical to deny MPs a free vote, and he believed it would assist his management of the party if he could avoid having to dragoon reluctant Conservatives to vote with the government.

Labour had their response out instantly. Robin Cook, the shadow Foreign Secretary, said Major had effectively thrown in the towel and abdicated all pretence at leadership. 'He has admitted that he cannot command the support of his party and that he does not expect them to vote for government policy.' More worryingly in the immediate future, Major had apparently miscalculated in failing to appreciate the speed with which the news media would start seeking the reaction of his Cabinet colleagues. The difficulty which Major's unexpected answer created for them was all too evident when *The World at One* caught up with Kenneth Clarke, who was campaigning in the West Country. He said straight away, and in a rather pointed fashion, that he had not been consulted by Major about the possibility of a free vote but he supported the idea. 'I think it will help address the present difficulty . . . The offer of a free vote should take off all the pressure, unless people are completely driven by the editors of some right-wing newspapers to come to a firm decision now.' Having been caught off guard by Major the day before, Labour were anxious to play up any possible signs of Tory dissent, and within minutes of the Chancellor's admission that he had not been consulted about the idea of a free vote, Gordon Brown issued a statement taunting Clarke with the fact that he was no longer even being informed of vital economic decisions by a Prime Minister who was 'making policy on the hoof'.

Labour were not to know it, but the trail of misfortune which Major had laid would keep the spin doctors at Millbank Tower busy for hours. By mid-afternoon it was open house. Paddy Ashdown said that if Major was not even talking to his Chancellor then the government was in 'free fall'. Press officers at Central Office tried their hand at damage limitation but succeeded only in causing further confusion. Their line initially was that Major was only acknowledging in his answer that a free vote was an option and that, as it would eventually be a decision for the Prime Minister, he had not felt the need to consult his colleagues. But later the briefing changed and journalists were advised that if Major had been asked the same question at the news conference the day before, when he urged Tory MPs not to bind his hands, he would have announced the offer of a free vote then. Unfortunately for the Tory spin doctors, that raised another unanswered question, namely, why Major had not informed Clarke of this at the pre-meeting when he briefed ministers and his campaign team about his intention to launch his appeal to the party to support his policy of negotiate and decide. Major himself, visiting the Cheshire Oaks shopping centre in Ellesmere Port, seemed oblivious to the consternation he had caused earlier in London and, when challenged by reporters, happily turned the possibility of a free vote into a probability. 'It would really be rather odd, wouldn't it, to say you are going to have a referendum of every adult in the country on whether to join a single currency, but then say backbenchers are going to be groomed in a particular way to vote. So clearly, the same principle must apply to them.'

Major's gay abandon seemed to know no bounds. When asked why he had not consulted the Chancellor about how he would respond to the question of a free vote, he came back with a flippant answer which would cost him dearly: 'If I had replied to the questioner and said, "I'm fright-fully sorry, that's a very interesting question, but I'd better go and ask Ken Clarke or Joe Bloggs or somebody else about it before I give you an answer," that may be the way that the Labour Party operates, but it's not the way I operate.' Labour could hardly believe their good fortune. Instead of calming his party through his concession of a free vote, Major had allowed his gesture to become a source of ridicule. Gordon Brown issued yet another statement, declaring that the Prime Minister really was making policy on the hoof if he was saying that he was as likely to consult Joe Bloggs as his Chancellor on the most important economic issue facing the country. If Charles Lewington had been hoping that a hurriedly arranged radio interview with the Deputy Prime Minister might succeed in pacifying the news media he was badly mistaken, for Michael Heseltine's appearance on *PM* succeeded only in compounding a day of disastrous news management. He bridled instantly when the presenter, Charlie Lee-Potter, suggested that the Prime Minister had been making policy on the hoof. It was perfectly clear, he said, that Major was answering a question about a free vote, not giving a prepared statement. 'That's why Cabinet wasn't consulted, colleagues weren't consulted. He wasn't making a policy announcement.' But Ms Lee-Potter persisted, saying that Major's answers during the day had indicated a shift in government policy. Heseltine became quite heated: 'He's not making policy on the hoof. He has said that is a decision to be taken at the time. That's the fourth time I've told you that . . . The moment he gives you an honest answer which indicates a possibility, you turn it into a commitment as though it is in tablets of stone and you then rush round and say, "Did everybody else know this? Was everybody else consulted?" And this becomes the issue of the day. Journalists should stop trivialising.'

Part of the problem for Heseltine on this occasion was that he had been extremely late arriving. The production team at Broadcasting House had been shouting down the line, asking where he was, and as the interview was just about due to start the producer was still trying anxiously to get him seated in the studio at Millbank. I had prepared a report for the top of *PM* which went chronologically through the day's developments, pointing out that Major had already consulted the Chief Whip about a possible free vote, and it was fairly evident from Heseltine's answers to Ms Lee-Potter's questions that he had not heard an up-to-date account of what had happened, because he kept quoting from the transcript of that morning's news conference, which had of course been overtaken by events. Unlike the Home Secretary, Michael Howard, who always made a point of allowing himself enough time to listen to news reports which preceded live interviews, Heseltine frequently cut it rather fine. Only the week before there had been something of a panic in the television studio being used for the hour-long phone-in, *Election Call*. With only five minutes to go before the programme was due to go on air, Heseltine was still at Central Office, and although it was just a short walk away, he arrived with less than two minutes to spare for make-up and the necessary camera adjustments.

Heseltine clearly regretted his outburst on *PM*, because he spent the rest of the evening doing television and radio interviews and was at pains to sound far more conciliatory. In her report for *Channel Four News*, Elinor Goodman used footage of a news conference earlier in the week at which Heseltine had ruled out the possibility of a free vote, saying it was 'not an issue for the election campaign'. But, despite having a dig at Ms Goodman for 'building a great castle in the air on the most flimsy of straws', he acknowledged that the 'probability of a free vote' was the most likely course of action when the House of Commons was asked to consider the single currency. On *Newsnight* he acknowledged that the Prime Minister had been thinking for some time that a free vote might be needed, and Major confirmed this himself on *Question Time*, saying that if he had been asked, he would probably have offered it a couple of years ago.

Next morning's newspapers had a field day with their reports of the confusion surrounding Major's impromptu offer and his failure to alert his Cabinet colleagues. Over a large colour photograph of Ken Clarke drinking a pint of beer, the *Guardian* ran the headline: 'Meet Joe Bloggs, Major's Chancellor'. But the *Daily Telegraph* led its front page with reaction to the Conservatives' latest advertisement which, it said, was the 'most ferocious' onslaught on the Labour leader since the 'demon eyes' campaign. The full-page advertisement in three national newspapers showed a picture of a tiny Tony Blair sitting like a child or a ventriloquist's dummy on the knee of a large, smiling Chancellor Kohl, with the message underneath: 'Don't send a boy to do a man's job'. The inspiration for the portrayal of Blair as the puppet of the German Chancellor came from Michael Heseltine, who drew it as a rough sketch at a Tory party strategy meeting, and it was developed into an advertisement by the Conservatives' agency, M&C Saatchi. The image of a president or prime minister sitting on the knee of a rival politician had appeared before in cartoons, in both Britain and the United States, but the depiction of Blair had notable similarities with the *Spitting Image* portrayal of Sir David Steel as the puppet of the SDP leader David Owen, which had done such damage to Sir David's credibility in the 1987 general election. The advertisement infuriated pro-European Conservative MPs. Edwina Currie said that while it might provoke guffaws in Central Office the public would not approve, and she thought it was puerile for the Conservatives to be depicting Chancellor Kohl as an 'ogre of any kind'.

My reports for the Radio 4 news bulletins that morning reflected the continuing divisions within the Tory party, but nevertheless the BBC's headline, to the effect that Europe continued to dominate the campaign, provoked criticism from Peter Mandelson when I reached Labour's news conference. He said I should not have given so much prominence to a story based on a Conservative advertising campaign. 'The BBC is not entitled to say that Europe is "dominating" the campaign. How can the BBC decide that on the basis of a newspaper advertisement? It might be that crime or health are the issues which concern people most.' Mandelson's admonishment served a useful purpose because it alerted me to the line Labour intended to take in responding to the Conservatives' suggestion that Blair was not a skilled negotiator and would be at a disadvantage up against the 'immensely experienced leaders of Germany and France'. On balance, Mandelson thought an advertisement which contrasted Major's leadership qualities with Blair's suited their strategy and could only benefit Labour. Accordingly Gordon Brown, who was chairing the news conference, made six references to leadership in his first answer. It developed into a rather repetitive recitation, but we certainly got the message: 'It is a question of leadership and John Major has to explain if he makes an issue of leadership, how he has failed to show leadership in Europe. Tony Blair has shown he can lead, and has shown by his magnificent reform of the Labour Party that he can lead and get results, if the issue is one of leadership.' Reporters who kept a running total said that by the end of the news conference the shadow Chancellor had made a total of twenty-four separate references to leadership.

Along at Central Office, Major and Heseltine were enjoying the fuss generated by the advertisement, anxious to show they were the best of friends after all the confusion over the free vote. Without being prompted, the Deputy Prime Minister took up the challenge which had been made at Labour's news conference. 'Gordon Brown said this is a question of leadership.' Here Heseltine paused and pointed at the Prime Minister, before continuing: 'This guy would never let Britain down.' Major insisted their advertisement had been trying to make a serious point. Blair had indicated in advance of the Amsterdam summit that he would make concessions to the European Union on issues like the social chapter. By contrast, 'Chancellor Kohl has not surrendered his negotiating position. Kohl will be fighting for the German people. He's not said, here are my six surrenders. He's not saying, "I'm going off to Amsterdam and I have changed the red flag for the white flag and here are my surrenders, and if you don't have a seat, I'll have a knee." Blair has thrown away his position.'

Danny Finkelstein was delighted their advertisement had kept Europe in the news. 'The ad is very much Heseltine's own view of Europe, that Britain should be in there to fight for her national interest and that you should be big enough to take on other countries. So you should sit tall in your seat and if Hezza had his way Kohl would be sitting on his knee.' Finkelstein and his research team at Central Office were convinced that the way Major had dramatised the issue of Europe was working in the Conservatives' favour, despite the news media's concentration on splits within the party. 'Journalists who are writing about this election being over are wrong. It's like a football match. We may be trailing 1–0 with five minutes to go but the game's not over yet. There's unmistakable evidence out on the ground that Europe is working in our favour. It is now getting through to people that the Conservatives will hold a referendum and that we won't take Britain into a federal Europe. Our tracking groups show there's actually very little switching from Conservative to Labour and that we have raised the salience on Europe as an issue and it is positive and it is helping us connect with our core voters, which is why we're not going to close it down.' Finkelstein believed the day Major switched tactics would be seen retrospectively as the moment the campaign moved in the Conservatives' favour. 'Even if we don't win this election, people who say Major's intervention on Europe was the moment events moved against us will be wrong. We're not bananas and whatever the result of the election, I'll prove to you that far from losing a week of the campaign because of Europe, we've gained from it. The Prime Minister has told me he's no intention of leaving Europe alone. This'll go right up to polling day.'

One convulsion which Finkelstein had not bargained for when he talked up their prospects and enthused about Heseltine's doodling was the impact Major's strategy might have on the pro-European wing of the party. A majority of the fifty Tory MPs who made up the group known as the Positive Europeans had agreed that while the election campaign was under way they would observe a self-denying ordinance to avoid publicity and would refrain from responding to attacks by the Euro-sceptics. However, many of them regarded the Blair–Kohl advertisement as so offensive that they felt they had no alternative but to voice their criticism. Lord Howe, the former Foreign Secretary, told *The Times* that he was disappointed Major had 'gone against his natural instincts' in putting party before nation and running the risk of damaging the partnership with Germany that Britain would need in the future. If people were led to believe in a false antagonism with Germany, it could harm relations with

Britain's European partners. Once Lord Howe had spoken, the pro-European science minister, Ian Taylor, felt able to break his silence and told *Today* that he disliked the advertisement because it suggested that Europe was a threat to Britain. The fiercest criticism came from Sir Edward Heath, who described the image Heseltine had created as a 'pitiful piece of publicity' which encouraged anti-German feeling rather than ridiculing Blair. 'How can we hope to influence other members of the European Union when they see this sort of thing happening? I believe it was absolutely contemptible . . . We are not getting our points across as a party or on our policies. This belief that Europe is the one thing people are concerned about is wrong. The party should drop that entirely.'

Heseltine, interviewed on *The World this Weekend*, defended the advertisement and insisted his sketch was 'very complimentary' to Chancellor Kohl. He then rounded on James Cox, the programme's presenter: 'These stories which diminish the campaign are a gross insult to the British people . . . I think the way the campaign is being reported means we are sleepwalking into a disaster.'

As perhaps was only to be expected, Kenneth Clarke also became embroiled in the repercussions after the *Guardian* reported, in a follow-up story, that the Chancellor had 'let it be known' through an aide that he had not been consulted before the advertisement was published. Gordon Brown's press officer, Charlie Whelan, who had done so much throughout the campaign to cause trouble for the Chancellor, claimed that whenever he 'let it be known' that he had not been consulted it was obvious he felt he had been insulted. Clarke's explanation of why he had not been informed was that on the day the advertisement was approved he was campaigning in the High Peak constituency where there was very poor reception for mobile phones. He told the morning news conference that the advertisement, in the 'long-hallowed tradition of political caricature', made the entirely valid point that Blair was not in the first division of European statesmen. 'Helmut Kohl has been a very good friend of this country on a number of occasions. He is a formidable political figure, a great European statesman . . . Tony Blair does not bat in that league and he should not be representing Britain at major conferences.'

The image of a politician as a ventriloquist's dummy was parodied mercilessly by the cartoonists and immediately copied in an advertisement for the Referendum Party which put a tiny Blair and Major on each of Kohl's knees, twinning it with a quote from the German Chancellor to the effect that he wanted to 'make the process of European integration irreversible' within two years. Labour, too, had succeeded in injecting some humour into their campaign advertising by deploying another long-standing political symbol, the British bulldog, in a starring role in one of its party election broadcasts.

Labour's pitch for the patriotic high ground had begun with Blair's speech to the party conference the previous October. Within weeks it became strongly evident, with the Union flag appearing on party litera-ture and as part of the platform backdrop at news conferences and other events. Attempting to identify Labour with the British bulldog, a symbol long associated with Conservative Prime Ministers, was a challenge Peter Mandelson could not resist. In his view, the bulldog was a strong symbol which conveyed history and tradition, and there was no reason why Labour should not make use of it, just as they had reclaimed the Union flag which the Conservatives had 'used and abused as if they owned it'.

The broadcast featured Fitz, a fifteen-month-old pedigree. After being shown looking tired and listless to begin with, Fitz pricks up his ears as Blair talks of the way he has transformed his party, and then leaps to his feet as the Labour leader starts to explain his policy objectives on issues like law and order, health and education. Soon the dog is straining at the leash, anticipating Blair's punch-line: 'I am a British patriot and I want the best out of Europe for Britain.' Clearly convinced that Britain could do better under a Labour government, the bulldog eventually breaks free.

With his customary skill, Mandelson turned the election broadcast into something of a publicity coup. An advance showing was arranged for journalists so as to generate newspaper stories on the day of transmission. Mandelson and Fitz had a joint photo-call. A smiling spin doctor was photographed gingerly placing his hand on the back of what the *Mirror* dubbed Mandelson's 'pure-bred pedigree chum'. Jo Gibbons, one of Labour's press officers, told me the event ended up being quite a 'love-in' between her boss and the dog. Mandelson did all he could to take advantage of the British love of animals, and footage from the broadcast was supplied for use in television news bulletins. In an interview on GMTV, shots of Fitz breaking free and wandering off into the distance were floated up on to the screen as Blair described the changes which New Labour had made. Another spin-off was an article in the *Sun* under Blair's by-line which sported the headline: 'Labour will give bulldog Britain a new leash of life'. Not to be outdone, the *Evening Standard* searched its photograph library and printed pictures of Winston Churchill and Margaret Thatcher, each holding a bulldog on the lead when out campaigning.

Labour continued their smash-and-grab raid on Tory political tradition in their next election broadcast. This one was set to the music of the patriotic hymn 'Land of Hope and Glory', which the Conservatives had come to regard as their party anthem and always sang during the finale to their annual conference. In place of a voice commentary, captions on the screen put over Labour's themes. The impact of the sequence on law and order was heightened by the inclusion of footage from closed-circuit television cameras in shopping centres which showed youths snatching handbags and breaking into cars. The captions were blunt: 'Under the Tories there are 50,000 fewer nurses . . . The Tories would sell off homes for the elderly and abolish the state pension . . . VAT on heating . . . They would put VAT on other essentials like food.'

Not all the attention gained by this appropriation of patriotic resonances was favourable. The jingoistic tone of Labour's publicity caused unease in some sections of the party, and the decision to feature a bulldog gave rise to particular consternation given the use of the same symbol by the overtly racist National Front. Bernie Grant, Labour MP for Tottenham, who was born in Guyana and chaired the parliamentary Black Caucus, found it offensive because, he said, his memory of bulldogs when he was growing up was that they were 'used to keep people in their place'. Nevertheless, Labour's broadcasts undoubtedly caused a stir, and this irritated the Tory spin doctors. Danny Finkelstein was scathing: 'Mandelson thinks playing "Land of Hope and Glory" and bringing on a bulldog is clever, but Labour are just abandoning any consistency or principle. People just don't trust New Labour. Only they could come up with a dog called Fitz. What will Blair do next, turn up in a skirt and handbag and call himself Thatcher?' David Willetts was sure Labour would not dent the message that only the Conservatives could be trusted on Europe. 'We took that decision and we got Europe running as an issue. Labour aren't putting up a real bulldog against that, just an Andrex puppy, and we're offering red meat, so no wonder the news agenda is working to our advantage.'

The repeated predictions of Finkelstein and Willetts that Europe would continue to play well for the Conservatives gained a degree of credibility after an ill-judged intervention by the European Commission President, Jacques Santer, who condemned the 'unjustified and misplaced' outbursts of the Euro-sceptics. The original text of a speech he gave in the Netherlands included a scathing reference to the advertisement showing Blair on Kohl's knee, but this passage was removed from the version delivered for – it was said – diplomatic reasons. Nevertheless there was no doubt about the target of Santer's scathing attack on the voices which seemed intent on demeaning the formidable success of the European Union and scoring cheap points by caricaturing European legislation. 'Do these doom merchants want us to step backwards to a Europe only composed of simple trading arrangements?' He set out his vision of a federalist Europe which should include a new chapter on employment, to give an 'even stronger signal that the Union cares', the extension of majority voting and progressive moves to build a military capability.

The Foreign Secretary, Malcolm Rifkind, tried to use the speech to attack Labour, saying Santer's vision of Europe was 'disturbingly similar' to that of Blair, who would drag Britain down the road of deeper integration. Major believed Santer's prescription of more majority voting would trap member states in a 'vicious circle of paralysis' and that the speech was a signal to Blair to 'put the foot on the accelerator' towards a federal Europe. 'Blair accuses us of making a fetish out of isolation. It's not isolation, it's called the British national interest.'

The ease with which Santer's intervention was exploited by the Conservatives forced Labour to harden their opposition to wider use of majority voting and support for preservation of the British veto. Blair had already toughened up his language in response to Major. As early as the October 1996 party conference he had declared that under his leadership he would 'never allow this country to get isolated', but as the campaign progressed and Blair faced the Conservatives' onslaught head-on this line changed. A Labour government, he now said, was 'perfectly prepared to be isolated but we won't pursue a policy of isolation.' Nor did he mince words in responding to Santer's speech. He made it clear that he disagreed with a lot of what the European President had said. 'What Santer says, with all due respect, is neither here nor there . . . If I am elected I will represent Britain.' Taxation, defence and immigration would remain subject to the British veto and were not open to negotiation. In an article in the *Sun*, Blair was categoric: 'I will have no truck with a European superstate. If there are moves to create that dragon, I will slay it.'

For all these confident pronouncements in public, behind the scenes at Labour's media centre there was a fair degree of agitation about the effectiveness of the Conservatives' propaganda, and again the BBC was in the firing line. David Hill took issue with my report on reaction to Santer's speech, and he wanted to know why news bulletins and programmes were not putting pressure on Major to say what he meant when he talked of not ruling out extensions of qualified majority voting. 'We really are pissed off again and it gets to the heart of our long-running complaint against the BBC. You are not analysing what you should analyse. Why aren't you analysing what would happen under a fifth term of Tory government? Major says he can't rule out changes to qualified majority voting but no one in the BBC is asking him about that.' Once Hill had got his complaint off his chest, he acknowledged rather grudgingly that by hitting Europe so hard the Conservatives were having an effect. 'I agree Europe is firming up Conservative supporters but it's only among their traditional voters and the Tories are deluding themselves if they think this will have any wider impact on the electorate.' Nevertheless, party strategists in Millbank Tower were taking no chances and for the final week of the campaign Labour's pledge of 'No single currency without a referendum' was moved swiftly to the top of the list of the promises which appeared in newspaper advertisements. The undertaking to hold a referendum had not even been included in the five promises which were printed on Labour's much vaunted pledge cards, but now, as polling day approached, it was mentioned repeatedly.

Labour's spin doctors had clearly not anticipated that the Conservatives would decide to fight quite so ferociously on Europe, which by all accounts was their weakest point. The Tories had not rolled over in the face of Labour's superior campaign strategy. Instead, they had picked up the most difficult issue they faced and used it to attack their opponents. Even though it was too early say who would gain, Major had succeeded in taking control of the news agenda for at least some of the time, and as a result issues like the health service and law and order had not generated as much coverage as Labour would have liked. And yet, although the Prime Minister might have won some plaudits from the Euro-sceptics for his concession in offering a free vote on the single currency, and although he was convinced he had enhanced his credentials as a tough negotiator, there was no sign that he was doing anything other than shoring up the traditional Tory vote. As the last few days of campaigning approached, the Conservatives turned their attention increasingly to ways of appealing to the 30 per cent of voters who were said to be still undecided. For it was in their hands that the outcome of polling day rested.

7

Storming the Citadel

Polling day was only eight days away when the Conservatives heard the news they had been longing for: an ICM opinion poll suggested that Labour's previously unshakeable lead had been cut dramatically to 5 per cent. Until the publication of that survey in the *Guardian* on 23 April, the Wednesday of the last full week of the campaign, the pollsters had been pretty well unanimous in reporting little sign of any significant shift in public opinion. Labour's commanding lead over the Conservatives had seemed totally secure. While the margin varied, all the surveys had been consistent in giving Labour a lead of well into double figures, and some were indicating that the gap between the two main parties could be as high as 20 per cent. The ICM poll that Wednesday morning suggested that Labour's support had dropped by three points to 42 per cent while the Conservatives' had risen to 37 per cent, up six points on their previous figure and their highest level of the campaign. On ICM's calculations, Labour's lead had fallen from fourteen points to five.

This was startling news, because the rest of the opinion surveys had been relatively stable, showing the Conservatives stuck for weeks at around 30 per cent of the vote, while Labour were nudging up towards 50 per cent. Nevertheless, although the polls had been predicting a landslide victory for Labour since the start of the campaign, Tony Blair and the rest of the party leadership had refused consistently to believe them. They expected their lead to be reduced, perhaps quite substantially, the closer polling day came – an expectation shared by Tory strategists, who had been waiting impatiently for the gap to start narrowing. Therefore the first sign of real movement, even though it had been picked up in only one opinion poll, was pounced on with glee at Conservative Central Office.

John Major, who was campaigning in Scotland, thought that at last he might be in with a chance. The reporters who were accompanying the Prime Minister said the news cheered him up no end and that on the way to his next campaign stop in Inverness he was full of fun, cracking jokes and at one point ruffling the hair of the BBC correspondent, Jon Sopel, and tweaking the nose of his ITN colleague, Tom Bradby. But the journalists noticed Major's mood changing as the day progressed and it became clear that Labour was being proved correct in asserting that the ICM survey was a rogue poll. Three opinion surveys being prepared for publication in the newspapers next day all showed the same picture as before: Labour's share in the high forties, approaching 50 per cent, and the Conservatives stuck at around 30 per cent.

Although the initial euphoria at Central Office waned once it was obvious that there had been no change in the overall pattern, the ICM poll in the *Guardian* was regarded as a highly significant portent of what might be happening out around the country. ICM were also employed to carry out private polling for the Conservatives and, while the results of these surveys were never published, it was being suggested that they too were showing a fall in Labour's lead and that it could be down to 6 or 7 per cent. Danny Finkelstein, the Conservatives' head of research, thought highly of ICM's leading pollster, Nick Sparrow, and the Central Office strategists considered the polling data they were being supplied with justified their belief that the opinion survey for the *Guardian* was not an aberration but confirmed the shift in opinion which they were convinced was in fact taking place.

When Finkelstein expounded on his theory after the morning news conference that Wednesday I sensed that most of the journalists who were with me thought he was whistling in the wind. I had heard him make the same case before, though, and his conviction that most of the polls were wrong had brought him into conflict with Bob Worcester, chairman of MORI, who, on *Breakfast with Frost* the previous Sunday, had challenged the Tory spin doctors to publish their figures. Worcester was adamant that the polls were static and that the Conservatives' share of the vote remained constant at around 31 to 32 per cent. 'If you ask me can the Tories catch up, I'd say I don't think they have a prayer.' Worcester dismissed out of hand reports that the Conservatives' private polling was showing a shift in their direction and he considered it was time the Tory spin doctors either 'shut up or put up'. Finkelstein would not release any statistics, but he was confident they were catching up on Labour. 'I think Nick Sparrow's figures are correct. Labour know that over the last week we have been gaining ground and that our prospects have been transformed. Bob Worcester says we are facing the biggest swing against us this century, that Conservative MPs with 18,000 majorities will be swept away; well, if he thinks that he's wildly out.'

Fuelling this professed sense of optimism that the Tory vote on polling day would be far higher than the grim predictions of the pollsters was another factor which was just as difficult to quantify or verify. The Conservatives were convinced that they could rely on a high proportion of the vast reserve of undecided voters, who, once inside the privacy of a polling booth, would definitely put their cross against the Tory candidate on the ballot paper. The problem which the Conservatives faced in substantiating this thesis was the 'spiral silence' which they admitted canvassers were encountering when they tried to find out what uncommitted voters were thinking. Most journalists find that although they rarely have much trouble interpreting the headline figures in an opinion poll, the statistical detail can be fiendishly difficult to understand, and the more I tried to test out the Conservatives' contention that they would end up with most of the 'don't knows', the more complicated it got.

For a start, how many undecided voters were there? Estimates ranged from three million to four million, or more – and those figures apparently excluded the ten million or so people who did not bother to vote in the 1992 election. Clearly, for a party in deep trouble, this massive pool of potential voters presented a tantalising prospect, and in their desperation to talk up their chances as they counted off the days to 1 May, the Conservative high command floated all sorts of fanciful theories. Andrew Cooper, Finkelstein's deputy, told me that on their calculations 15 per cent of the people who would vote were undecided and another 12 per cent would not answer the question or say anything at all about their intentions. 'We're convinced the spiral of silence is much greater than in the 1992 election and that many of the people who are disinclined to give their views to pollsters and canvassers are more likely to vote Conservative than anything else. If Bob Worcester goes on predicting a landslide for Labour right up to polling day, he'll lose in spades.' Finkelstein was clearly irritated by the way political commentators were writing the Conservatives out of the race. 'We're already getting journalists speculating about a Tory leadership contest having started when there's no evidence for that, and what we're having to contend with is that when Major is on the television saying he wants to win, we have some tosser talking over him, prattling on about a leadership election. The message we want to get out is to make people realise they have a choice, and we know a lot of the undecideds are sliding our way. I am absolutely stone cold certain Bob Worcester will be looking ridiculous on the Friday after polling day.' Finkelstein's fighting talk was reinforced by Charles

Lewington, who insisted Tory party managers were in good heart. 'We think the ground is shifting all the time. We test the doubtfuls and the undecideds all the time and we think that up to 50 per cent of voters are soft, uncommitted or won't say.'

However, neither Labour nor the Liberal Democrats had detected any movement in the polls. Alastair Campbell said their figures showed no sign of a shift. The problem they had to address was the prospect of votes being wasted on Liberal Democrat or fringe party candidates and how to convince electors that the only guarantee of getting the Tories out was to vote Labour. 'We do think the Liberal Democrats have a credibility problem, because Paddy Ashdown gets into the slipstream every day of whatever is the bad story for Labour. But we think the people the Liberal Democrats have got from us, we can get back. But if the Conservatives are saying they can detect a shift because of Europe, it's bullshit. All our polls are showing that the impact of Europe is division, division and that's bad for the Tories.' The Liberal Democrats' campaign manager, Lord Holme, agreed with Labour that there was not the slightest sign of the Conservatives' share of the vote lifting off and that it was stuck at 31 per cent, or 32 per cent at the most. But he did accept the Conservatives' assessment that the number of uncommitted voters was higher than in 1992. The Liberal Democrats' estimate was that one in four were undecided and that of those who were saying which way they would vote, three out of four were soft in their intentions – in other words, still worth wooing. 'But there is one thing we are confident about: after polling day we will see a significantly larger number of Liberal Democrat MPs than at any time since the war.'

Uncertainty over the accuracy of the opinion polls, speculation about the likely size of Labour's majority, predictions for the share-out of jobs in Tony Blair's first Cabinet and forecasts for the likely line-up in a Tory leadership election – these tended to be the dominant talking points among journalists in the final week of the campaign. Politicians from the three main national parties had talked themselves to a virtual standstill on the main policy issues and the Conservatives, having decided to build the whole of their election strategy around Major, appeared to be totally bereft of ideas for putting fresh life into their final push to polling day. One surprise story, which emerged late in the afternoon of the day the *Guardian* had carried the controversial ICM poll, concerned the unexpected publication of an early version of Labour's election war book, which set out the strategy and likely battle lines for the period leading up to the start of the campaign. A copy of this document, somehow obtained by Central Office towards the end of 1996, gave the Conservatives an indication not only of the tactics which Labour intended to adopt but also an assessment of what Labour considered to be their own strengths and weaknesses. Brian Mawhinney's calculation in deciding when to release the war book to the news media seemed to have been that while it was still relevant to Labour's tactics it would be best kept under wraps, but that once the information was out of date it should be published at a moment that would cause Tony Blair the maximum embarrassment.

Labour had made two significant policy announcements that day, both designed to generate positive publicity. In the morning there had been a celebrity line-up for the launch of a four-year plan to divert £1 billion from the proceeds of the midweek national lottery draw towards projects in health and education. Blair said he wanted to make sure that 'the people's lottery met the people's priorities', and he believed their announcement would be 'as important as well as popular as any initiative taken by any political party in the course of this campaign'. An endorsement for Labour's plan to establish 'healthy living centres' was given by writer and broadcaster Dr Miriam Stoppard, and then, in another publicity coup, Anthony Minghella, director of the Oscar-winning film *The English Patient*, spoke in support of the party's proposal for a national endowment for science and the arts. The initiative on the lottery was followed in the afternoon by an undertaking from the shadow Chancellor, Gordon Brown, that if Labour were elected their pledged 3 per cent reduction in the rate of value added tax on domestic fuel would take effect in time to cut winter bills for gas and electricity.

Labour's ability to come up with announcements which had popular appeal so close to polling day was intended to provide a sharp contrast with the lack of fresh policy proposals from the government. For the Conservatives to counter by suddenly releasing copies of the war book to the news media, with no prior warning and without even holding a news conference, suggested that Mawhinney and his colleagues were frantically trying to find some way of diverting attention from Labour's proclamations and of playing on the uncertainty generated that morning by the ICM poll. Secret strategy documents are always of great fascination to journalists, and as Mawhinney toured the television and radio studios late that afternoon he played up suggestions of skulduggery, saying the war book arrived at Central Office six months ago in a 'plain brown paper envelope' and that he thought it was sent by a disenchanted Labour Party worker. The reason he gave for publishing it was to expose Labour's 'smear and scare tactics'.

In a section headed the 'Threat of another Tory term', Labour set out a strategy to warn voters that if the Conservatives were re-elected, government policy would include 'putting VAT on food' and 'paying to see a general practitioner': Mawhinney claimed this indicated that months before writing their manifesto, Labour had 'cynically decided to scare people about VAT on food'. He maintained that the cynicism revealed in the war book had been demonstrated in other ways during the campaign itself, citing as an example what he called Labour's attempt to frighten pensioners into believing their existing income would be affected by the government's plans for long-term reform of the state pension.

Mawhinney knew he was hardly likely to cause his opponents much discomfort in revealing Labour's attack strategy, because most of the campaigns were already up and running; but where he hoped he could cause more mischief was by exposing the weaknesses which were causing Blair's spin doctors most concern. This section of the war book showed that Labour believed they were weak on economic issues like interest rates, inflation and tax; issues which aroused 'fear of Labour', like the hidden left, unions and inexperience; issues affecting Labour's ability to pay for their plans and concerns about Labour's evasiveness; issues which could be said to involve the break-up of Britain, like Labour plans on devolution and Europe; and the role of Labour councils. Equally revealing were Labour's judgements on the Conservatives' strengths, which included the fact that Major was seen as being 'decent and honest' and that the Tories were considered to be stronger on patriotism, because of the way they campaigned against the break-up of the United Kingdom and European federalism. The other area of potential embarrassment was the war book's references to the target audiences which Labour felt they should address. One group who were seen as 'weak Labour identifiers' were women aged from twenty-five to forty who were nervous about a Labour government; thought Major was 'decent and honest', and were probably prone to vote Conservative on the grounds of 'better the devil you know'.

Alastair Campbell, faced with the task of trying to limit the damage which the war book's revelations might inflict on Labour's campaign, called reporters together to a briefing. He was clearly annoyed that Mawhinney had come up with a story which looked like leading the political news and overshadowing their two policy launches. He said the war book was a year old and they had already suspected the Tories had a copy of it because Major's New Year broadcast appeared to have drawn on phrases from it. 'We're quite happy for the Tories to be highlighting Labour's fears of a fifth Tory term of government and if Dr Mawhinney, in his usual sophisticated way, has helped us, then that's fine by us.' Campbell admitted that the attack strategy of suggesting the Conservatives would impose a charge for visiting a general practitioner had been dropped because it was 'not credible'. But he denied that Labour had in effect admitted 'weaknesses': what the document did, he said, was summarise the Conservatives' descriptions of Labour's failings.

The war book was prepared by the unit headed by Philip Gould, Labour's leading adviser on polling strategy, and this was the second time one of his confidential documents had been leaked at an awkward moment. A similar flurry had occurred at the 1995 party conference when the *Guardian* obtained a copy of his report entitled 'The Unfinished Revolution', which said Labour were not 'ready for government' and suggested that Blair needed to establish a 'unitary command structure' in the party. Charlie Whelan told me that Gordon Brown repeatedly told Gould that as he 'never read any of this stuff anyway' it was stupid to go on writing these reports as they kept getting leaked. Whelan considered Mawhinney had made a tactical mistake in publishing the war book late in the afternoon. 'It was a good story, but if the Tories had let it out overnight then it would have dominated the morning news conferences and that could have caused us real trouble.'

Charles Lewington acknowledged quite openly that publication of the war book had been timed to try to sabotage coverage of Labour's policy announcements. The deciding factor for Mawhinney in releasing the document was the claim made by Blair the previous weekend that the state pension was no longer safe with the Conservatives. 'This really is worrying old age pensioners, and the sheer anger which Dr Mawhinney felt over the extent to which Labour were preying on the fears of the elderly made him determined to expose Labour's lies.' Lewington was as surprised as Whelan that Gould had been so naïve as to prepare a report listing Labour's weaknesses; staff at Central Office, he said, unlike Labour, had learned from their mistakes and were careful not to commit a devastating critique of that kind to paper. Shortly before their 1994 conference, the Conservatives had been embarrassed by the leaking of what became known as the Maples memo, in which a former minister, John Maples, wrote about the inadequacy of Tory publicity and the lack of effective coordination between party and government. Lewington said the Conservatives' war book was in the form of a rolling programme, rather like a diary of events, and it certainly did not list their weaknesses. Mawhinney had taken a gamble in drawing attention so pointedly to the effectiveness of Labour's warnings about the threat which the Conservatives' plans posed to the future of the state pension. As Whelan had explained to me, Labour knew they must be hitting the Tories hard on pensions if the party chairman was prepared to admit publicly that they were rattled and, needing no further encouragement, Labour did all they could to highlight their concerns.

Blair opened his news conference next morning by emphasising what he said was the stark choice voters faced in choosing between a new government with fresh ideas and a divided country under 'the same old Tories who have got away with everything they have wanted to do'. Either side of the platform were panels listing the alternatives and setting out six threats facing the country if the Conservatives were re-elected. One of them was 'state pensions abolished'. Despite the government's categoric assurances that their reforms would apply only to people now entering the labour market and would not affect existing pensioners, Blair insisted it would mean the privatising of the old age pension. 'They say it's only for young people. Look at the small print and look at how they're going to cost it and fund it, and then ask yourself whether they're not going to do that for older people as well. And that's why we are perfectly entitled to warn people of what the Tories' pensions proposals mean.'

Labour's renewed attack on pensions provoked an outraged response from Brian Mawhinney. At a hurriedly arranged news conference the Secretary of State for Health, Stephen Dorrell, accused Blair and his 'cronies' of inventing a litany of the worst lies they could think of about the Conservatives. Dorrell said that when the government launched Basic Pension Plus in March, the Labour leader had described the proposals as 'bold' and thought they would allow the debate about pension reform to be conducted 'more sensibly'; but now Blair was whipping up fears among pensioners through a deception. 'A rabbit caught in the headlights looks positively relaxed when compared with Blair answering a question on economics. The tougher the questioning, the more he panics; the more he panics the more he lies, telling bare-faced, despicable lies.' As Dorrell was speaking a picture of Blair on the set behind him kept changing in colour, like a chameleon, from red to blue and then to purple, which was the colour Labour had started using that week on some of their promotional material. The caption at the top read 'You can't believe a word Blair says' and, to back up Dorrell's allegations, documents were handed out entitled 'Labour's purple poison' and 'The Labour lie machine', listing what were said to be Labour's lies.

The ferocity of the attack took journalists by surprise but Danny Finkelstein was unrepentant about the way it had been so sharply personalised against Blair. 'The feeling is we should go hard after Blair, leave no stone unturned, and after what he's said on pensions he'll never recover, because it's a deception.' Finkelstein said he was very angry because Labour were refusing to accept government assurances that existing pensioners and contributors were not affected by Basic Pension Plus. 'When we've made charges against Labour which have been categorically denied we've dropped them. I think we should have gone on saying Labour have made spending pledges worth £30 billion, but Labour denied it completely. I stand by that calculation but we've dropped it.' David Willetts thought Labour's pensions allegations were so manifestly bogus that they would end up rebounding on their authors, somewhat as Labour's 'Jennifer's ear' election broadcast had backfired in the 1992 election.

By any standards it had been a pretty venomous occasion, and while the row over pensions was given as the ostensible reason for the news conference, the subtext was that the Tory spin doctors were doing all they could to get pictures and soundbites into the evening news bulletins that attacked Blair for being a liar. The aim was to try to puncture the effect of a ten-minute election broadcast which was to be transmitted that evening showing the Labour leader talking informally but passionately about his beliefs and objectives.

For this broadcast Blair had been interviewed wearing an open-necked shirt and filmed in fly-on-the-wall style at the family home in Islington by the celebrated documentary maker Molly Dineen, whose award-winning films included *Home from the Hill* and *The Ark*. Footage included shots of Blair in the kitchen making tea and sitting at the table having a meal, chatting to his children. At one point he was filmed standing by the refrigerator talking about 'all the rubbish' politicians have to get up to, and as he spoke this image was mixed with a shot of him signing a Labour poster as a publicity stunt. As a teenager, he said, he had never wanted to enter politics. 'I thought politicians were complete pains in the backsides.'

Labour hoped this portrayal would counter the 'phoney Tony' jibes of the Tories and help to convince the public that once in No. 10 Downing Street Blair would, as he said, act as a 'galvanising force' in driving through change. Journalists dubbed it 'Blair: The Home Movie' as its raw presentation was in complete contrast to Hugh Hudson's 'Kinnock: The Movie', a glossily produced election broadcast for the 1987 general election, which showed Neil and Glenys Kinnock walking along a cliff top to the strains of Brahms. Labour were flattered when in the 1992 campaign the Conservatives followed their example and commissioned an election broadcast by John Schlesinger (which became known as 'John Major: The Journey'), showing Major being driven through the streets of south London to Brixton Market where, as a young politician, he erected his first soap box. During the 1997 campaign Major deliberately made a point of avoiding over-produced election broadcasts, preferring a conversational style, direct to camera, which he thought was more effective.

The pensions row produced more lively exchanges at the next morning's news conferences. Blair was challenged head-on as to whether he could justify sending Labour canvassers out on to the doorsteps to tell elderly people their pensions were at risk. Adam Boulton, political editor of Sky News, could hardly have been more forthright in his question: 'Isn't this a pathetic attack, a scare tactic? Everyone knows there is no threat to existing pensioners, but Labour people are saying on the doorstep that the state pension will be abolished.' Blair had rarely faced such hard-hitting, sustained interrogation at a news conference. Although he did not answer the point about what was being said by Labour's canvassers, he stood his ground, arguing that the introduction of a privately managed pension scheme was one of the Conservatives' key proposals at the election and therefore it was entirely right that Labour scrutinised it carefully. 'There is no doubt that when up and running, the purpose of this is to replace the present basic state pension with a private pension.' In responding at his news conference, the Prime Minister was as angry as Dorrell had been the day before. He accused Labour of mounting a carefully calculated campaign to frighten pensioners by repeating an untruth on the doorstep when Blair knew no Conservative government would threaten the security of old age pensioners. If ever a proposal to damage the state retirement pension was countenanced by the Cabinet or prevailed, Major would have no part of it. 'I would not only leave Downing Street, I would leave politics and I would call a general election. This is just the politics of crude fantasy, scurrilous, unscrupulous campaigning in order to win votes from people whom they wish to frighten.'

Far from being chastened by the Conservatives' attack, Labour had restated in briefings after their news conference that their canvassers would go on warning the elderly that the state pension was at risk. In a renewed attempt to persuade journalists to denounce this as scaremongering, the Conservatives arranged a briefing with the Secretary of State for Social Security, Peter Lilley. We had to wait outside for a time, and I discussed Labour's tactics with two other political correspondents, Jill Sherman of *The Times* and the *Daily Mail*'s Paul Eastham. It became apparent as we talked that all three of us felt uneasy at the way elderly people were being alarmed about a proposal which, even if it were implemented, would not be fully in place until the year 2040. Eastham told me there was no doubt that Labour were scoring on pensions, but he thought their conduct was outrageous. Pensioners had been frightened by an untruth, and he felt that reporting the story had been his lowest point in six years as a political journalist.

Lilley tried valiantly to nail what he said was Blair's 'monstrous lie' that existing pensioners would be affected when Labour knew that Basic Pension Plus was designed for people now in their twenties. Yet although he had a clear command of the proposed changes in pensions, his hesitant, diffident manner suggested a lack of urgency and I thought he was hardly the right minister to have been given the task of rebutting Labour's propaganda. He kept insisting that he was not privatising the state retirement pension because, although the funds would be managed privately rather than by the government, there was no transfer of state assets to the private sector. I felt I had to query this and pointed out that the delivery of all sorts of public services had been transferred to the private sector and the public knew this as privatisation. He looked puzzled and merely repeated his point that no assets were being transferred, but when I tried again and said private contractors provided all sorts of services without taking over state assets, he did not bother to answer. This element of detachment in his manner was characteristic of his approach. Lilley was one of the few ministers in the Cabinet who appeared to have taken a calculated decision to try to get on in politics without having to rely on promoting himself through a constant round of television and radio appearances. Government press officers had told me that he frequently made a point of refusing to do interviews where there was no overriding justification for them as he doubted the value of personal media exposure. He was happy to talk to journalists and provide them with stories, but preferred to concentrate on his speeches in the House of Commons, which he prepared in great detail.

Danny Finkelstein sat through the pensions briefing and I could see he looked unhappy. He must have realised that Lilley was failing to inspire us and not providing much of a fight-back against Labour. Afterwards I sensed Finkelstein's genuine disappointment that the Conservatives' Basic Pension Plus had been turned against them so successfully by Labour. I asked if he thought it was a tactical error to have launched the scheme so close to the election when there was every likelihood it would become a political football. He said that at the time they were certain their proposals would be popular and that people would see them as an imaginative way to provide better pensions for young people. 'When we announced Basic Pension Plus we got the best response of any day since I joined Central Office. It was described as one of the most attractive ideas in our manifesto.' David Willetts believed Labour had attacked hard on pensions because they feared the Conservatives' vote was firming up over Europe. When it became an issue of trust, Major had to take it head-on. The original thinking behind the launch of Basic Pension Plus was to show that the Tories had not run out of ideas. 'We judged that it would be attractive to young people. We never thought Labour were seriously going to suggest that existing pensioners were at risk. We thought cost would be the issue.' He conceded that the Conservatives had lost not only several days of campaigning but also some crucial support among pensioners.

Labour's determination to go on hammering home their warning was demonstrated that afternoon while Blair was campaigning in Kent. Carole Walker, the BBC correspondent who covered the visit, asked the Labour candidate in Folkestone and Hythe, Peter Doherty, if she could follow and film a canvasser to assess the reaction of old age pensioners. After contacting the Millbank Tower media centre, which Doherty described as a slick machine, a party worker, who was also a local Labour councillor, was lined up to go out with the television crew, and they soon found an elderly resident who was worried about the possibility of a threat to her pension. The conversation was filmed and part of it used in Ms Walker's report for the *Six o'Clock News*. In the question and answer which was broadcast, the woman pensioner spoke first: 'If it's going to be privatised, like everything else under the Tories, what will happen?' The canvasser replied: 'I think you're right. You can't trust the Tories on pensions. After what they did with VAT on fuel, you can't really trust them whatever they say now, can you?' Alastair Campbell, who was travelling with Blair, complimented Ms Walker on her report and he said he thought the contribution of their party worker had been most effective.

David Hill had told me earlier that day that Labour intended to take every opportunity to step up their attack. 'There's nothing like a good scrap with the Tories and we know the government are in a total panic over pensions. Yes, our warnings are aimed at people drawing a pension today, as well as at future pensioners, because the Conservatives want to get the green light to pension reform and it would lead to the abolition of the state pension.' Whenever Blair was asked in interviews or at news conferences about Labour's campaigning techniques, and whether he approved of what was being done in his name to promote the party, he always gave the same well-rehearsed reply. Either way, he said, he could not win: Labour had been criticised in the past for having a woefully inadequate campaigning structure and yet, when he had ensured the creation of a professional organisation which was capable of taking on the Tories, he faced fresh complaints. Whenever I heard Blair respond in that way I could not help feeling that he was always skirting round the real point of the question. I knew from my own experience that the party machine he controlled was not only effective but ruthless, and that his answer was an astute way of taking some of the credit for what had been achieved while skilfully giving the impression that he was not aware of the practices which were being queried. The point on which I considered Blair had really become a touch hypocritical was his constant criticism of broadcasters for reporting what he termed 'tit for tat' politics, when he knew full well that the Millbank Tower media centre was doing all it could to fuel such coverage in the confident knowledge that the more they could expose on television and radio the tired and unpopular faces and voices of Tory ministers, the better it would be for Labour. Blair gave a clear exposition of his complaint on *The World this Weekend*: 'Nothing is more frustrating for me than seeing those Tory divisions on television night after night. It squeezes out what we want to say.' He returned to the theme during a question-and-answer session organised by the *Sunday Times*, repeating his criticism of television and radio for allowing political debate to descend into the tit-for-tat reporting which was driving everyone mad. 'I know it is a function of the way we communicate. Everything gets concertinaed into news slots. Maybe in time we can have a different debate. But it is not our design which has made it so, but the way modern politics communicates itself to the public. It is not our desire that this happens and if a way to change it could be found, I would be the first to say yes to it.'

Unfortunately I failed to find an opportunity during the campaign to ask the question which I would have liked Blair to address, namely: did he think Labour were the principal beneficiaries of tit for tat reporting? My firm conclusion was that the ingenuity of Labour's spin doctors in finding ways to put Tory ministers on the defensive and to get them on to the television screens night after night, reminding the public of their mistakes and gaffes, paid handsome dividends. The country was in the mood for a change, but it was the diligence of those who worked in Labour's media centre that ensured the government's unpopularity was an ever-present theme of the daily news coverage; and the most reliable method of achieving that was to encourage and utilise the tit for tat reporting of politics from which Blair was publicly seeking to distance himself.

As I again discovered to my cost, the persistence of Labour's spin doctors secured them a notable victory in the final week of the campaign when they succeeded in persuading the newsroom to drop a pre-recorded report which I had left overnight for use in the 7 a.m. Radio 4 news bulletin. My report had referred to Major's intention to launch an offensive against what he was going to say was Labour's plan for an 'emergency budget' in July 1997, should they win the election.

As the campaign had progressed, Gordon Brown had made it clear that it would be his intention as Chancellor to bring in an immediate budget, in order to introduce the windfall tax and cut the rate of VAT on domestic fuel; but although the newspapers had been referring to it as an 'emergency budget' this was the first time Major had described it thus, and as the phrase appeared to give credence to Tory claims that Brown's tax-and-spend plans did not add up, Labour were none too keen for it to be repeated. I was interviewed about the running order for the day's campaigning in a pre-recorded discussion to be broadcast at 5 a.m. in *Morning Reports* on Radio 5 Live, and I then recorded the item for the news bulletin. In the middle of my report was this reference to the day's campaign themes: 'The Conservatives will attack Labour over the threat of higher taxes, suggesting that Labour's plan for an emergency budget in July would mean tax increases to fill a £12 billion black hole in their spending plans. It's an accusation which Labour have rejected repeatedly. They in turn will warn of the dangers of a fifth term of Tory government. Labour say that if the Tories got back it would mean VAT on food.'

The first I knew of the trouble in store was being woken at home at 6.54 a.m. by a pager message from Charlie Whelan telling me my report had been dropped from Radio 4 because the words 'emergency budget' were 'Tory talk' and should not be used. Whelan had apparently complained to Radio 4 well before the 7 a.m. news bulletin, demanding that my report should not be broadcast. I could only assume that he must have been alerted after Labour's monitoring unit picked up the phrase in my 5 a.m. broadcast. The newsroom thought that I had constructed my sentence in such a way as not to pin the word 'emergency' firmly enough on to the Conservatives – and on reading back the sentence, I could see that some form of additional attribution of the word 'emergency' to the Tories would have been advisable. The report did not go out. The incident showed not only Labour's thoroughness in checking what the BBC was saying but their persistence in following through a complaint.

Whelan whooped with delight when he saw me at the afternoon news conference and reminded me gleefully of his success in getting my report dropped from the 7 a.m. bulletin. 'That shows bullying the BBC does work. And don't forget to put that in your next book.' David Hill, who was standing beside him, told the assembled group of journalists that he had just faxed off a complaint to the *One o'Clock News*. 'Of course bullying the BBC works. That's why we do it. We know it works. Obviously, in the end, the newsrooms give in, that's why we keep it up.' George Parker, political correspondent of the *Financial Times*, was among the journalists who looked on bemused as the spin doctors gloated about their prowess in berating the BBC.

In those final few days of the campaign the contrast between the Labour and Conservative media operations could not have been greater. At Millbank Tower, the spin doctors were like coiled springs, ready to pounce on the slightest mistake or omission, so fearful were they that an unexpected or uncontrolled event might deprive them of almost certain victory. At Central Office, on the other hand, there was no longer any aggression towards reporters but instead signs of a growing realisation that it was all over, and an acceptance of the fact that the only point at issue was the size of Labour's likely majority. Another significant change was also becoming apparent: briefings and conversations were no longer being projected forward to what might happen on polling day but were becoming reflective, and increasingly they seemed to be centred on attempts to explain and justify the tactics used in the campaign. I could not help feeling that the task of trying to prepare a soft landing for John Major had already begun; and, almost without prompting, Major must have sensed the change himself, because his responses now appeared to be more about defending his achievements than about looking ahead to the challenges of a possible fifth term.

Major gave every impression of starting to wind down during the final weekend. On completing a Saturday morning news conference he returned to Huntingdon, adopting a somewhat leisurely pace of campaigning. He was filmed with his wife Norma chatting to some of his constituents in the Market Inn. Blair, meanwhile, had taken the train to Manchester on what turned out to be a whistle-stop tour. At stations on the way north he was photographed with local candidates. Richard Branson, head of the Virgin organisation, which had the franchise for the privatised west coast line, travelled with Blair for part of the journey. When the teatime television news bulletin included a script line to the effect that the party leaders were having a busy day, David Hill rang in to complain, saying it hardly looked like a hectic day for the Prime Minister if the only picture the BBC had to broadcast was of a shot of him having a pint with his wife.

Major's frustration at the Conservatives' failure to get their policy messages across to the electorate in the face of Labour's skill in influencing the news agenda was strongly apparent in the comments he made anticipating defeat. In answer to a question on *Election Call* on the last day of the campaign, he blamed the news media for filtering out what he wanted to say. Although he did not acknowledge the part Labour played in generating many of the story lines about which he complained, he said that all too frequently he had been pushed off the news agenda by the 'squabble of the day, by the gaffe of the day and the speculation of the day'. The problem he faced as Prime Minister was that one could not encapsulate the complexities of government into a soundbite. That evening he was asked by Jon Snow on *Channel Four News* if he regretted having opted for a long campaign because it seemed to have highlighted the terrible divisions within his party. Major acknowledged that he had deliberately sought a long campaign because he feared Labour would obscure the main issues for the first week or two, which they had done 'extremely successfully'. In making that judgement, he considered it would only be through staging a long campaign that the Conservatives would be likely to get a rational debate on issues like education, health, employment and welfare. 'But, no, we didn't get entirely the rational debate I wanted. My judgement was right, that our opponents would try to block off most of the last fortnight as well, and my judgement was right that they would try to avoid debate on specific issues. The debate was partly engaged, but personally not as fully as I would have wished.'

Major's references to the fact that key decisions were based on his judgement, and the impression this gave of the campaign having been fought entirely the way he directed it should be, was backed up by briefings at Central Office during the last few days. David Willetts and Danny Finkelstein told journalists that Major was uneasy about some of the attacking strategies which had been prepared by Central Office. He felt that personal attacks against Blair were not in keeping with his personality, or the office of Prime Minister, and there were a number which he would neither make himself nor allow others to use. Another source of friction were the advertising campaigns being prepared by M&C Saatchi which did not always fit in with the personal style of campaigning which Major had favoured. Several advertisements were rejected, including one which was apparently based on the theme 'New Labour, new mortgage danger' and included an illustration of a house falling off a cliff. Brian Mawhinney's aim all along was to run a campaign with which Major felt comfortable, and that had meant jettisoning some of their earlier ideas and advertising projects, which in turn meant upsetting Lord Saatchi.

Sir Tim Bell, another of the Conservatives' media advisers, believed the tactics adopted by the party chairman were correct. 'Dr Mawhinney set out from the start to organise the campaign in the way the Prime Minister wanted it to be run. What John Major decided, we did, and there was no conflict about the choices because the party chairman was determined it would be a campaign which the leader was comfortable with. It was always going to be a very personal campaign, because that's what John Major ran in the 1992 election and I don't think there is a single thing in the campaign which we have organised for him in this election which he has been unhappy about.' Sir Tim said long experience had taught him that if commercial clients went ahead with an advertising presentation against their better judgement it often led to a drop in sales; and the same applied when a party leader was forced by his campaign team to do things he was unhappy with, because the politician would not put his heart into a strategy which did not suit his style. Major had demonstrated this in the 1992 election when, after resisting attempts to make him perch on a bar stool and answer questions in the round, he came up with the idea of a soap box. The personal style of the 1997 campaign was also reflected in Major's decision to do the election broadcasts himself, in a conversational style, straight to camera. Sir Tim was full of praise for the way Mawhinney had handled meetings of the strategy group at Central Office. 'The chairman was determined from the start to avoid splits in the camp. There were some very frank discussions, but he really did all he could to get a consensus. He also worked hard on bringing Lady Thatcher back on board. Don't forget we went into the campaign twenty points behind in the polls with virtually all the newspaper hacks against us. Yes, some press guys came back, but most of the damage was done in the previous four years.'

Sir Tim shared the conviction of the Central Office spin doctors that the high proportion of uncommitted voters would have a significant impact on the result. The number who were undecided, or who would not say how they would vote, had grown in every election since the 1970s. 'The political tribes are much smaller. People don't go to political meetings any more because they can watch it on television, but when people are bombarded by messages in their own homes you can't be sure how they'll vote.' Michael Heseltine expounded at length at the last but one news conference on his theory why the Conservatives' vote would be higher than the opinion polls were predicting. He said that of 2,000 people who were approached for a telephone poll, only 1,000 ever agreed to take part and a quarter of them would not say how they would vote, so that meant that on his calculation opinion surveys were based on only 36 per cent of those who were originally approached. 'I know that none of you are going to print this, or analyse the truth behind it, because newspapers have invested so much on surveys based on that 36 per cent sample. The public don't take the polls as seriously as the media do. For most people they're a great big joke.' Heseltine was confident that a majority of those who would not say, or did not know, would vote Conservative, and when asked again if he thought Major would win, he replied: 'Yes, I think the Conservative majority will be more than sixty.' Steven Norris reinforced the message, telling me he could not believe that the polls were correct in suggesting that Major had been deserted by a quarter of the party's traditional supporters. 'I can't find 25 per cent of Tory voters who are not with us this time. I can find one in ten, but not one in four. Our canvas returns all say the same thing: there are lots of shy Tories and silent Tories. But we haven't had a lot of stick out there in the constituencies and our instincts, of everyone who's been doing this since we were kids, are that if what we're finding on the doorsteps is right, it isn't going to be as bad as the polls predict.'

Although the Tory hierarchy and their strategists were still happily spinning away, Norma Major appeared to have no illusions. On the return flight to London after her husband's last regional tour on the Monday before polling day there was quite a party atmosphere on board. Champagne and cakes had been laid on by the cabin crew, together with carnations for everyone's buttonhole. Brian Mawhinney, who had been with Major as they had flown to Belfast, Edinburgh and then Anglesey, assured the journalists who had been covering the trip that Central Office had information from eighty constituencies, including key marginals, which flew in the face of the opinion polls. Clarence Mitchell, the BBC's correspondent on the flight, told me that although party officials appeared to believe what Mawhinney was saying, he noticed that Norma Major was taking her own snaps of the party as though she knew it was her husband's final flight as Prime Minister and realised it would be her last opportunity to get some pictures for the family album. Mitchell also said that the journalists were surprised at the access Major afforded them during the campaign and flattered by the way he remembered their first names. They found his command of policy detail, and his ability to speak coherently off the cuff, without repeating himself, most impressive.

On landing at RAF Northolt, Major went straight to College Green at Westminster for a photo-call with staff from Central Office. He shook hands with many of the party workers; then, just as he started to speak, Big Ben struck six o'clock. After the first of the chimes, realising that they were going to go on interrupting him, he said to the laughter of those crowding in a circle around him that every election had its own special character and dangers. 'I know how hard so many people have worked,' he went on. 'This election has been a lot of fun. It has had its moments . . . Now we have seventy-two hours in which to save the union, to make sure the system of government which has prevailed in this country is protected and enshrined. It's not just a question of who governs for the next five years, it's a question of what that government will do in the next five years. We will protect the unity of the United Kingdom and draw a line in the sand of where we won't surrender to the European Union, on the veto and the social chapter. These are the fundamental choices for the British nation.'

That evening Major was in the BBC's Millbank studios for a *Panorama* interview with David Dimbleby. On the way out he stopped off in the newsroom to look at the report being shown in the *Nine o'Clock News* of his day's campaigning in Belfast, Edinburgh and North Wales. He was full of fun, cracking jokes and chatting away to Jon Sopel and Clarence Mitchell, the two correspondents who had travelled with him. Once he had left, Dimbleby told me that Major had been extremely affable but that what had struck him during both the interview and their conver-sation afterwards was that he was not talking about winning or what he would do in government, but instead had wanted to defend his record as Prime Minister. When Major appeared on the election edition of *Question Time*, Dimbleby had noticed the same sort of responses; when that programme was off the air, Major had stayed on for three-quarters of an hour, chatting away about his success in gaining the British opt-out on the single European currency.

The last of the Prime Minister's events which I attended was his eve-of-poll news conference, at which he urged voters to accept that the transformation which had taken place in Britain was nothing less than an economic miracle. 'It's too good to give up' was his repeated refrain. I was struck by the way he chose to phrase his attack, because although he meant it to tell against Labour, he seemed to put his finger on the three principal reasons for his own plight. After listing his achievements and his aims for a fifth term, he turned his fire on his opponents: 'It would be a tragedy if these opportunities were lost by the false attraction of a well-packaged marketing scam. Because that's what the Labour Party is. A coalition of interests whose sole purpose is the pursuit of power.' Inadvertently he seemed to have hit on the three characteristics which had been the hallmarks of the governments of Margaret Thatcher and which I knew were also the driving forces behind Tony Blair and New Labour. The resolute pursuit of power under Blair's leadership had transformed the Labour Party, just as it had propelled Thatcher forward in her early years. Blair had succeeded, as had Thatcher, in moulding together and then controlling the coalition of interests which made up his party. And the success of New Labour derived in part from the way Blair and his advisers, through skilful presentation, had won over large sections of the news media, a strength which had proved invaluable to Thatcher in her first years in power. Major's parlous position was underlined by the weariness and lack of purpose which were evident in many of his Cabinet colleagues, who had palpably lost all interest in the pursuit of power; by his failure to control the Tory party's rival interest groups, whose gory infighting had been exposed time and again in the splits on Europe; and by the withdrawal of support by newspapers which had loyally backed the Conservatives in the four previous elections.

If the final week of the Conservatives' campaign had given the impression of being a free fall to polling day, Labour stuck rigidly to a programme drawn up by the five-day campaign unit at Millbank Tower, which had mapped out a tight schedule for Blair's last round of visits to key seats. Labour had targeted 110 marginal constituencies, which included the ninety they hoped to win and twenty which required defending because of small majorities. David Hill told me their last week of campaigning had gone exactly to plan, and indeed throughout the election they had kept to around 80 per cent of their original programme. A number of events had been changed, as had some of the topics at news conferences, but except for the few days when, he admitted, Labour had been forced on to the defensive, the Conservatives had failed to cause them serious trouble for any real length of time.

Not to be outdone by Major's campaign finale of a 1,000-mile flight to the four corners of the United Kingdom, Paddy Ashdown hired a helicopter for a whirlwind tour of the Liberal Democrats' target seats in his last few days of electioneering. Lord Holme was sure that out of the three party leaders, Ashdown had come across as the one who had listened and paid attention to what the voters were saying. 'We purposely did not package him too heavily. He has not been the face hidden behind media spin and image-making, but he got out there and engaged with people and his rating as leader rose as the campaign went on, especially on trust and openness.' The Liberal Democrats' aim in the final week of the campaign, as Ashdown criss-crossed the country in his helicopter, was to try to encourage the biggest possible vote in every constituency, and in this way to get the public's endorsement for the policy of spending more on education and health. Although the Liberal Democrats remained cautious about the outcome, they were encouraged by opinion poll evidence suggesting that they were ahead of the Conservatives in many of their target seats. This was Lord Holme's eighth election campaign in over thirty years of active political involvement, and he had never known one when the Liberal Democrats' policies had been focused so clearly and when they had succeeded in communicating them so effectively to the public. 'The teachers said we had the best education policy, nearly half of all doctors said our health policy was the best and we ended up in the polls second to Labour on both education and health. So voters got a clear picture of what we were offering and they don't see us any more as being a party that's just about electoral reform.'

Lord Holme had chaired their morning news conferences and although he had enjoyed them, he disliked the way they had been dominated by journalists from radio and television who were always trying to catch his attention. 'I think it is a loss to politics that newspaper correspondents seem cowed by the eye of television and they didn't ask as many questions as I would have expected or liked. All the broadcasters ever want to do is play a simple game of one-day cricket, but the print journalists like to get engaged in a complicated tennis match and that can be far more interesting politically.'

The Liberal Democrats may have come a distant third of the main parties in respect of technological infrastructure for their campaign, but they could be quick on their feet. Lord Holme himself had a deft touch under questioning, which he demonstrated to good effect on the day the Conservatives released Labour's war book. Asked if the Liberal Democrats had a secret strategy document, he replied: 'When I took on the job I was handed a rather dusty folder, but knowing the Liberal Democrats, I think it was called a peace plan, or something like that.' Jane Bonham Carter, the party's director of communications, enjoyed the day earlier in the campaign when they succeeded in tweaking the tail of Excalibur, the computerised information retrieval system which was at the heart of Labour's high-tech media centre. At a news conference to launch Labour's policy for the National Health Service, the shadow health secretary, Chris Smith, said their aim was to cut bureaucracy and stop the development of a two-tier service. Smith quoted from a speech the previous November by Dr Evan Harris of the British Medical Association, who said that if patients had a fundholding general practitioner they could get quicker treatment, but if not they were stuffed.

Despite Labour's much vaunted procedures for using Excalibur to check political facts and figures as part of their rebuttal strategy, Smith and his advisers had failed to think of running a search on Dr Harris, who was in fact the Liberal Democrats' candidate in Oxford West and Abingdon. Ms Bonham Carter told me they worked fast to exploit Smith's gaffe and used it to highlight their argument that Labour's health policy was unsustainable in view of Blair's refusal to commit extra cash. Dr Harris put out a statement accusing Smith of conveniently having forgotten to point out that his speech had also called for significant extra resources as the only way to address the NHS funding crisis. The episode was, Ms Bonham Carter said, a classic demonstration that the most expensive computer systems were of no use unless those who operated them knew what to look for. She was dismayed by the lack of vision in Labour's campaign. 'We've had the Tories talking to themselves and yet Labour were a real disappointment and just bottled out when asked how they'd pay for things. The only real political story of the campaign was that we were perceived as the only party which was actually saying anything and we had the policies to carry through what we were promising.'

My task on election night was to report reaction from Labour's campaign headquarters at Millbank Tower. The atmosphere was decidedly friendlier than it had been at some of the morning news conferences. Blair had set the tone the previous evening when he arrived in his Sedgefield constituency ready to vote next day. On a visit to the local Trimdon Labour Club, he made a short speech in which he acknowledged the efforts of the broadcasters and reporters who had been accompanying him throughout the election period. 'The media have been following us around in the campaign. A word of thanks to them. It's not always been easy, but there you are guys, the Labour Party congratulating the media.' His speech was punctuated by applause from local party workers and there was another round of clapping for the media contingent.

As we waited in the media centre for the first results to come through, David Hill, who was master of ceremonies for the evening, told me he was convinced Blair had won by a comfortable margin. I had rarely seen Labour's press officers looking so relaxed and so pleased with themselves, and there was a real sense of anticipation. However, there was no clue then that we were in for one of the most momentous nights in the history of the Labour Party. Among the party workers who had experienced the harrowing defeat of 1992, there was still a modicum of caution in conversation and a determination to maintain the self-discipline which Blair had shown at a news conference earlier in the week when he had insisted that he did not think Britain was 'landslide country'.

There was less restraint in the polling day editions of the morning newspapers. Although the *Sun* had backed Labour from the start of the campaign, its front page was as imaginative in support of Blair as it had been destructive of Neil Kinnock in 1992. The star-studded lucky finger used in commercials for the national lottery was pointing directly at a large colour photograph of the Labour leader, with alongside it the headline 'It must be you'. Readers were told they had a unique opportunity to join the 'greatest jackpot syndicate ever' and the guaranteed prize was a 'share in our country's future, a brighter tomorrow'. But there was no gamble, it cost nothing; and yet everyone would be a winner. 'All you must do is vote Labour.' For students of political journalism the contrast was staggering. In the 1992 election the *Sun*'s front page had carried a large picture of a light bulb on which had been superimposed a photograph of Kinnock's face, together with a large headline which said: 'If Kinnock wins today, will the last person to leave Britain please turn out the lights.'

If the Conservatives had been hoping for unequivocal endorsements from the two tabloids which in the past had been among their strongest supporters, there was fresh disappointment. The front page of the *Express* took a neutral stance under the banner headline 'Now it's up to you' –

though it did remain loyal to the Tories, saying that, like true conservatives, it would stick to 'the devil we know'. The *Daily Mail* had headlined what it claimed was 'The great don't know factor' and said the Tories were praying that the army of an estimated four million don't know voters could still sink Blair's chances and 'provide the biggest political upset this century'. But in its comment column the *Mail* studiously avoided giving its support to the Conservatives. The previous day it had warned that if Blair got a 'massive Euro-friendly Commons majority' the pound could be sacrificed, and if voters wanted Britain to retain its independence they must 'however reluctantly, vote Conservative'. All it would say this morning, however, was that the voters were sovereign.

The other great contrast with the last election lay in the final opinion polls, which on election day in 1992 were just beginning to pick up the late swing to the Conservatives which carried Major to victory. Of the four polls published that day, Gallup put the Conservatives half a point ahead; ICM showed the two main parties as neck and neck; MORI had Labour in front by one point; and NOP gave Labour a lead of three points. On election day in 1997, the polls were not only unanimous in putting Labour way out in front but suggested they had the largest ever lead enjoyed by an opposition party challenging for power since serious polling began after the Second World War. Of the five polling companies with surveys out that day NOP put Labour 22 points ahead; MORI, 20; Harris, 17; Gallup, 13; and ICM, 10. When exit polls commissioned by the BBC and ITV were released at ten o'clock that evening, they provided further confirmation that Labour were heading for a landslide victory. It was almost as if an electric charge had gone through Labour's media centre, so great was the excitement. The BBC's poll gave Labour a 47 per cent share of the vote, 18 points ahead of the Conservatives. The projected Labour majority was approaching 200 on a swing of 13 per cent, which indicated the worst result for the Tories since the Duke of Wellington was hammered in 1832.

As in 1992, the first constituency to declare was Sunderland South. Here Chris Mullin was returned again for Labour with a 10.5 per cent swing, up dramatically on the 2.5 per cent swing he had achieved five years earlier. As Mullin delivered his acceptance speech, promising that Labour would 'govern for the many, not the few', David Hill started smiling and told me he was pleased to see that the re-elected MP's remarks had been totally on message as far as New Labour was concerned.

Soon the results were coming in thick and fast. As we crowded round the television sets in the media centre, watching the election programmes,

Hill could not believe the gains Labour were making and the staggering size of the swings. As he hailed from the West Midlands he was almost speechless when, in their first gain of the evening, Birmingham Edgbaston, which had been Conservative for seventy-five years and was sixty-seventh on Labour's list of target seats, was taken by Gisela Stuart on a 10 per cent swing. Portsmouth North, Labour's hundredth target seat, was secured on a swing of 13.5 per cent; Basildon was lost by the Conservatives to Labour's Angela Smith on a swing of 15 per cent; and Crosby fell to Labour on an 18 per cent swing. Hill could hardly contain himself. 'Look, these swings are now so high, we've got a world event on our hands. Everyone will be asking who is this man who's grabbed his party and the country by the scruff of the neck and won a landslide. That's something the world will want to know more about and it'll be our job to tell them how it happened.'

Looking back, the event which Hill thought was probably the most telling harbinger of their sensational success was the Staffordshire South East by-election, which Labour won in April 1996 on a huge 22 per cent swing. 'That by-election followed the abandoning of Clause Four and the creation of New Labour, and it was that which gave Tony Blair the chance to prove his leadership and show that he could be trusted. Then of course we gave the pledges, not extreme promises, nothing earth-shattering, but positive, solid pledges on education and health.' Edwina Currie, who lost Derbyshire South to Labour on a 13 per cent swing, was being interviewed almost simultaneously on *Election '97*. She said the reason the Conservatives had done so badly was that once Blair changed his party, people started going over to Labour and they just kept moving that way. Peter Mandelson, who appeared on the programme a little later, agreed instantly with that analysis. Blair's transformation of the Labour Party had been the key to their success. 'Yes, it was New Labour wot did it.' But Mandelson said it had taken ten years for the people of Britain to be persuaded to put their faith and trust in a Labour government. When Alastair Campbell was interviewed, while waiting for Blair's declaration in Sedgefield, he was still surprisingly cautious. He was beginning to think the campaign had not made a great difference after all, because it was clear that support for Labour had been tremendously strong all along. 'The Conservatives did make a great mistake, though, in trying to target Tony and the long campaign rebounded against them. We had a fantastic operation out on the ground, in the constituencies, and we have supplanted the Conservatives as the most professional political party.'

Almost as riveting as the declarations themselves were the various predictions of Labour's likely majority in the House of Commons. The prospect that it could be over 180 or even higher suggested a triumph of even greater proportions than the 1945 Labour landslide when Clement Attlee swept to power with a 146-seat majority. Soon the broadcasters and journalists at Labour's media centre were feeling somewhat redundant. The results being announced in constituencies around the country were so electrifying that the last thing any of the programmes wanted to broadcast was a round-up of the spin doctors' reaction at party headquarters. Back in the BBC's newsroom in Millbank, preparing for the morning output, I had a chance to begin assessing the carnage in the Conservative Party. Labour and the Liberal Democrats had rampaged their way through some of the safest Tory seats in the country; ministers had been defeated left, right and centre; and the Euro-sceptics had not been spared as Tory MPs who were household names had gone down like ninepins.

Martin Bell had become the first Independent MP elected to the Commons since before the Second World War. He had taken Tatton with a majority of just over 11,000, easily defeating Neil Hamilton, and told local voters he believed they had 'lit a beacon which will shed a light in some dark corners and illuminate the mother of parliaments itself'. In a moment of high drama in Wandsworth Town Hall, the former Conservative minister David Mellor, who was giving his speech at the declaration and acknowledging his defeat by Labour in Putney, suddenly found he was being heckled with shouts of 'out, out, out' and a slow handclap from Sir James Goldsmith, who had stood against him in the same constituency and had lost his deposit. Mellor, never short of a cutting response, told the Referendum Party's billionaire leader that he should 'get off back to Mexico knowing that your attempt to buy the British political system has failed' and that the people of Putney had said 'Up your hacienda, Jimmy.' When asked on *Election '97* about his defeat and the mounting mayhem in his party, Mellor's instant imagery in describing the disaster which had befallen his colleagues could hardly have been bettered: 'A tidal wave has burst over the Conservative Party tonight, and it's not a matter of putting your finger in the dike. The sea wall is collapsing all around us.' David Evans lost Welwyn Hatfield on an 11 per cent swing to the Labour candidate Melanie Johnson, whom he had offended eight weeks before polling day by claiming she had 'three bastard children'. He told *Election '97* that he was not sure whether his remarks were the cause of his defeat: 'Yes, people said to me in the constituency that they didn't like what I said about her, but then they said they agreed with me.' Evans thought the reason the Conservatives had done so badly was because Blair came across as a 'good Tory leader with good Tory policies'. Piers Merchant survived a 15 per cent swing to Labour in Beckenham, holding his seat with a majority of nearly 5,000, but Jerry Hayes was roundly beaten in the Conservative marginal of Harlow, which Labour took with a majority of 10,500 on a 12.5 per cent swing.

The defeat of seven Cabinet ministers was just one of the many devastating statistics of the night. Michael Forsyth, the Secretary of State for Scotland, was the first to go soon after 1.00 a.m. when his majority of 703 in Stirling disappeared under a swing of nearly 8 per cent to Labour, who took the seat with a majority of over 6,000. He said reports of his 'political demise have not, in fact, been exaggerated'. An hour later the President of the Board of Trade, Ian Lang, lost Galloway and Upper Nithsdale to the Scottish National Party on a swing of 9.5 per cent. Malcolm Rifkind, the Foreign Secretary, was beaten by Labour in Edinburgh Pentlands on a swing of nearly 10 per cent, and with the loss of the other seven Tory-held Scottish seats the Conservatives finished the night without a single MP in Scotland – a wipeout which was mirrored in Wales, where the party's six seats were all lost. In Essex, where Labour did particularly well, Tony Newton, the Leader of the House, lost Braintree on a swing of nearly 13 per cent. William Waldegrave, the Chief Secretary to the Treasury, had to relinquish Bristol West to Labour on a swing of 12 per cent, and the Chancellor of the Duchy of Lancaster, Roger Freeman, who faced a swing to Labour of 10.5 per cent, was beaten in Kettering by a mere 189 votes.

Of the seven defeats inflicted on Cabinet ministers, the most spectacular was the fall of the Secretary of State for Defence, Michael Portillo, in Enfield Southgate, his 1992 majority of 15,545 turned into a majority of 1,433 for Stephen Twigg on a 17.4 per cent swing to Labour. Twigg, general secretary of the Fabian Society and a former president of the National Union of Students, had the backing of an army of young Labour campaign workers, drawn from all over London. Enfield Southgate – by far the safest of the seven seats lost by Cabinet ministers – was one of the constituencies identified in the *Observer* as a target for tactical voting by potential Liberal Democrat supporters. This advice appeared to have been highly effective because the Liberal Democrat share of the vote dropped to 10.6 per cent, down from 14.4 per cent in 1992. As the count was declared, Portillo looked mortified, as if he could not take in the devastation or come to terms with the way the Tory party had been slaughtered by Labour. 'I am weeping for the Conservative Party . . . It has been a terrible evening for us. I dearly hope they will be able to put things back together.'

Portillo's humiliation was all the more significant because he had been seen as the front-runner for the Tory right in the leadership contest for which Conservative MPs had been bracing themselves, in view of what was regarded as the near-certainty of John Major's defeat in the general election. The newspapers on election morning had been full of speculation about his chances. 'Portillo poised to seize victory from defeat' was the *Daily Mail*'s headline over a report by the paper's political editor, David Hughes, who considered the Secretary of State for Defence was fast emerging as favourite to succeed Major if the Tories were beaten. Portillo had won new friends after fighting what was seen as a good campaign; his allies were quoted as saying that he had 'not put a foot wrong and grown significantly in stature' after a series of punchy and effective performances on radio and television. In his political notebook in the *Financial Times*, Robert Peston had taken a swipe at Portillo for using the election campaign to heighten his exposure and promote his bid for the leadership. A 'clique of courtiers', he said, had been working assiduously to extend the defence secretary's power base, and he described the kind of conversation which he assumed had taken place between Portillo and Charles Lewington at Central Office: 'Charles, it's Michael here, Michael Portillo. Just wanted to mention that, as a London MP, it's terribly easy for me to get over to the Beeb if you need someone at a moment's notice to do the *Today* programme or breakfast television. It's really not an inconvenience, don't hesitate to ask.' In fact, I had not detected any attempt by Portillo to take personal advantage of BBC interviews; but certainly he had spared no effort during the election in attacking Labour. One evening, when interviewing him at Central Office for *Breakfast News*, it took ten minutes to set up the shot. We were told that the interview had to be filmed in front of the platform used for news conferences and, because of difficulties with the computerised graphics, we were asked to wait until the technicians were satisfied with the placing of the slogan on the backdrop, which said 'Blair's running from the truth'. Portillo's persistence paid off: when the interview was recorded, the slogan was a clear visual reinforcement of the answers he gave, rebutting Labour's statements at its news conference earlier in the day.

The speculation that Portillo would make a challenge for the leadership had inevitably increased in view of the ominous predictions of the government's imminent defeat. Nevertheless Portillo had shown great loyalty to the Prime Minister since the unexpected leadership contest in July 1995 when Major was re-elected, defeating John Redwood by 218 votes to 89. Portillo was uncertain at the time whether to stand, and although he eventually indicated he would enter the contest only if Major were defeated and it went to a second round, he did not escape charges of disloyalty because it emerged that extra telephone lines had already been installed in his likely campaign headquarters. This had been arranged by David Hart, a former aide to Margaret Thatcher and one of Portillo's closest confidants. When I spoke to Hart on the afternoon of polling day he confirmed to me that Portillo would stand for the leadership if the Conservatives lost the election and Major resigned. Hart thought Portillo might well declare his hand that weekend, perhaps by making use of an article which was already being prepared for possible publication in the *Sunday Telegraph* and which would set out his vision for the future of the Tory party. 'He doesn't want to come out too early, or be provoked, but he has earned a lot of support because of the loyalty he's shown Major. But there is no need to hurry; he is the front-runner . . . it should be much easier for Portillo as the party is likely to be 99 per cent Euro-sceptic in the next parliament.'

I asked Hart if he saw any danger of Portillo being defeated in Enfield Southgate, in view of the push being made against him by Stephen Twigg's supporters. He played down the possibility, saying he thought that would require an unprecedented collapse in the Tory vote. 'John Major has fought an honourable and decent campaign and I think a lot of people will hold their nose and vote Tory. Labour ran a technically brilliant campaign but Blair doesn't realise the electorate is grown up. People can see through New Labour. Two weeks into the campaign, after what Labour said on privatisation, I advised Major to do a poster which should have told electors that "Labour think you're stupid". People don't like being treated with contempt and the voters aren't idiots.' Hart was convinced that even if Labour were elected they would soon be in trouble. 'I think Labour will be behind in the polls within six months. Most of the newspapers are Conservative at heart. Labour's honeymoon in the press will last ten days at most and once the Conservatives are saying sensible things, and once Michael is saying sensible things, the newspapers will be behind him all the way.'

Hart had always impressed me by the extent of his knowledge about the activities of the Tory right and the accuracy of his predictions. I had known him since the 1984–5 pit strike when he advised Thatcher and the National Coal Board's chairman, Ian MacGregor, and secretly assisted efforts to encourage a return to work through the National Working Miners' Committee. Therefore, on election night, as I saw the television pictures of the agonised look on Portillo's face at the declaration of the Enfield Southgate result, I realised the shock that his defeat would cause among those who regarded him as the true heir to the Thatcherite inheritance and Thatcher's anointed successor. However, there was no time to dwell on the likely repercussions because my next assignment awaited me. After his declaration in Sedgefield, Blair was due to speak at Labour's victory celebrations at the Royal Festival Hall some time after 4 a.m. and we had heard that a party to end all parties was already under way on the South Bank.

My request to gain admission had been flatly rejected in advance by Labour's spin doctors. They said the number of tickets for journalists was strictly limited and no further passes were available. In the event it was of no consequence, because spilling out on to the Embankment was a political gathering of a kind I had never witnessed before in my thirty-seven years working as a reporter. Hundreds of young people, many in their early twenties, who had also been unable to gain access to the party, were milling about in front of the enormous stage from which Blair would speak. I had seen youth rallies in support of Margaret Thatcher during the early years of her premiership and I had marvelled at the enthusiasm with which she was greeted by members of the Young Conservatives and Conservative Students. But, as I began talking to Labour's young activists while their election theme song, 'Things Can Only Get Better', blared out from loudspeakers, I discovered not just admiration but adoration for Blair, and I had to force myself to remember that they were talking not about a pop star but a politician.

On Blair's arrival, the applause seemed endless. As he expounded his vision for Britain and the responsibilities their victory had placed on New Labour, every sentence was punctuated by another burst of cheers and clapping from the young people all around me: 'We always said that if we had the courage to change, we could do it, and we did it. [applause] The British people have put their trust in us and it is a unique and humbling experience and the size of our likely majority will now impose a special sort of responsibility upon us. [applause] We have been elected as New Labour and we will govern as New Labour. [applause and shouts of yes, yes] We were elected because as a party today we represent the whole of this nation and we will govern for the whole of this nation. [applause] We will speak up for that decent, hard-working majority of the British people [applause] and we will set about doing the good, practical things that need to be done in this country, extending educational opportunity, not to an elite but all our children, modernising our welfare state and rebuilding the National Health Service as a proper national health service [applause].'

Dawn was breaking over the Thames and my first report was due on air within the hour so I set about my task, looking for party workers to interview from among the great throng of young people who had cheered Blair so enthusiastically. I stopped a group of three Labour activists, young women in their early twenties; as there was so much noise they thrust themselves forward to get closer to the microphone, so eager were they to give me their reaction: 'I think Tony Blair is the greatest thing that's ever happened to Britain and I've got the greatest hope in the world for the future with Tony Blair.' His speech had captivated the second of the three: 'I think it was absolutely brilliant. He's the best thing that's happened to this country. I'm so looking forward to the next five years when he can put all what he said into action.' The third of the group was equally ecstatic: 'I've just had the time of my life. This is the best moment in my life. I think Tony Blair is the only person who can lead us into the future.' Over the years I had recorded plenty of gushing political soundbites but these three young women seemed refreshingly honest and gave me the impression that they felt they had participated in what they regarded as an historic moment for the country. I knew personally how deeply New Labour's crusade to sweep away the Conservatives had touched young people. My own daughter Hannah, a twenty-five-year-old newly qualified teacher at a secondary school in south London, had been out canvassing for Labour in Mitcham and Morden, where Dame Angela Rumbold lost her seat on a 16 per cent swing. After Blair had toured the constituency in support of the Labour candidate, Siobhain McDonagh, I was taken aback when Hannah telephoned me that evening to say she had been there for his visit and 'I touched him'.

On the other side of the Thames from Blair's celebrations, the change in government was becoming a reality. After his constituency declaration, John Major and his wife Norma returned to London and were met on their arrival at Central Office by applause from a crowd of around 200 which included party officials and other members of the election team. Michael Portillo, fresh from his defeat in north London, was among those who greeted them. Major thanked party workers for all they had sacrificed during the campaign in the hope and dream of a different outcome. But the task ahead was to regroup and prepare for the job that had to be done in opposition. He hoped there would not be any immediate recriminations. 'I don't think there was much we left undone that we could have done. There are times in politics when the ball just rolls in the opposite direction and there is a not a great deal you can do about it. Politics is a rough old trade, sometimes you win and sometimes you don't. When you don't, you just ask yourself why you didn't, and put yourself in a position where next time you get it right and you do win. We have suffered a very bad defeat, let's not pretend to ourselves it is anything other than it is. Unless we accept it, we will be less able to put it right.'

Major then left for Downing Street to prepare for his resignation. Shortly after 11.00 a.m., before leaving for Buckingham Palace and an audience with the Queen, he spoke for the last time from the steps of No. 10. He reflected on the state of affairs that greeted the new government, saying that the economy was in a far better shape than when he first entered Downing Street and that Labour would inherit the 'most benevolent set of economic statistics of any incoming government since before the First World War'. He also announced that he was stepping down as party leader. 'I have been an MP for eighteen years. I have been a member of the government for fourteen years, a member of the Cabinet for ten years, and Prime Minister since 1990. When the curtain falls it is time to get off the stage, and that is what I propose to do. I shall therefore advise my parliamentary colleagues that it would be appropriate for them to consider the selection of a new leader of the Conservative Party to lead the party through opposition, through the years that lie immediately ahead.'

The stupendous scale of Labour's victory took time to absorb and, as the final declarations were announced while we all waited for Blair's arrival in Downing Street, the statistics made compelling reading. By the final count Labour had taken 418 seats and had secured a majority of 179 on a 44.4 per cent share of the vote, which represented a swing to Labour of 10.5 per cent. The Conservatives finished with 165 seats, on a 31.4 per cent share of the vote. The Liberal Democrats had also made sensational inroads into Conservative heartlands, more than doubling their number of seats and achieving the best result of any third party since 1929. On a 17.2 per cent share of the vote, they gained a total of 46 seats. Paddy Ashdown said the Liberal Democrats intended to be the constructive voice of opposition in what they hoped would be a parliament of historic reform. His party intended to hold Labour to their manifesto commitment to implement an ambitious programme of constitutional change, including devolution to Scotland and Wales and a commission on electoral reform. 'Tony Blair and the Labour Party have entered into an agreement with the Liberal Democrats. I expect that to be delivered.' Lord Holme said he thought the result had buried the conventional wisdom that a vote for the Liberal Democrats was a wasted vote.

On revisiting Labour's media centre in the short lull before Major and Blair had their audiences with the Queen I was struck by the almost chastened tone of Peter Mandelson, who was giving a series of radio and television interviews. It was almost as though he still could not believe the magnitude of their success. He told *Election '97* that he had predicted a Labour majority of fifty in the Millbank Tower sweepstake. In the end they had taken ninety-eight of their 110 target seats and won many others as well. His immediate conclusion was that people were so tired of the Conservatives they had simply turned their back on them. Mandelson said he was certainly not going to take the credit for their success: it had been Neil Kinnock who began moving the party towards victory, John Smith who then took those efforts an extra length and finally Tony Blair who had gone the final distance to create New Labour, in which people could put their trust. He praised the efforts of all those who had worked in the election team at Millbank Tower. 'We had a tremendous team and we did not really come under any serious pressure. Indeed, the campaign has been one of great joy.' Although Mandelson was keen to get away after his interviews, he smiled as the journalists who had been waiting at the media centre crowded round and expressed their amazement at the enormity of Labour's majority of 179. It was Mandelson's grandfather, the former Labour Home Secretary Herbert Morrison, who had run the post-war campaign which produced the 1945 landslide and a Labour majority of 146. Mandelson told me of the importance his family would attach to the 1997 result. 'I never thought I would beat my grandfather. Everyone always said the 1945 result would never be revisited. So you can see what it means in family terms.'

David Hill told me he thought that his first post-election task as chief media spokesperson would be to look ahead to ways of ensuring that the expertise which had been built up at Millbank Tower for the campaign was used to play a role in supporting Tony Blair and his Cabinet. 'From now on we'll operate the party's media centre as an arm of a Labour government, so that we can help Tony Blair deliver the message which he wants his government to deliver. We will continue to have a very high-level media operation here at Millbank Tower, and yes, we'll continue our role attacking the Conservatives, but we want to ensure that the way the whole party cooperated in the election is maintained now that Labour are in government. We saw what happened under the Conservatives, that a divided party loses, so we must make take steps to maintain the unity that Blair has created.' Clearly, Labour's high command were determined to avoid a repetition of the breakdown in cooperation and trust which had bedevilled the Conservative Party at regular intervals under both Margaret Thatcher and John Major, when soured relations between the Prime Minister's advisers in Downing Street and party staff at Central Office had hampered efforts to coordinate publicity on behalf of the Conservatives.

Labour party workers who had been manning the media centre on the morning of 2 May were called up to the privacy of the Millbank Tower war room to be given their instructions on how to prepare for Blair's arrival at No. 10 after his audience with the Queen. There were 150 passes available for Downing Street, and staff were asked to wave the Union flags they would be issued with but not to carry Labour Party signs, posters or balloons. They were told that the leadership wanted Blair's welcome to look like a 'spontaneous outpouring from offices and factories to greet the new Prime Minister' and that they should remember that the Union flag was now Labour's flag. Stewards would advise staff where to stand, and those with children would be directed to the best places for camera shots. Blair's arrival was a masterpiece of choreography. He and Cherie walked along the lines of wellwishers as they made their triumphal progress to No. 10's front door, where they were joined by their three children, Nicky, Kathryn and Euan, for a family photograph which filled the front pages of next morning's newspapers. Blair stood waving to the crowd, his other hand resting on Nicky's shoulder. 'The new kids on the block' was the *Daily Mail*'s headline, while the *Express* had as its caption just two words in capital letters: 'Our House'.

In his first speech on the steps of No. 10, Blair paid tribute to John Major for the dignity and courage he had shown and for the manner in which he had handed over power. He realised the great trust which the British people had placed in him as their new Prime Minister. 'This is not a mandate for dogma or doctrine, or a return to the past, but it was a mandate to get those things done . . . that desperately need doing for the future of Britain. This new Labour government will govern in the interests of all our people . . . And it will be a government that seeks to restore trust in politics in this country, that cleans it up, that decentralises it, that gives people hope once again that politics is . . . about the service of the public . . . Today we are charged with the deep responsibility of government. Today, enough of talking, it is time now to do.'

Two hours later Blair announced his first seven Cabinet appointments: Deputy Prime Minister, John Prescott, with responsibility for environment, transport and the regions; Chancellor of the Exchequer, Gordon Brown; Foreign Secretary, Robin Cook; Home Secretary, Jack Straw; Secretary of State for Education and Employment, David Blunkett; President of the Board of Trade, Margaret Beckett; Lord Chancellor, Lord Irvine. The citadel had been won; now the generals had to turn their hands to farming.

8

Winning the Peace

After a landslide of the magnitude achieved by the Labour Party in 1997, attempting to determine the role played by the news media in the election, and to assess the impact it might have had on the outcome, is no easy task. Any judgement on whether the reporting of the campaign influenced the electorate will probably be regarded as pure conjecture. Weariness with the evasions and excuses of Conservative ministers, the longing for a change of government after eighteen years of Tory administration, and the inspiration and drive of a transformed Labour Party are far more likely to be cited as factors which had a tangible impact on the verdict of the voters. Nevertheless, I would suggest that Labour's relentless and imaginative efforts to guide and shape political coverage on television and radio and in the newspapers were partly responsible for turning their already near-certain victory into a record-breaking triumph.

Labour succeeded where the Conservatives so palpably failed. They used the news media to attack the government and raise their own profile, while at the same time avoiding most of the potential harm which unfavourable exposure could have inflicted on their own electoral chances. This was no mean accomplishment, bearing in mind the competitive environment in which broadcasters and journalists have to work and the commercial pressures they face, which put a premium on constructing a good story at anyone's expense. By finding ways to encourage the news media to hound ministers and expose Tory splits, Labour snuffed out the Conservatives' dwindling chances of gaining credit for the government's achievements. And, by dint of their own dedication and ingenuity, Labour proved far more effective in the art of political propaganda. The feeling that it was time for a change was deep-seated in the electorate, but the publicity Labour contrived to generate, and their expertise in arousing a sense of political excitement in their 110 target seats, seemed to create the kind of atmosphere nationally which is usually seen only in high profile by-elections; and once that enthusiasm had been unleashed, the determination to kick the government where it hurt seemed to develop a momentum of its own.

The forces seen at work during the election campaign, which, I believe, were to prove so influential, originated in the culture which had been imbued in Labour during the long years of opposition. Often, it seemed, the top priority – above all other activity – was the need to manufacture news stories which attacked and ridiculed the efforts of Conservative ministers. Of course, a posture of attack is more appealing to the news media and easier to sustain than one of justification; all governments are regularly forced into a defensive posture; and divided and tired Conservative MPs were willing accomplices in their own downfall. Nevertheless, Labour's well-rehearsed routines for capturing the news agenda, and their calculated policy of wooing Tory-supporting newspapers, had been in place for years, not just for the few weeks of the election campaign, and the confidence that comes from long practice added an edge to their efficacy. Therefore, when looking at the reasons for Labour's landslide victory, one should not ignore the cumulative effect of their sustained efforts to cajole the news media into denigrating the Conservative Party, whether the target was government incompetence or the sleaze which tarnished individual MPs. I would suggest that the massive fall in the Conservatives' vote can be attributed in part to the disenchantment Labour had helped to generate. Shy and silent Tories stayed at home because they could not bring themselves to vote for a party which, in the public's mind, had become so discredited and so tainted. Voting Conservative in the 1997 election, even in the privacy of the polling booth, was not just unfashionable but, even for many of their traditional supporters, an act impossible to contemplate.

I have tried in this book to give an insight into Labour's ruthless efficiency in propagating the type of news which damaged John Major's government and exacerbated the divisions within his party. Journalistic endeavour and political ambition are two powerful but separate forces, and I am not suggesting that in addressing the activities of the Labour Party the former was in hock to the latter. But there can be no doubting the effectiveness of Labour's news factory, which churned out a non-stop supply of stories aimed at enticing the media away from an agenda which the government would have preferred them to follow. Shadow ministers and their aides became undoubted masters in the black art of exploiting leaks of confidential government documents; commercial secrets or embarrassing statistics involving the privatised industries and the financial affairs of their 'fat-cat' directors were perpetually being spirited, somewhat mysteriously, into the public domain; Labour's spin doctors had the uncanniest knack of spotting ministerial gaffes which had originally escaped the attention of the media; and if there was a government slip-up to be exposed, Labour's timing was immaculate in revealing it at the optimum moment so as to block out favourable publicity for the Conservatives. Of equal importance was an ability to bamboozle broadcasters, journalists and their editors into downplaying or dropping stories which harmed Labour's image. Self-discipline had become the watchword of New Labour, and only rarely was there public dissent within the party itself; but swift measures were always taken to try to limit unfavourable coverage from whatever quarter it came. The difficulties I encountered when reporting issues involving the trade unions illustrated the assiduity with which Labour's guardian spirits applied themselves to eliminating all reference to stories which might re-awaken or reinforce anti-Labour prejudices.

In seeking to sustain my argument about the superiority of Labour's media operation and the party's ability to outwit the combined forces of the Whitehall information service and Conservative Central Office, and then to move on to an examination of how Labour might try to manipulate the news media now that they are in government, at no stage do I wish to diminish the importance electorally of Tony Blair's achievements in creating the concept of New Labour. The crucial support which his party received from newspapers like the *Sun*, and the toning down of anti-Labour propaganda in the *Daily Mail* and the *Express*, was not achieved with a wave of the wand by Peter Mandelson. A succession of dramatic shifts in party policy had transformed Labour's standing among newspaper executives, business leaders and other influential groups. If Labour had not cut loose from the philosophy of tax and spend; if the party had not promised to keep all the Conservatives' employment laws; if it had not shown a readiness to embrace the private sector; then no amount of spin doctoring could have secured the unprecedented endorsements the party was receiving by the time the formal campaign got under way. Blair's boldness as leader and the overwhelming support he was given for the steps he was advocating, from the rewriting of Clause Four of the party's constitution to the abandonment of outdated commitments, provided a telling contrast with the inability of John Major either to discipline his MPs or to cajole them into line. The Labour leadership's thirst for power and the professionalism of their party machine gave them an air of invincibility which was barely dented during the six-week campaign. Nevertheless, my contention that an ability to command the news agenda was a significant factor in the Conservatives' humiliating defeat was borne out by the steps which Labour took immediately on taking office to ensure that the government of Prime Minister Blair would maintain far greater control over the news media than was ever exercised by his predecessor.

Margaret Thatcher demonstrated with devastating effect how, once a new government has secured control of the news agenda, the enthusiastic backing of the media can be of incalculable value in achieving political objectives. The trick she performed was to ensure that her own enemies became the enemies of the journalists and the broadcasters. In the early 1980s strikers and trade union leaders were vilified by large sections of the news media, as were the Argentine generals during the Falklands War. The Winter of Discontent which preceded the 1979 general election had lined up Thatcher's targets for all to see, and the anti-union fervour of her rhetoric was mirrored in the news coverage of the day. One only has to think of the media hype in support of the 'new faces' who braved the mineworkers' picket lines and began the return to work in the 1984–5 pit strike to grasp the powerful emotions which she let loose.

The lessons of these years were clearly not lost on Labour. When in opposition, they pilloried the 'fat-cat' directors of the privatised utilities to demonstrate the corruption and unfairness of a Conservative administration. Once Blair gained power, those very same business leaders became a target of the policy objectives of a Labour government; and within a matter of weeks they had, by their own ineptitude, felt the lash of hostile publicity, in the same way that union leaders had a decade earlier. A windfall tax on the profits of the privatised utilities and measures to ensure that the national lottery became the 'people's lottery' were seen by the Labour leadership as two of the most popular promises on which they fought the election. Both proposals had wide support in the news media; yet within weeks of the election the British Telecom chairman, Sir Iain Vallance, threatened a legal challenge to the windfall tax, and the directors of the lottery operators, Camelot, awarded themselves massive bonuses. They were surprised and hurt by the public backlash they provoked, apparently oblivious both to the result of the election and to the way in which even those newspapers which had previously supported the Conservatives were now identifying themselves with Labour's objectives. After the new Secretary of State for National Heritage, Chris Smith,

called in the Camelot directors and told them they should give their
bonuses to charity, two newspaper front pages provided one small illustration of the way the media were reflecting the government's determination
to turn what had come to look like a runaway profit-making enterprise into
a 'people's lottery'. 'Smirking Camelot fatcats told: give your cash back',
was the *Mirror*'s headline, a sentiment fully shared by the *Express*, whose
front page was headlined 'Give us back your bonus'. Within days the
Camelot directors had agreed to make contributions to charity from their
long-term bonuses.

Any incoming government elected on the kind of mandate achieved by
Labour in 1997 would rightly expect an extended honeymoon in the
media and a recognition by journalists that the decision of the electorate
could not be ignored. Newspaper proprietors and programme editors
would be foolish to take any other line because, at least to begin with, they
would be anxious to keep in step with the widely acknowledged opinion of
the public that a new Prime Minister should be given every chance to
prove him- or herself. In politics at least, honeymoons generally come to
an end. However, one notable feature of the 1980s was that Thatcher
proved highly adept at retaining the support of the popular newspapers
long after her expected period of grace, and it was not until the 1997
election, when the Conservatives were attempting to get re-elected for a
fifth term, that they finally lost the enthusiastic backing they had enjoyed
for so long. My impression is that Labour will turn out to be just as astute
in their efforts to retain the backing of the press. A prerequisite for the
successful orchestration of news coverage, as Thatcher and subsequently
Blair have demonstrated, is to build up a network of friendly media
magnates. Their support can be critical at times of crisis in government.
Blair took the trouble to establish friendly relations with Rupert Murdoch
well before the election, and shortly after it his policy of wooing
newspaper proprietors paid off handsomely when he got the backing of
Viscount Rothermere, chairman of the *Daily Mail*.

By far the most significant move which the new Blair administration
made towards ensuring that Labour remained the masters of manipula-
tion was the attempt to embed deep in the heart of the government
machine not just the media personnel but also the procedures and
techniques which helped deliver victory in the general election. The two
key appointments were no real surprise: Peter Mandelson was made
minister without portfolio, responsible for 'implementing government
policy and presenting it effectively', and Alastair Campbell followed Blair

into No. 10 Downing Street to become the new Prime Minister's press secretary. A raft of other appointments metamorphosed many of the press officers and aides who had been attached to members of the shadow Cabinet into political advisers and installed them in the departmental private offices of the new Cabinet. As expected, Charlie Whelan became special adviser to the Chancellor of the Exchequer, Gordon Brown; and Tim Allan and Hilary Coffman, two of Campbell's assistants, joined him as Downing Street press officers, as did Campbell's partner Fiona Millar, who became an assistant to Cherie Blair, a role she had also performed during the campaign. Within a month of the election a total of fifty-three political advisers had been appointed, including eighteen in Downing Street – more than double the number under John Major, who expressed his reservations about the scale of these party appointments. Blair defended his recruitment of political advisers, denying that their arrival would herald the politicisation of the government machine: 'I believe it is important to bolster the centre of government and bring in fresh ideas, while at the same time maintaining and supporting a politically neutral civil service'.

Peter Mandelson, who had a seat on most of the key Cabinet committees, was immediately seen as the linchpin of the new structure, with a role comparable to that exercised by Michael Heseltine when he was Deputy Prime Minister and had responsibility for coordinating government publicity. However, there could hardly have been a greater contrast between the circumstances in which Heseltine had to operate and the new environment which Labour had established. Mandelson inherited the Deputy Prime Minister's daily routine of an early morning meeting in the Cabinet Office for the key personnel involved in government publicity, but the new minister without portfolio had one immediate advantage: unlike Heseltine, who had to sit round a table with the changing faces of civil servants and other ministers, Mandelson could get straight down to business with tried and tested colleagues like Alastair Campbell with whom he had worked for over two years and been through an election.

Blair's anxiety to act swiftly and get his party appointees in place was prompted by a concern not only to maintain the momentum of their success on the publicity front, but also to avoid the pitfalls of the past when government and party have gone their separate ways. Over the years, both Conservative and Labour administrations have faced difficulties when relations between their advisers in Downing Street and staff at party headquarters have deteriorated. The gulf that can open up between the two centres can sometimes be so troublesome as to jeopardise the very survival of the government. Thatcher's tempestuous dealings with Central Office have been well chronicled, as have the turbulent times through which Labour governments have had to navigate when the national executive committee has effectively established a rival power base at party headquarters. Well before the election campaign, Blair began a process of reforming Labour's internal structures; the likely outcomes of this include a diminished role for the national executive, so as reduce the potential for friction, and a shorter and far less confrontational party conference. Once the election was won, the transfer of Labour's key election press officers straight into the private offices of Cabinet ministers was backed up by moves to cement the closest possible cooperation between the government's promotional efforts and the continuing work of the party's media centre at Millbank Tower. As David Hill, the chief media spokesperson, told me on the morning after polling day, he intended to operate the media centre as 'an arm of the Labour government'.

Blair has gone further than any other Prime Minister in his attempts to mesh together government and party publicity. If he succeeds he will stand a good chance of preventing the problems which have dogged successive governments in the past, problems that have invariably been rooted in the inability of the civil servants who make up the government's information service to speak about the political activities of ministers or the intricate party problems which sometimes beset them. Under John Major, Downing Street press secretaries were either unable or reluctant to brief journalists on the ramifications of internal disputes like the split with the Euro-sceptics and the removal of the party whip from the rebel Conservative MPs. By contrast, Alastair Campbell and his two assistants, Tim Allan and Hilary Coffman, as party appointees face no such constraints when briefing journalists; similarly, Charlie Whelan can talk about the political repercussions of decisions being made by Gordon Brown with a freedom which would be out of the question for civil servants in the Treasury's press office. The downside of this otherwise felicitous arrangement is the potential for the scale of Labour's political appointments to become a source of tension in the future if situations arise in which conflicting guidance is being given by the political advisers and the departmental press officers. Political journalists would have no inhibitions about exploiting such discrepancies if newsworthy issues were involved.

The attention which Blair has paid to the task of establishing a hands-on approach to publicity suggests that he wants his party in government to remain on a permanent campaign footing. Indeed, he has made no secret of the fact that he wants preparations for winning a second term to have the highest priority. The early months of a new government tend to be the most straightforward in terms of news management, and the almost breathless pace taken by Blair and his ministers assured them a steady succession of favourable headlines in the immediate aftermath of the election. After the Queen's Speech setting out Labour's first legislative programme at the State Opening of Parliament in mid-May, Blair spoke confidently of the progress they had already achieved: 'We will not put right the damage of eighteen years in eighteen days or even eighteen months. But in twelve days we have already shown we can make a difference.'

Blair rapidly demonstrated his flair for publicity through a high-profile visit to Northern Ireland and by the welcome he gave to President Clinton, who sat in on a Cabinet meeting in No. 10, but too much should not be inferred from the ease with which he garnered flattering attention. After all, it mirrored the start of John Major's premiership, when the freshness of his appeal after the very different style of Margaret Thatcher won similar plaudits. Unlike some previous Labour leaders, Blair entered government without having first been tested under severe fire from the news media. While he had a few damaging moments as Leader of the Opposition, they paled into insignificance when compared with the sustained criticism and derision which Major was forced to endure for much of his time in No. 10. Most of the difficulties which Blair encountered arose from personality clashes or policy disagreements within the shadow Cabinet, and there were few occasions on which he had to withstand serious pressure – for example in January 1996, when he supported the then shadow health secretary, Harriet Harman, who had become embroiled in controversy after deciding to send her son to an opted-out grammar school. Now, Blair has the great advantage of being able to dictate the timing of events, and the flair and expertise of Alastair Campbell and Peter Mandelson will ensure that full advantage is taken of this, so that even if unpopular announcements have to be made, ways will be found to minimise their impact.

The defensive mechanisms which Blair has put in place have been designed to forestall and deflect the media pressures which would inevitably develop should a real calamity strike his government. So soon in the life of a new administration, only the foolhardy would hazard a guess about the potential disasters which might lie in the path of the new Prime Minister. Given his massive parliamentary majority and the expertise his closest advisers have developed in handling adverse publicity during Labour's long years of opposition, it will take a catastrophe akin to the 1992 withdrawal from the exchange rate mechanism or the 1967 devaluation of the pound to throw New Labour violently off course. The referendums on Scottish and Welsh devolution pose perhaps the greatest presentational challenges in the short term, but the severest test in Blair's first few years in office looks almost certain to be a decision on British membership of the European single currency.

In view of the much reduced size of their parliamentary party, the chances of the Conservatives posing any serious threat to the new government seem slim, to say the least. The Tories face a daunting challenge in repairing the devastation of their cataclysmic defeat and a rapid recovery looks highly unlikely. Charles Lewington, their director of communications, resigned within days of the election; his departure had been expected, whatever the outcome, and his contract was about to expire. He gave his version of what had been a 'spin doctor's nightmare' when assessing the campaign for the *Sunday Telegraph*. For him, the defining moment had been sixteen days before polling day (15 April), or 'D minus 16 in our confusing campaign jargon', when John Major 'smelt defeat in the spring air' and confided that the 'game was up', telling a trusted aide: 'You know we can't win it.' Lewington said he was 'the messenger everyone wanted to shoot' that night because he had to report that two ministers, John Horam and James Paice, had both strayed from the official line on the single currency. He acknowledged the impotence of the leadership's position once years of division and contradiction in Conservative European policy had burst on to the campaign stage. 'My instinct, as with the attempted deselection of Hamilton and Merchant earlier, was to insist that the two junior ministers should be made to resign. I felt Tony Blair's charge of weak leadership was killing our man ... The Prime Minister was dispirited and deflated to learn of this fresh setback. No, they couldn't be sacked, he said quickly. "I can't sack two ministers in the middle of an election campaign. And sacking them over Europe would send the right of the party into orbit." ... Incontrovertible arguments, but a spin doctor's nightmare.' Yet despite Lewington's frustration over the continued splits within the Tory party and Major's failure to maintain a consistent approach towards disciplining recalcitrant MPs, he rarely revealed the true state of his own melancholy feelings when briefing journalists during the final stages of the campaign; nor did he let slip the obvious short-comings of the message he had to offer.

As the Conservatives have lost much of the press support they once took for granted, and in view of the fact that there is no guarantee it can be recovered in the immediate future, a newly elected party leader should rethink the party's media strategy in its entirety. Because of the Tories' traditional links with the newspaper proprietors and the loyalty they were once shown, Central Office has always leant more heavily towards the press than television or radio. As a consequence, the Conservatives have had both less understanding of broadcasters' needs and less ability to influence their output than Labour. They would do well to address this imbalance.

Changes afoot within the broadcasting industry could also assist the new government as it prepares to withstand media pressure. Some comment and current affairs programmes are consciously adopting a less confrontational style in the belief that audiences have tired of the tit for tat approach which Blair complained about during the election. If, as a result, there are fewer television and radio appearances by politicians and interviewing is less strident than of late, the government is likely to be the beneficiary. John Major's ministers often had no option but to subject themselves to a constant round of interviews, so desperate were they to defend themselves against Labour's attacks; but in doing so they repeatedly tripped themselves up and contradicted one another, under-lining the need for such appearances to be effectively coordinated. The point will not have been not lost on Mandelson and Campbell. The mismanagement of the last administration's publicity will remain a constant reminder to Labour's spin doctors who, after the rigours of opposition, now have the chance to control the government machine which they have hitherto dedicated themselves to attacking.

Index